ACCELERATION
for ALL

A How-To Guide for Overcoming Learning Gaps

SHARON V. KRAMER   SARAH SCHUHL

Solution Tree | Press

555 North Morton Street
Bloomington, IN 47404
800.733.6786 (toll free) / 812.336.7700
FAX: 812.336.7790

email: info@SolutionTree.com
SolutionTree.com

Visit **go.SolutionTree.com/priorityschools** to download the free reproducibles in this book.

Printed in the United States of America

Library of Congress Cataloging-in-Publication Data

Names: Kramer, Sharon V., author. | Schuhl, Sarah, author.
Title: Acceleration for all : a how-to guide for overcoming learning gaps /
  Sharon V. Kramer, Sarah Schuhl.
Description: Bloomington, IN : Solution Tree Press, [2023] | Includes
  bibliographical references and index.
Identifiers: LCCN 2022053249 (print) | LCCN 2022053250 (ebook) | ISBN
  9781954631014 (paperback) | ISBN 9781954631021 (ebook)
Subjects: LCSH: Academic achievement. | Curriculum enrichment. | Learning.
Classification: LCC LB1062.6 .K73 2023 (print) | LCC LB1062.6 (ebook) |
  DDC 370.15--dc23/eng/20230216
LC record available at https://lccn.loc.gov/2022053249
LC ebook record available at https://lccn.loc.gov/2022053250

Solution Tree
Jeffrey C. Jones, CEO
Edmund M. Ackerman, President

Solution Tree Press
President and Publisher: Douglas M. Rife
Associate Publisher: Sarah Payne-Mills
Managing Production Editor: Kendra Slayton
Editorial Director: Todd Brakke
Art Director: Rian Anderson
Copy Chief: Jessi Finn
Senior Production Editor: Laurel Hecker
Content Development Specialist: Amy Rubenstein
Copy Editor: Evie Madsen
Proofreader: Charlotte Jones
Text and Cover Designer: Abigail Bowen
Associate Editor: Sarah Ludwig
Editorial Assistants: Charlotte Jones and Elijah Oates

Acknowledgments

This book is the result of almost two decades of work in schools and districts across the United States and beyond. It could not have been written without the endless work of the educators who invited us on their continuous-improvement journeys. These educators are a constant inspiration and their tireless focus on students is what keeps us going. We learn so much from these educators as they work through the challenges and struggles their schools serving underserved populations at risk face.

Although there are too many schools and districts to name them all, we want to convey our deep appreciation for the opportunity to partner with the Glendale Elementary School District in Arizona, Huntsville Independent School District in Texas, and Anna Strong Learning Academy in Arkansas. The passion and persistence of all these schools and districts remind us of our *why*, or our purpose. When you know your *why*, there is a clear pathway toward your *what* to do. These are gap-closing schools and districts because their investment in each student is evident. This is really their story.

We are also appreciative of the constant support of Jeff Jones, the chief executive officer of Solution Tree, and the entire Solution Tree family. Jeff's vision and passionate focus on educators and students has changed education around the world. We are especially indebted to Douglas Rife, president and publisher of Solution Tree Press, for his unending encouragement and belief in this work. Countless others on the Solution Tree team support us every day, and their efforts are immensely appreciated.

In addition, we also appreciate our team of priority schools associates who coach, guide, mentor, and challenge schools to push forward. They encourage us with their dedication, stories of celebrations, and never-give-up attitude. This amazing team is making a difference in the lives of students. Because of them, lives are being saved and doors of opportunity continue to open.

Finally, we had the amazing opportunity of working together and coauthoring this second book. We are grateful to our families for their support and understanding as we navigated our way. We believe equity of opportunity for all students is a fight worth fighting! This book represents a clear pathway to equity and is our contribution to learning for all when *all* really does mean *all*.

—Sharon V. Kramer and Sarah Schuhl

Solution Tree Press would like to thank the following reviewers:

Doug Crowley
Assistant Principal
DeForest Area High School
DeForest, Wisconsin

Connie Debes
Kindergarten Teacher
Lincoln Consolidated Schools
Lincoln, Arkansas

John D. Ewald
Education Consultant
Frederick, Maryland

Jenna Fanshier
Sixth-Grade Language Arts Teacher
Hesston Middle School
Hesston, Kansas

Jed Kees
Principal
Onalaska Middle School
Onalaska, Wisconsin

Lindsey Matkin
Principal
Kinard Middle School
Fort Collins, Colorado

Sheryl Walters
Instructional Design Lead
Calgary, Alberta, Canada

Steven Weber
Associate Superintendent for Teaching
    and Learning
Fayetteville Public Schools
Fayetteville, Arkansas

Visit **go.SolutionTree.com/priorityschools** to download the free reproducibles in this book.

Table of Contents

About the Authors ix

Introduction 1

CHAPTER 1
The Case for Acceleration 5

    Acceleration as an Alternative to Remediation 6

    The Shift to Acceleration. 8

    Acceleration Strategies Based on New Mindsets 10

        Mindset One: Schools and Districts Are Learning Organizations 11

        Mindset Two: All Students Can Learn Grade- and Course-Level Standards 12

        Mindset Three: Formative Assessment Is Integral to Learning. 12

        Mindset Four: Schools Must Systematically Intervene to Accelerate Learning 12

        Mindset Five: Instructional Strategies Should Create Forward-Moving Learning 13

        Mindset Six: Everyone Is a Leader of Learning 14

    Conclusion 15

    Discussion Questions for Reflection and Action 15

CHAPTER 2
Culture That Accelerates Learning 17

    The Shift to a Culture of Learning 17

    Cultural Practices to Accelerate Learning 18

        Students Co-Create Learning Contracts 18

        Teachers Engage and Learn in Collaborative Teams 21

        Administrators Stay Focused on Learning. 22

        Parents and Community Members Shift Their Thinking to Learning 22

        Symbols and Artifacts Show Learning Is Required 25

        SMART Goals Are Audaciously Attainable 25

    Conclusion 30

    Discussion Questions for Reflection and Action 32

CHAPTER 3

Priority Standards and Learning Cycles That Accelerate Learning......... **33**

The Shift to Focusing on Priority Standards and Learning Cycles........................ 34

Acceleration Strategies for Priority Standards and Learning Cycles 34

    Identify Priority Standards... 35

    Unpack Priority Standards to Create Learning Progressions 38

    Embed Prior-Knowledge Standards Into Units............................... 43

    Focus Acceleration in Ten-Day Learning Cycles Within Units 45

Conclusion 59

Discussion Questions for Reflection and Action 59

CHAPTER 4

An Assessment System That Accelerates Learning **61**

The Shift to Learning From Assessments..................................... 62

Acceleration Strategies Through Assessments.................................. 64

    Audit Current Assessment Practices...................................... 64

    Create a Balanced Assessment System.................................... 66

    Create Common Assessments Unit by Unit 68

    Implement Common Formative Assessment Strategies........................ 71

Conclusion 86

Discussion Questions for Reflection and Action 86

CHAPTER 5

Daily Grade-Level Instruction That Accelerates Learning **87**

The Shift to Grade-Level Learning Every Day 88

Acceleration Strategies as Part of Instruction 89

    Design Quality Lessons Tied to Grade-Level Learning Every Day 90

    Plan for Massed and Spaced Practice 93

    Utilize Whole-Group and Small-Group Learning 95

    Teach Conceptually.. 96

    Incorporate Reading and Writing Every Day............................... 99

    Engage Students Actively 101

    Utilize Error Analysis 102

    Give Meaningful Feedback.. 103

    Empower Student Learning Through Reflection and Goal Setting................ 104

Conclusion 105

Discussion Questions for Reflection and Action 106

CHAPTER 6

An Intervention System That Accelerates Learning. **107**

    The Shift to Multitiered Systems of Support 109

    Acceleration Strategies for Intervention. 111

        Repurpose Time in the Master Schedule for Intervention. .112

        Respond as a Team to Student Learning Data 114

        Focus on Student Growth. 120

        Utilize Blended Learning 122

        Create Small Groups. 122

        Develop and Use Peer Tutors 123

        Implement Support Classes or Learning Labs. 125

        Engage Students in Learning Behavior Expectations 125

    Conclusion 126

    Discussion Questions for Reflection and Action 127

CHAPTER 7

Leadership Practices That Accelerate Learning **129**

    The Shift to Shared Leadership. 130

    Leadership Practices to Accelerate Learning. 130

        Create a Guiding Coalition or Learning Team 131

        Utilize Instructional Coaches. 134

        Build a System of Instructional Support. 140

        Engage the Community and Stakeholders 145

    Conclusion 146

    Discussion Questions for Reflection and Action 147

CHAPTER 8

Continuous Improvement That Accelerates Learning **149**

    The Shift to Continuous Improvement. 151

    Acceleration Strategies in Continuous Improvement. 152

        Archive Team Products Systematically 153

        Teach Until the Last Day of School 156

        Engage in Step-Up Transition Planning. 156

        Apply Learning at Vertical Step-Up Transition Meetings 158

        Celebrate! 160

    Conclusion 162

    Discussion Questions for Reflection and Action 164

EPILOGUE
Dare to Dream and Then Dare to Do **165**

References and Resources 171

Index 177

About the Authors

 **Sharon V. Kramer, PhD,** knows firsthand the demands and rewards of working in a professional learning community (PLC). As a leader in the field, she has done priority schools work with districts across the United States, emphasizing the importance of creating and using quality assessments and utilizing the PLC continuous-improvement process to raise student achievement. Sharon served as assistant superintendent for curriculum and instruction of Kildeer Countryside Community Consolidated School District 96 in Illinois. In this position, she ensured all students were prepared to enter Adlai E. Stevenson High School, a Model PLC School PLC at Work® architect Richard DuFour started and formerly led.

A seasoned educator, Sharon has taught in elementary and middle school classrooms and served as a principal, director of elementary education, and university professor. In addition to her PLC experience, Sharon completed assessment training from Rick Stiggins, Steve Chappuis, Larry Ainsworth, and the Center for Performance Assessment (now the Leadership and Learning Center). She has presented a variety of assessment workshops at institutes and summits and for state departments of education. Sharon has also worked with school districts across the United States to determine their power standards and develop assessments.

Sharon has been a Comprehensive School Reform consultant to schools that received grant funding to implement the PLC process for schoolwide reform, and her customized PLC coaching academies have empowered school and district leadership teams across the United States. Sharon has presented at state and national conferences sponsored by Learning Forward, the National Association for Gifted Children, the American Federation of Teachers, and California State University. She has been instrumental in facilitating professional development initiatives focused on standards-based learning and teaching, improved understanding and utilization of assessment data, interventions and differentiation that meet the needs of all learners, and strengthened efforts to ensure K–12 literacy.

Sharon is the author of *How to Leverage PLCs for School Improvement* and coauthor of *School Improvement for All: A How-to Guide for Doing the Right Work*; *Best Practices at Tier 2: Supplemental Interventions for Additional Student Support, Elementary*; and *Best Practices at Tier 2: Supplemental Interventions for Additional Student Support, Secondary*. In addition, she served as editor of *Charting the Course for Leaders: Lessons From Priority Schools in a PLC at Work* and *Charting the Course for Collaborative Teams: Lessons From Priority Schools in a PLC at Work*. She also contributed to the books *It's About Time: Planning Interventions and Extensions in Elementary School*, *The Teacher as Assessment Leader*, and *The Collaborative Teacher: Working Together as a Professional Learning Community*.

Sharon earned a doctorate in educational leadership and policy studies from Loyola University Chicago.

To learn more about Sharon's work, follow @DrKramer1 on Twitter.

Sarah Schuhl, MS, is an educational coach and consultant specializing in mathematics, professional learning communities (PLCs), common formative and summative assessments, priority school improvement, and response to intervention (RTI). She has worked in schools as a secondary mathematics teacher, high school instructional coach, and K–12 mathematics specialist.

Sarah was instrumental in the creation of a PLC in the Centennial School District in Oregon, helping teachers make large gains in student achievement. She earned the Centennial School District Triple C Award in 2012.

Sarah grows learning in districts throughout the United States through professional development to larger groups or small-group coaching. Her work focuses on strengthening the teaching and learning of mathematics, having teachers learn from one another when working effectively as collaborative teams in a PLC, and striving to ensure the learning of each student through assessment practices and intervention. Her practical approach includes working with teachers and administrators to implement assessments for learning, analyze data, collectively respond to student learning, and map standards.

Since 2015, Sarah has coauthored the books *Engage in the Mathematical Practices: Strategies to Build Numeracy and Literacy With K–5 Learners* and *School Improvement for All: A How-To Guide for Doing the Right Work.* She is a coauthor (with Timothy D. Kanold) of the *Every Student Can Learn Mathematics* series and *Mathematics at Work™ Plan Book,* and editor of the *Mathematics Unit Planning in a PLC at Work* series. She contributed to *Charting the Course for Leaders: Lessons From Priority Schools in a PLC at Work* and *Charting the Course for Collaborative Teams: Lessons From Priority Schools in a PLC at Work.*

Previously, Sarah served as a member and chair of the National Council of Teachers of Mathematics (NCTM) editorial panel for the journal *Mathematics Teacher* and secretary of the National Council of Supervisors of Mathematics (NCSM). Her work with the Oregon Department of Education includes designing mathematics assessment items, test specifications and blueprints, and rubrics for achievement-level descriptors. She has also contributed to a middle school mathematics series and an elementary mathematics intervention program.

Sarah earned a bachelor of science in mathematics from Eastern Oregon University and a master of science in mathematics education from Portland State University.

To learn more about Sarah's work, follow @SSchuhl on Twitter.

To book Sharon V. Kramer or Sarah Schuhl for professional development, contact pd@SolutionTree.com.

Introduction

There is no shortage of books, articles, blogs, speeches, podcasts, and webinars expounding on the need to close or eliminate student achievement gaps. The need to address students falling below grade level in their learning is not a new phenomenon. Unfortunately, the COVID-19 pandemic exacerbated the amount of unfinished learning all students experienced and created an even greater sense of urgency to address the problem. This urgency is most felt in marginalized communities: students of color, multilingual students, students with learning and thinking differences, and students in lower-income areas. Schools in these communities feel the magnitude of the need to overcome achievement gaps. Some of these schools have been designated *priority schools* or *improvement required*, graded *D* or *F*, or given other such indicators by their state or nation. Most schools have some under-achieving students or groups of students. The major difference in a priority school is the number of students who need support to achieve at grade level or beyond. Until schools address learning gaps in achievement, learning for all students remains out of reach.

In priority and non-priority schools, it is all too common for students to enter the classroom not yet knowing the prerequisite concepts and skills they need to learn grade-level standards. There are many reasons why a student may not have learned the standards needed in the previous grade level or course. Some students have a history of struggling, and each year their need to accelerate learning to grade level grows. Some students have personal situations that impact their schooling, and others may not have engaged in learning as much as required. Perhaps teachers ran out of time to teach grade-level stan-dards last year. Perhaps teachers tried to cover every grade-level standard and taught quickly without checking on student learning along the way. Whatever the reason, gaps exist in student learning that require a systematic and comprehensive response.

Despite ever-present discussions of learning gaps, the process and progress in closing the gaps have been slow and, in some instances, nonexistent. This is not because schools and districts have not tried to increase student achievement. Nor is it due to a lack of effort or caring on the part of educators. Achievement gaps are a complex, multifaceted problem that requires educators to shift deeply ingrained systems and practices. Doing so will be challenging, but it is critically important work: "Closing the achievement and opportunity gaps that exist within our schools is a foundational civil rights issue" (Westover & Steinhauser, 2022, p. 29).

The usual approach is to try to help students catch up by reviewing and reteaching content from previous years. Although this may help fill some of students' learning gaps,

> "Achievement gaps" are caused by a system, not students. The best news is we know everything we need to know to rebuild a system that benefits EVERY learner.
> —PAULA MAEKER

it does not help them reach grade-level knowledge and skill fast enough. As each school year and course marches on, the gap between those students who are achieving grade-level learning and those who are not gets wider and wider. This creates a system of winners and losers rather than a system in which all students are taught—and expected to learn—at high levels.

The system that will eliminate achievement gaps for all students *accelerates* learning. If students are behind, they must learn more than a year's worth of content to get back on grade level. Instead of moving backward by reviewing and reteaching, acceleration helps students catch up while making forward progress in their learning. Acceleration works by integrating foundational and prerequisite knowledge into current units of instruction so students continue to learn grade-level content while filling in learning gaps. This just-in-time instruction means the prior content immediately connects to each day's grade-level learning. Acceleration requires timely assessment practices to gauge learning on a frequent or daily basis so targeted interventions occur immediately. Acceleration spirals learning in a continual cycle so students can learn current and prerequisite skills and knowledge all year, not just in a specific unit of instruction.

Acceleration is not a program, a new initiative, or even something that happens at a separate school for gifted students or students at risk. Acceleration is a *mindset*, or a way of thinking about learning in each lesson, every day. It represents a shift in approach necessary to ensure improved results. It is a shift away from the institutionalized approach of *remediation*, or the belief that students cannot go forward until they learn a set of predetermined prerequisite skills. Acceleration does not require new curricular materials or specialty training to implement. It is not necessary to plan a year of staff development before acceleration can begin. It is not something new or magical. However, acceleration does demand that educators view students through the lens of assets, not deficits—what students can do now, instead of what they're missing. It also requires teachers and collaborative teams to build their collective efficacy and accept the charge to accelerate learning. It calls on the entire school community to build confidence and student efficacy so all students believe they can and will succeed. Acceleration is proactive rather than reactive. It challenges current thinking and traditional practice.

This book details a systems approach to learning that supports all students as they learn grade-level knowledge, skills, and dispositions. This approach also supports collaborative teams of teachers as they craft instruction, assessments, and interventions that accelerate learning. The acceleration strategies we describe in this book draw on the professional learning community (PLC) process for teacher teams and schoolwide collaboration. In a school that operates as a PLC, educators adopt a focus on learning, a collaborative culture and collective responsibility, and a results orientation (DuFour, DuFour, Eaker, Many, & Mattos, 2016). Teachers work in interdependent teams to plan, instruct, and assess cycles of teaching and learning unit by unit. The following four questions guide their work (DuFour et al., 2016).

1. What do we want all students to know and be able to do?

2. How will we know if they learned it?

3. How will we respond when some students do not learn?

4. How will we extend the learning for students who are already proficient?

These collaborative structures are the foundation of acceleration. The core of acceleration—the process of grade- or course-level learning every day—already exists in the collaborative work of teams. It is a shift in thinking about this work that results in acceleration for all.

We wrote this book to provide a framework of practical, hands-on strategies that move learning forward. When an entire school or district accepts and implements these strategies, all students experience high levels of learning—at grade level or beyond. Learning for all, not just some, becomes a reality. Acceleration is equity in action.

Chapter 1, "The Case for Acceleration," establishes the rationale for taking the path less traveled, that of acceleration over remediation. We introduce a set of specific mindsets or beliefs about education that teachers and leaders must adopt as a basis for acceleration.

In chapter 2, "Culture That Accelerates Learning," we address the importance of a healthy school culture focused on the learning of adults and students. This chapter describes the process for developing a learning-focused culture by creating a community of learners across the school campus and within each classroom.

Chapter 3, "Priority Standards and Learning Cycles That Accelerate Learning," examines the concept of a guaranteed and viable curriculum—a curriculum that is consistent across classrooms and contains a manageable amount of content for the time available to teach it (Marzano, 2017). It focuses on determining the priority standards all students will learn and embedding the prerequisite knowledge and skills into learning progressions and grade-level unit plans.

Assessment is the key to acceleration, but not just any type of assessments. Chapter 4, "An Assessment System That Accelerates Learning," presents formative assessment practices that provide information to both the teacher and student to move learning forward. We emphasize providing many opportunities for students to show what they know in the classroom and on common assessments and using external assessments strategically.

In chapter 5, "Daily Grade-Level Instruction That Accelerates Learning," the focus shifts to planning lessons and delivering instruction that accelerate learning. This is the practical application of acceleration: meaningful lessons tied to grade-level learning every day is the only way to close the achievement gap for all students.

Even with an effective system of acceleration, students will still learn at different rates. Chapter 6, "An Intervention System That Accelerates Learning," considers tiered systems for responding when students need extra support to reach grade-level expectations.

Chapter 7, "Leadership Practices That Accelerate Learning," shows how critical leadership is when shifting mindsets and ensuring every student learns grade-level standards. Leadership is essential in improving any school or district, but no one person can do the work required to close achievement gaps alone. In a learning-focused school, everyone is a learner and a leader.

Chapter 8, "Continuous Improvement That Accelerates Learning," explores how teachers and teams can learn from their experiences each school year and use that learning to inform the work the following year. In this manner, a school's system of acceleration will be built on the strategies, lessons, assessments, and resources proven successful in promoting and ensuring learning for all.

Throughout each chapter you will read about common traditional strategies to reconsider in the shift from remediation to acceleration. You will also learn numerous strategies to adopt and customize as you implement acceleration to grow student learning to grade level or beyond. At the end of each chapter are reflection questions to use for discussion, learning, and action at your site.

Equity in learning happens when every student learns grade- or course-level standards (or higher) from one year to the next. This requires educators to take intentional actions every day. As you begin your journey to accelerate learning for all students, it is our hope you will have many additional suggestions, strategies, and ideas for moving learning forward and closing student achievement gaps beyond those we share. It is our belief that as educators engage in acceleration work, they will become better, stronger, and more effective as they build their skills at supporting and accelerating student learning. It is time for a mind shift! New mindsets will produce new results.

CHAPTER 1

The Case for Acceleration

Every year in Sharon's long and storied career as an educator, she began the school year by reviewing much of the important learning from the previous year or course to ensure her students were ready for the new standards they were about to tackle. The idea was to build a strong foundation for the new learning. In theory, it also provided an opportunity for students who were below grade level to catch up, and allowed time to establish classroom routines and structures. In some years, reviewing and reteaching content took as many as four to six weeks of instructional time—almost an entire quarter of the year.

Other school practices validated Sharon's approach to starting the school year. The school library rarely opened for student use until nearly a month into the school year. Academic interventions waited until the beginning-of-the-year diagnostic testing was complete, usually sometime in mid- or late-October. Small-group reading, writing, and mathematics instruction were not delivered until all students had tested and could be placed into groups. The start of the year was instead used to get acquainted with students, build relationships, and establish rules and procedures. Although these activities are essential to supporting increased student learning, they could have occurred in an ongoing manner throughout the year *along with* grade-level instruction, rather than *instead of* grade-level instruction during the first month of school. There just seemed to be no rush or sense of urgency to begin learning.

Sharon was well intentioned and, like every educator, she wanted her students to succeed, but this approach was not working. In fact, students often did not seem any better prepared for grade-level learning; they still had difficulty retaining and applying the review information later in the year. Reteaching at the start of the school year also sent a message: students did not have to retain information because there would be a significant opportunity for review at the start of each year. In addition, it communicated to students that they were unprepared for the current grade level or course, causing them to lose confidence rather than feel their teachers believed in their ability to learn and grow.

Not surprisingly, Sharon never finished her grade-level curriculum and there were always priority standards her students went to the next grade never having an opportunity to learn. This put students even further behind the next year when they entered their new classrooms. Unfortunately, this process creates a cycle of remediation that students almost never escape. Students fall further and further behind each year they matriculate through the grade levels and courses. Sharon's experience—common to many

> How we think about the impact of what we do is more important than what we do.
>
> —JOHN HATTIE AND KLAUS ZIERER

educators—illustrates why the endless cycle of review and remediation fails to improve student learning. If students are to catch up to where they need to be in their learning, schools must instead embrace acceleration.

Acceleration as an Alternative to Remediation

Let's begin with a more detailed understanding of what has been the traditional response when students are not learning at grade level: remediation. Often, *remediation* means reteaching content students previously failed to learn—reviewing standards or units from lower grade levels or prerequisite courses—before beginning new learning. There is heavy emphasis on mastering the previous content to be ready for the current grade-level standards. In other words, *remediation* means going backward to go forward. But how is that working so far? Are remediation strategies moving the learning forward or fostering inequities for some students? Are they perpetuating the achievement gap or closing it? Is this a culture of learning for *all* or learning for *some*?

Data from Zearn, a nonprofit organization whose online mathematics platform one in four U.S. elementary students use, provide a direct comparison of remediation and acceleration. The following findings were revealed in data on more than two million students in more than a hundred thousand classrooms:

- Students who experienced learning acceleration struggled less and learned more than students who started at the same level but experienced remediation instead.
- Students of color and those from low-income backgrounds were more likely than their white, wealthier peers to experience remediation—even when they had already demonstrated success on grade-level content.
- Learning acceleration was particularly effective for students of color and those from low-income families. (as cited in TNTP, 2021, p. 1)

Although remediation may help fill some students' learning gaps, it does not help students reach grade-level knowledge and skill proficiency fast enough to catch up with their peers. Remediation purports to support students who have fallen behind, but these students can never catch up if they keep working on below-grade-level content. Remediation is entrenched in the past: what students missed last year and what they need to redo. As students matriculate through each school year, the gap between those students who are achieving grade-level learning and those who are not gets wider and wider. Furthermore, students see remediation as failure to advance or being part of the "slow" class or group. Students often have a sense of futility, which leads to low levels of engagement and a lack of improvement.

On the other hand, acceleration focuses on the present: what students need right now to excel this year in this course or grade level. There are many definitions of the term *acceleration* as educators use it to describe learning. It is often defined as advancing learning faster than the typical grade-level expectations, such as taking a ninth-grade Algebra 1 course in eighth grade or enrolling in an honors track in high school. In elementary schools, it can mean learning higher-grade-level standards and compacting the curriculum to learn more in a shortened period. Accelerated learning is not new or novel, just not widely practiced or understood. In many cases, its use has been restricted to students who have already achieved the grade-level standards and are ready for additional challenges, as evidenced by this definition: "to progress from grade to grade more rapidly than usual: to follow a speeded-up educational program" (Accelerate, n.d.). This definition implies that acceleration will not increase the learning of all students, only some. It focuses on moving already-strong students beyond grade-level understanding.

Similarly, there have been efforts to accelerate learning for other targeted populations of students. The Accelerated Schools Project began at Stanford University in 1986 to improve schools for students at risk of academic failure. The focus was on replacing academic remediation for these students with what was termed *academic enrichment* (Accelerated Schools Plus, 2006). Too often, acceleration is limited to high-achieving students or students at risk; this book focuses on acceleration strategies for *all* students.

Acceleration is not just the smart thing to do. Acceleration is a matter of equity: "Opportunity gaps have long disproportionately affected students of color, those impacted by poverty, and other vulnerable populations such as ELL students and those receiving special education services" (Takabori, 2021). These marginalized students are routinely denied challenging work. Furthermore, the COVID-19 pandemic exacerbated these trends and learning gaps themselves. During the COVID-19 pandemic, schools offered varied learning experiences. In some regions, students spent most of the year learning virtually. In others, students attended schools with masks and social distancing. In some schools, students attended through a hybrid model or learned asynchronously. And in some schools, students had choice about how they would learn. These interruptions in education affected learning opportunities and achievement rates. A joint study from The New Teacher Project and ReadWorks (a free digital repository of texts and question sets for English language arts classes) examined what kind of assignments teachers gave through the ReadWorks platform (TNTP, 2022). They examined patterns of assignments in seventy-five thousand public and private schools serving more than twelve million students across the United States. The data indicate that prior to the pandemic, students were assigned below-grade-level work about a quarter of the time. During the 2020–2021 school year, that proportion increased to nearly one-third of the time. In schools where most students were from low-income families, students spent 65 percent more time on below-grade-level work than students in predominantly wealthy schools, even when these students demonstrated they could be successful at grade-level work (TNTP, 2022). These findings suggest the circumstances of the pandemic deepened existing inequities in access to grade-level learning.

Unfortunately, assessment data show that the achievement gap also increased for many students. In particular, a working paper titled *Test Score Patterns Across Three COVID-19-Impacted School Years* finds, "Achievement gaps between low- and high-poverty schools widened in elementary grades and gaps increased primarily during the 2020–21 school year" (Kuhfeld, Soland, & Lewis, 2022, p. 7). Additionally, the study reveals significant drops in reading and mathematics data from 2019 to 2021 (Kuhfeld et al., 2022). The first *Nation's Report Card* since the start of the pandemic echoed these results (Mollenkamp, 2022). Compared to the previous report, eighth-grade average mathematics scores dropped by eight points and indicate 38 percent of grade 8 students were performing below the basic achievement level on the National Assessment of Educational Progress. None of the states posted gains in mathematics. Reading scores in grades 4 and 8 declined by three points, with 37 percent of fourth graders scoring below basic level in this area. In addition, the inequity between higher- and lower-performing students widened (Mollenkamp, 2022). The need for acceleration strategies has always been strong, but the pandemic has expanded the number of students not yet at grade level and brought a new level of urgency to acceleration.

When given the opportunity, students—including students from marginalized backgrounds—are just as successful on grade-level work as they are on below-grade-level work (TNTP, 2022).

Students are up to the challenge, but they cannot learn grade-level standards if educators do not give them equitable opportunities to engage in grade-level learning. Equity is important work and requires action, not merely talk. Accelerating learning for all students is equity in action. To be perfectly clear, going backward to move forward is not working for educators or the students they serve. We believe accelerating learning, rather than remediating learning, is the most promising approach for ensuring all students learn at grade level or beyond.

The Shift to Acceleration

In this book, we describe *acceleration* as the systematic process of bringing all student learning to grade level or beyond. The practices that generate accelerated learning are not wholly new; they are built from best practices many teachers and collaborative teams already employ. Acceleration does, however, require shifts in educators' thinking about learning. It demands that educators view students through the lens of assets, not deficits. It calls on the entire school community to build student confidence and efficacy so each student believes in making important and significant progress. Table 1.1 shows some of the shifts schools need to employ acceleration.

TABLE 1.1: Remediation Versus Acceleration

SHIFT FROM . . .	SHIFT TO . . .
Deficit-based instruction	Strengths-based learning
Curriculum-based learning	Student-centered learning
Reviews of previous content before learning any grade-level standards	Instruction on grade-level standards every day, starting on the first day of school
Increased pace to cover more standards	Learning progressions developed for grade-level priority standards
Leveled groups for core instruction	Heterogeneous groups for grade-level priority standards along with differentiation as needed
A focus on coverage and teaching lessons or standards	A diagnostic approach to each unit, standard, and lesson that includes gathering information about student learning and making instructional adjustments as needed with the outcome of grade-level learning

Acceleration focuses on students' strengths or assets, not deficits. Instead of looking at how far away students are from mastery or proficiency, it seeks to find out how close they are based on what they already know. Although it can be difficult to ascertain exactly what a student does and does not understand, each student brings a wealth of experience and knowledge into the classroom. It becomes the teacher's job to connect new learning to what a student already knows. In many cases, teachers can accomplish this by teaching social-emotional learning skills such as empathy for others. For example, when teaching science concepts related to weather (tornadoes, hurricanes, fires, earthquakes, climate change, and so on), a teacher might start by making connections between severe weather events and their impact on peoples' lives.

Activating prior knowledge is essential to acceleration because students are better learners of something new if they can connect to something they already know. One common metric for the power of instructional strategies to generate student growth is *effect size*. According John Hattie (2009, 2012, 2017), an award-winning educational researcher and author, an effect size of 0.4 equates to a year's growth in a year's time, or normal expected growth. Any strategy or practice with an effect size greater than 0.4 means student growth is occurring faster than expected, or accelerating. Linking grade-level learning to prior knowledge has an effect size of 0.98 (Hattie, 2017). Determining what students know and then making connections is central to their learning.

Another important shift for acceleration is from curriculum-centered learning to student-centered learning. Most schools and districts have a set of grade-level and course-specific standards as well as a schedule to follow. Traditionally, teachers have tried to rigidly stick to that schedule to cover the required curriculum before the end of the year. Acceleration paces instruction based on student needs within the grade-level requirements. While teachers still have a plan for the year (such as a proficiency map; see chapter 3, page 33), that plan is a guide, not a prescription for the learning of all students regardless of their specific needs. Teachers must teach the students in their classes. When teachers adjust the curriculum to meet the needs of students, there is less struggle and more learning. This requires a shift to knowing what each student needs, fostering more active learning, and emphasizing differentiation, all while keeping grade-level learning in focus.

As we alluded to at the beginning of the chapter, *acceleration* means starting grade-level or course-specific instruction on day one of class instead of reviewing previous content before beginning the new learning. Many teachers would argue that this is impossible, given that so much of what students need to learn depends on prerequisite skills and learning. We agree! It is *how* teachers deal with prerequisite skills that we take exception to. The best way to approach the recovery of prerequisite skills is to embed the most important concepts students need to know into the current grade-level learning. This is just-in-time instruction teachers provide at the point of need. For example, a fifth-grade mathematics unit on fractions assumes that students have prior knowledge of the third- and fourth-grade fraction standards. As fifth-grade teachers design lessons and units on fractions, they embed review of that prerequisite content into new instruction to fill gaps in students' learning during the unit as needed. This is much more efficient and effective than spending weeks covering missing knowledge at the start of the year only to address the grade-level content months later. Students immediately apply the prior knowledge related to fractions to what they need to know today instead of later in the school year. Rather than hold students back to recover learning, accelerate learning to help students fill in gaps at the point of need.

Educators cannot accomplish acceleration by covering more content even faster. This only results in fewer students learning, deep frustration, and feelings of hopelessness and despair. *Acceleration* means focusing on the most essential standards—*priority standards*. Most districts and schools determine the essential standards for each grade level or course of study. Acceleration requires a deeper dive into this set of essentials to find those most important to learning *at this point in time*.

After teams determine the priority standards, it is important they clearly understand the learning progression of each standard. Teams build a ladder of skills and concepts from least complex to most complex that ensures students learn the standard. Each rung on the ladder represents a grade-level learning target on the way to learning the standard and simultaneously builds prerequisite learning. Teams home in on those concepts and understandings absolutely necessary to move learning forward. Focusing on conceptual understandings that underpin student learning is the key to determining which standards to designate as priority. For example, the concept of place value in mathematics underpins telling time, counting money, calculating with fractions and decimals, and so on. Conceptual thinking allows deeper understanding that transfers across many standards and affects student learning long term.

In a school that uses acceleration, all students engage in grade-level learning every day with differentiation that scaffolds learning by specific needs. This is a strengths-based approach that does not categorize students into ability groups. Tracking or ability-grouping students for general instruction is detrimental; grouping for differentiation on specific learning targets, on the other hand, is helpful.

Again, moving from remediation to acceleration is a shift in mindset. It requires teachers, collaborative teams, schools, and districts to change their current mindsets about how to approach both teaching and learning. It is not about just teaching everything faster. Educators cannot continue following the curriculum schedule and hoping students will catch up or, worse, keeping students behind in retention or remedial classes.

The good news is that teachers already know how to accelerate learning because the practices are not new. It is just a matter of being intentional about how you approach the work of ensuring high levels of learning for all students. In the end, acceleration is a way of thinking about each unit, standard, lesson, and activity diagnostically: What do students know now and what do they need to know to learn the standard?

As collaborative teams address acceleration diagnostically, they answer some of the following questions.

- ▶ What will students need to learn more deeply? What is a priority?
- ▶ What gaps does our team need to fill?
- ▶ How will we connect students' current learning to grade-level standards and content?
- ▶ What is not essential to student success in this unit or lesson?
- ▶ Is this the most effective lesson, activity, or strategy right now?
- ▶ How can we allocate time for learning in the most effective and efficient manner?
- ▶ What level-up strategies will accelerate learning to grade level?

While teams and teachers may already be addressing many of these questions, *how* they answer each one when students are not yet at grade or course level is what requires a shift in mindset, as described in the next section.

Acceleration Strategies Based on New Mindsets

There are six specific mindsets that serve as the foundation for the acceleration strategies we describe in later chapters.

1. Schools and districts are learning organizations.
2. All students can learn grade- and course-level standards.
3. Formative assessment is integral to learning.
4. Schools must systematically intervene to accelerate learning.
5. Instructional strategies should create forward-moving learning.
6. Everyone is a leader of learning.

Mindset One: Schools and Districts Are Learning Organizations

Setting the foundation for acceleration requires everyone to agree on the purpose or mission of their work—*to collectively ensure students learn critical grade-level content.* To accomplish this mission, staff and students alike become learners, creating an organization focused on using inquiry and action research to grow the learning of everyone in the building. The mission to ensure grade- or course-level learning and the process for doing the real work of acceleration is clear to all. As educators implement acceleration strategies, the focus is on learning. Acceleration represents a shift from what teachers teach to what students learn. Teachers can plan and implement a lesson according to all the best teaching practices, but if the students do not learn, it really doesn't matter. Learning must be the intentional outcome of everything done in the classroom.

Schools cannot wait to get everyone on board or to agree. Acceleration cannot wait for everyone to embrace the idea in advance. In our experience, staff buy-in does not often occur before educators implement new programs or initiatives; buy-in usually follows successful implementation. Teachers get on board when they see evidence the new program or initiative works, and the results indicate students are growing to grade-level understanding. When collaborative teams see the connections to the work they already engage in and the progress of their students, their investment in the process will increase.

Figure 1.1 is a planning tool to consider your school's current evidence that learning is required and the evidence you aspire to. The responses in figure 1.1 are examples. Use this discussion tool to reflect on your individual school or district's thinking and next steps.

Directions: For each stakeholder, ask, "What current evidence do we have that learning is required? What data might we gather in the future to show strong evidence that learning is required?"

Stakeholder	Current Evidence That Learning Is Required	Future Evidence to Gather to Show Learning Is Required
Students	Most students attend and participate in class lessons.	All students complete assignments because learning is required, not optional.
Teachers	Collaborative teams have regularly scheduled meetings.	Teams learn together as they use student-assessment data to determine the most effective strategies to ensure learning for all.
Administrators	Administrators focus on organization so teachers can teach.	Administrators focus on learning and act as the lead learners of the school.
Classified Staff	Staff are dependable and take their work seriously.	Staff understand they are part of the learning process and often are the first point of contact for students daily.
Guardians	Guardians are engaged in school meetings and check on their child's progress.	Guardians know learning is required at this school and ensure their child attends and is on time to learn. They frequently ask learning questions.

FIGURE 1.1: Learning is required discussion tool.

*Visit **go.SolutionTree.com/priorityschools** for a free reproducible version of this figure.*

Mindset Two: All Students Can Learn Grade- and Course-Level Standards

Accepting the idea that all students can learn grade- or course-level standards is a challenging mental shift for most educators, given the academic diversity of students in each classroom. It can sometimes be too easy to give excuses for why students might not be learning based on educational labels or outside circumstances, instead of working to ensure every student learns and determining (as a team) how to make that happen.

Of course, it is important for this mindset to translate into real practices in classrooms. One practice that results from a mindset that all students can learn is building strong relationships with students. Strong, positive teacher-student and student-student relationships are among the greatest conditions for learning (Hattie, 2017; Marzano, 2017). Cultivating a community of learners within each classroom and throughout the school needs to be a continuous effort. Furthermore, teachers must share the belief that all students can learn with the students themselves. Student self-efficacy correlates to increasing student achievement. If students believe they can learn and feel capable, achievement increases. In Hattie's (2017) updated list of factors related to student achievement, student self-efficacy has an effect size of 0.92. Students must believe they can handle difficult grade- and course-specific work and be successful. This is essential to engaging students in their learning. Student self-efficacy is often the missing piece in learning. Students *owning* their learning—not just participating in learning—is the key to students accelerating their learning.

Mindset Three: Formative Assessment Is Integral to Learning

Without the information assessments provide, teachers would not be able to re-engage students and support their learning. Diagnostic teaching and learning require information from assessments to target specific student needs and misconceptions.

For too many students and adults, the word *assessment* implies a singular event for the purpose of evaluation and judgment. With acceleration, educators use assessments as part of the learning process and as a way to celebrate learning with students and grow their self-efficacy. But not all assessment practices are equal in promoting learning. A balanced assessment system of both formative and summative assessments is necessary—*formative assessments* for continued teacher and student learning, and *summative assessments* to gather data on learning after instruction. To effectively accelerate learning, teachers and collaborative teams focus on formative assessments that provide information about how to move student learning forward in a timely manner. We address specific formative assessment practices in chapter 4 (page 61). Acceleration occurs when students have frequent opportunities to show what they know through daily check-ins, formative assessments, and unit assessments.

Figure 1.2 is a discussion tool to reflect on how teachers and students currently view assessments in your school.

Mindset Four: Schools Must Systematically Intervene to Accelerate Learning

Students who lack the necessary skills and knowledge required for grade- or course-level learning need a support system that intervenes in a timely manner. Intervention typically involves placing students with similar needs into small groups for targeted instruction. Unfortunately, many schools and districts rely solely on large-scale diagnostic testing at the beginning of the year to determine these needs. Waiting to form intervention groups until *after* beginning-of-the-year

Directions: Answer the following questions individually and then share your answers with one another to discuss.

1. Think of the assessments students take at your school. What is the purpose of each?

2. Which assessments provide the most effective feedback so students can learn from their current thinking and grow?

3. How do students learn from assessments?

4. How do collaborative teacher teams learn from assessments?

5. How scary are assessments to students in your school? Use a scale of 1–10 (1 is not scary and 10 is very scary). Why?

FIGURE 1.2: Assessment discussion tool.

Visit **go.SolutionTree.com/priorityschools** *for a free reproducible version of this figure.*

testing feeds the remediation cycle because the time devoted to testing is subtracted from instruction and delays the response to students' immediate needs.

One strategy to begin accelerating learning at the beginning of the school year is to form small groups of students with like needs using data from the end of the previous year. This allows learning to begin immediately, with no loss of instructional time waiting for additional information. After educators have collected the new data, they can utilize the information to validate or revise the work already in progress. The new data come from diagnostic or high-stakes assessments *and* formative assessments educators give throughout each learning cycle. Both inform the intervention process throughout the year.

Figure 1.3 (page 14) is a discussion tool to brainstorm the data your school could use from the end of one school year to form targeted intervention groups at the start of the next school year.

Mindset Five: Instructional Strategies Should Create Forward-Moving Learning

Instructional strategies that accelerate learning to grade or course level focus on active, fast-paced, hands-on activities that advance learning. The goal is for students to learn on grade or course level with their peers. This contrasts traditional remediation, which focuses on backward movement with the goal for students to catch up to peers. During remediation, instruction focuses on reteaching every missing skill, often in isolation and not applied to current learning.

Directions: Discuss your answers to each question to form a plan for using data from the end of the school year to inform small-group intervention at the beginning of the next school year.

1. What data do you currently collect at the end of the year that give you targeted and specific information to use for small-group intervention learning at the beginning of the next year?

2. What data could you collect at the end of the year (if needed) to give the next grade-level or course educators the information they need to form small groups for intervention at the beginning of the next year?

3. How will you use the data to form the small groups or intervention groups at the beginning of the year?

4. When will you create the small groups or intervention groups for the first day or week of school?

FIGURE 1.3: Intervention discussion tool.

*Visit **go.SolutionTree.com/priorityschools** for a free reproducible version of this figure.*

Acceleration diagnostically selects skills just in time to connect to new learning and applies these skills in the very same lesson. Educators provide prerequisite knowledge just ahead of time in minilessons or microbursts of learning, enabling students to understand new information as the teacher presents it. Acceleration strategies intentionally make each skill and lesson during core instruction relevant. This is a critical component to student motivation and memory: "We learn more effectively when we see how ideas are conceptually connected to one another, when our minds are fully engaged, and when the tasks we encounter are motivating because they are interesting and accessible" (Darling-Hammond, Flook, Cook-Harvey, Barron, & Osher, 2020).

While remediation is typically isolated from core instruction, acceleration is connected to core instruction because teachers embed prerequisite knowledge into each unit and lesson. Through this relevance, instructional practices for acceleration build student self-efficacy and engagement. School is not something done *to* students, it is something done *with* students. You might ask, "Do I address prerequisite knowledge *with* grade-level learning every day, or is learning slowed with full days (especially at the start of the year) focused on prerequisite knowledge?" and "Is the learning of grade-level standards slowed so that not all priority grade-level standards are even an option for students to learn?"

Mindset Six: Everyone Is a Leader of Learning

Leadership really, really matters! No matter how knowledgeable or charismatic a principal is, a single individual can never effectively lead a school alone. Every person in a school is a leader and works to support student learning. The way the leadership communicates and supports learning makes a difference in the success of the students and the school staff. Everyone is all in for *all* students.

Leadership training and school-improvement consultant Jay Westover and former superintendent Christopher Steinhauser (2022) state, "The role then of a leader is to empower and grow the capacity of the group to co-lead improvement efforts and, in doing so, become less relevant and needed for sustaining the most critical work at hand" (p. 55). Each school and district may need to examine its leadership structure to ensure the system is growing leaders with a shared leadership model by teaching and modeling leading the work of acceleration. A leadership team must direct and support the charge. This team guides by example and supports collaborative teacher teams as they implement ongoing cycles of learning. Deeply implementing the work of teams to accelerate learning is the real work. Everyone in a school or district understands that it takes the entire school community to accelerate learning and reach the goal of learning for all.

Conclusion

Each of these mindsets represents a shift away from remediation toward acceleration and increased learning for all students. Shifting to new thinking is the only way to get new results. Educators already know what is not working—now it is time to do something different! Acceleration challenges long-standing thinking, assumptions, and past practices, which are often barriers to moving forward. A lack of action is part of the problem. As educators wait to change peoples' minds, more students are getting further and further behind. The remaining chapters of this book present strategies you can implement to begin accelerating learning now. This is a call to action!

Discussion Questions for Reflection and Action

As a team, discuss the following questions. Visit **go.SolutionTree.com/priorityschools** for a free reproducible version of these questions.

- ▶ What is acceleration and why is it necessary?
- ▶ What are the key differences between *remediation* and *acceleration*?
- ▶ What about the current mindset and culture of your school and district community need to change?
- ▶ How do the current practices of your teachers, collaborative teams, leadership team, students, and community members support acceleration?
- ▶ Which mindset will be most easy to shift? Why?
- ▶ Which mindset will be most challenging to shift? Why?

CHAPTER 2

Culture That Accelerates Learning

Sharon was seated on an airplane, traveling to a school in a different state to coach collaborative teams. As is often the case, the departure was delayed. After what seemed like an eternity, the pilot announced it was finally time to begin the trip. He explained to passengers that because of the delay, an on-time arrival at their destination was doubtful. But what he said next made Sharon want to stand up and applaud! The pilot stated that to avoid the tardy arrival, he had used his knowledge of geometry to determine a different flightpath that would make up the time of the delay. While she was delighted to arrive on time, the real reason Sharon was elated was because the pilot mentioned the importance of geometry in solving the flight-delay problem. He clearly understood that the purpose of his geometry class was to solve real-world difficulties such as delayed flights.

Learning is an ongoing, never-ending process not just in schools but also in life. The purpose or mission of schools is learning. However, as we travel throughout the United States and meet with educators and students, the purpose of schools is not always clear. In fact, if you ask individuals about the purpose of school, their answers vary.

If you ask typical high school students, "What is the purpose of going to school?" they might say it's to graduate and move on, or to see friends, or to participate in sports, music, clubs, or other activities. If you ask teachers, "Why do students take algebra as freshmen in high school?" the answer is usually that it is a required course. Rarely does the answer focus on the importance of algebra to students' learning or life. Such answers reveal the belief that the purpose of school is to reach the next grade level and eventually graduate. While graduation may be a goal so students can pursue their dreams, the real purpose of school is *learning*. Graduation is simply a celebration that follows the K–12 learning experience. A culture of learning is evident when students and teachers alike focus on learning every day.

The Shift to a Culture of Learning

Schools and districts are learning organizations, which means the purpose of schooling is learning. As such, learning must be required. Learning cannot be optional or happen accidentally or incidentally. The entire school and district must become a learning community that lives its purpose (DuFour et al., 2016). To clarify their purpose and describe their future,

> Learning is not attained by chance, it must be sought for with ardor and attended to with diligence.
>
> —ABIGAIL ADAMS

many schools and districts spend a great deal of time developing their mission and vision statements. In fact, some schools take up to a full year to gather input and craft their mission and vision statements. Often, the school or district partners with community stakeholders, which is an important process that creates a sense of community and gives voice to others. Although this can be a lengthy process, it doesn't need to be. In any case, the result is a mission statement that describes *why* the school exists and a vision statement that outlines the school's *desired future*. We believe the mission of a school or district is obviously *learning* and the vision is related to *more students learning more*. The mission statement answers the question, "Why do we exist?" while the vision statement answers the question, "What must we become to accomplish our fundamental purpose?" (DuFour et al., 2016, p. 39).

Just developing a mission and proclaiming it is merely a structural change. Unfortunately, structural changes without cultural changes amount to little change, if any at all. The value in a purpose or mission statement is not that one exists, but that it is clear to everyone and lived on campus. If the school truly requires learning, then what does it look like, sound like, and feel like? What specific actions does it require of students, teachers, administrators, parents, and community members? The mission must be more than a poster on the wall or a statement on the school's website; it must become part of the culture.

According to Kent D. Peterson (2002), professor emeritus of educational leadership and policy analysis at University of Wisconsin-Madison, "School culture is the set of norms, values, and beliefs, rituals, ceremonies, symbols, and stories that make up the 'persona' of the school" (p. 10). If the mission is *Learning is required*, the stories the school shares, the norms it puts in place, and the celebrations it conducts all reflect learning—both for students and staff. Additionally, acceleration would be an integral part of the school's culture to ensure the learning of every student.

A school with a strong learning culture knows its purpose, and educators within it actively collaborate to reach and celebrate goals. Teachers and students alike strive to learn, respect one another in the process, and celebrate their learning with one another. Table 2.1 shows some of the shifts schools need to develop a culture of learning that is lived, rather than simply written on paper.

The good news is there are specific and targeted strategies to create the learning-centered culture foundational to accelerating learning. The rest of this chapter describes specific cultural practices that move the entire organization to live its purpose of *learning is required*.

Cultural Practices to Accelerate Learning

To accelerate learning, the many stakeholders central to a school's success have critical roles in the process. Each stakeholder embraces actions designed to grow the culture of the school so anyone stepping on campus *feels* and *knows* the school is focused on its mission of learning. We share several of those actions in the following sections.

Students Co-Create Learning Contracts

In a school that requires learning, the role of the students is to partner with their teachers and classmates in the learning process. This partnership goes beyond just completing assignments on time. It manifests itself in active participation in the learning process. One way students and teachers can develop expectations for engagement and participation is to co-create learning contracts that describe the behaviors that will enhance learning.

A *learning contract* is an agreement between the students and the teacher. The contract specifies concrete behaviors that constitute the norms for learning. When students co-create learning contracts, they become inherently more involved in their own education, and the learning process

TABLE 2.1: Shifts to Develop a Culture of Learning

SHIFT FROM . . .	SHIFT TO . . .
Treating learning as optional	Treating learning as required
Existing as a school or district	Being a learning organization
Writing mission and vision statements and simply posting or storing them	Creating mission and vision statements that are lived on campus and focused on ensuring every student learns at high levels
Creating small SMART goals (Conzemius & O'Neill, 2014) with action plans that educators seldom, if ever, review or use	Creating stretch SMART goals and action plans that educators routinely monitor for effectiveness
Assigning work below grade or course level	Assigning work at grade level with scaffolding and strategic minilessons of previous content if needed
Telling students how to behave on campus, often by telling them what *not* to do	Teaching students how to behave on campus using clear expectations and intervention if needed
Allowing teachers to work in isolation with their own assigned students	Supporting teachers to work in collaborative teams to create learning cycles and taking collective responsibility for student learning (DuFour et al., 2016)
Telling students how to behave in class and what to learn	Co-creating with students classroom expectations and learning targets that provide a purpose for lessons
Needing administrators to rush from one urgent managerial matter to the next all day	Prioritizing what needs to be accomplished each day so administrators can focus on learning
Continuing a culture where guardians and community members are uninvolved or less knowledgeable about school	Inviting guardians and community members to be part of the school culture with high expectations and pride
Showcasing only clubs and athletics through symbols and artifacts	Reflecting the importance of learning as well as extracurricular experiences through symbols and artifacts

Source: Adapted from DuFour et al., 2016.

becomes more self-directed and reciprocal. This process builds a learning culture in each class-room that permeates the entire school. In addition, the responsibility teachers give to students as they engage in developing the learning contract very often increases motivation and accelerates learning (Greenwood & McCabe, 2008).

The process of co-creating learning contracts begins by discussing how people learn best and rec-ognizing one person may learn differently from another. To demonstrate, teachers can model their own personal learning styles and the way they enhance their learning. For example, a teacher might share that many individuals like to listen to music while they learn, but, for her, it is often more difficult to comprehend what she is reading if she is also listening to music. After further discussion and examples, students then write down the ways they learn best, then discuss their responses in small groups. The whole-class discussion that follows focuses on the following questions.

- ▶ Do we all learn in the same way?
- ▶ Do we all learn at the exact same time?
- ▶ Do individuals know a lot about some things and less about others?
- ▶ Do we all need to learn the same grade-level or course content this year?
- ▶ How can we ensure *all of us* will learn and be prepared for the next step toward crossing the same finish line?

As students begin to realize that people learn differently and at different rates, it becomes apparent that to learn together, the class must create the learning culture and environment by clarifying the behaviors needed for this to happen.

The next step is to engage students in thinking about the specific ways learning will occur during lessons. Most classrooms employ three types of instructional models: whole-group discussions, small-group work, and independent learning time. These may look different in elementary classrooms, high school science classrooms, or elective classes such as physical education and art, to name a few. The most important question for students to consider is, "How do you learn best in each of these settings in each class?" As students brainstorm how they learn best in whole-group discussions, small-group work, and independent learning, record their answers in positive language by category. These become the behavior agreements, or learning contracts, to which the class agrees to adhere so all students can learn and begin to shape their learning identities. Figure 2.1 is an example of a learning contract created with student input.

Whole-Group Discussion
We learn best when . . .
• We have some think time before the teacher asks a student to respond
• No one shouts out the answers
• The teacher calls on several students for a response so we can think about each answer
• Student-to-student talk is a part of the discussion
Small-Group Work
We learn best when . . .
• We can hear one another in our group
• We talk loud enough so our group can hear us but not so loud that other groups hear us
• Everyone participates and contributes to the work
• We understand the directions
• We know the best way to get answers to our questions if we are stuck
Independent Work
We learn best when . . .
• It is quiet
• We understand the work and know what it should look like when we finish
• We know how to get help if we are stuck or have a question
• We help one another and are not concerned with being the first one finished

FIGURE 2.1: Sample learning contract.

After the class creates a learning contract (with clearly defined behavior expectations for learning), the teacher posts it in a prominent place in the classroom and reviews the behavior agreements before engaging students in each of the learning settings. In addition, students must indicate their agreement to the behaviors by signing their own individual contract or the poster of classroom behaviors.

If teachers require learning, then they must teach students learning behaviors, not just expect them. A learning contract serves the same purpose as establishing classroom rules and routines. Traditionally, a teacher would just post a list of classroom rules (and warnings) and then spend a few minutes reading them aloud. Learning contracts that students co-create and commit to will take more time (although less than one full class period or block of time). However, it is worth taking this valuable instructional time because students need learning contracts to accelerate learning. When students understand how to behave in various instructional models, they can actively engage in learning and close gaps. They create a learning culture.

Teachers Engage and Learn in Collaborative Teams

In a learning-focused school, learning is required not just for students but also for the adults within the organization. Teachers partner with their students and colleagues to learn together. This means teachers work in collaborative teams to learn together and build shared knowledge and understanding. PLC experts and coauthors Richard DuFour, Rebecca DuFour, Robert Eaker, Thomas W. Many, and Mike Mattos (2016) identify the *collaborative team* as the engine of school improvement in the PLC process. They identify common team structures that include grade-level teams, course-specific teams, and vertical teams (DuFour et al., 2016). Teachers work together to make sense of the standards, assess student learning, and deeply investigate student data and information to determine the best strategies for students to learn more across the grade level or course. Teams answer four learning questions in recurring learning cycles, as figure 2.2 shows.

Critical Question One: What do we want all students to know and be able to do?
• Determine the priority standards and create a proficiency map (pacing guide) for the year.   • Unwrap the priority standards.   • Use a calendar to create a unit plan including when teachers will give assessments and when the team will respond to the data and information.
Critical Question Two: How will we know if they learned it?
• Create team common formative assessments to administer in a cycle of ten teaching days or less.   • Determine team scoring agreements and how teachers will administer the assessment.   • Complete a data-analysis protocol to determine trends in student work to create a team-targeted intervention and extension plan.
Critical Question Three: How will we respond when some students do not learn?   **Critical Question Four: How will we extend the learning for students who are already proficient?**
• Create a team response to target trends in the assessment by individual student and specific need.   • Extend the learning for students who demonstrate proficiency by including non-priority or nice-to-know standards or extend the thinking of the current priority standards with specific activities.

Source: Adapted from DuFour et al., 2016.

FIGURE 2.2: Work of teams in recurring learning cycles.

Visit go.SolutionTree.com/priorityschools for a free reproducible version of this figure.

As teams work through each learning cycle, their attention focuses on how to accelerate the learning for students who still need to develop certain prerequisite skills. Teachers collaborate to identify and embed specific prerequisite skills that lead to grade-level learning of priority standards in each unit, rather than teach all the prior-knowledge standards at the beginning of the year before addressing grade-level learning in learning cycles.

Learning cycles are results oriented. The focus on results forces teams to identify students by name and need in order to relentlessly attend to next steps when students do not learn, and achieve the teams' collective responsibility of learning for all (DuFour et al., 2016). Teams do not waste time on excuses; instead, their time is spent on action and next steps, creating a learning-focused culture. As teams engage in this work, they are never satisfied until all students have learned.

Administrators Stay Focused on Learning

In a learning-focused culture, the district and school create *guiding coalitions* or *learning teams* to lead the mission of learning (DuFour et al., 2016; see chapter 7, page 129). The role of these teams and the administrators on them is to build the capacity of the staff to effect positive change. Leaders utilize everyone in the building to raise the levels of achievement for all students. Not just any leader can improve a school or district, particularly an underperforming or priority school. It takes leaders who can harness the power within to improve the school or district. This most often means accelerating the learning of both staff and students.

Principals and superintendents are pulled in many directions every day. It is easy to get distracted and put aside the most important work of school improvement. Leaders must be intentional about what they focus on since what the leader focuses on is exactly what everyone in the school and district will focus on as well. Teachers don't have to wonder for long what matters at their schools or in their districts. They can tell by what leaders celebrate, what leaders confront, what leaders discuss or ask questions about, what leaders pay for, and how leaders spend their time. If the leaders are focused on learning, then the staff and students will concern themselves with learning too. The leaders must focus, focus, focus on the things that matter most! Figure 2.3 shows a planning tool leaders can use for focusing on learning.

Because schools and districts are learning organizations, their sole purpose or mission is to ensure high levels of learning for all students (DuFour et al., 2016). Leaders establish and reinforce a commitment to learning. This focus requires leadership at all levels to become the *lead learners* in the organization. In the role of lead learners, leaders create the foundation and supports to accelerate learning. Leaders promote a culture of learning by immersing themselves in learning with teachers. Leaders set the tone and example for a learning organization.

Parents and Community Members Shift Their Thinking to Learning

In a learning-focused school, parents or guardians and community members adopt the mindset of *learning is required*—often a shift in thinking for these stakeholders. The teachers, administrators, and students need to model a focus on learning so parents or guardians understand the specific actions important for them to undertake. The rationale must be clear and reinforced, often at the point of need. For example, students whose parents or guardians frequently drop them off at school late interrupt learning in the classroom and miss critical learning themselves. If learning is the focus, the person admitting late students to class must explain the rationale to the parents or guardians, as in the following example:

Directions: Reflect on the following questions to make a leadership plan focused on learning.

1. How will you routinely engage in classroom walkthroughs? How many classrooms will you visit each week?

2. How will teachers get formative feedback on their instruction?

3. When will you expect collaborative teams to meet each week (for at least one hour)? How will you monitor the work of collaborative teams and provide feedback to teams?

4. How often will the guiding coalition or learning team meet? How will you ensure team members focus on leading learning at each meeting?

5. When will you meet with your administrative team or instructional learning team (instructional coaches) each week?

6. When during the week will you address questions 1–5? Put each learning-focused action on a weekly planner.

7. How will your actions and conversations show staff and community members your relentless commitment to learning?

FIGURE 2.3: Administrator learning-focus planning tool.

*Visit **go.SolutionTree.com/priorityschools** for a free reproducible version of this figure.*

At our school, learning is required, so it is important for your child to arrive on time. When students miss the beginning of class, they miss the focus for the day and the directions and spend a great deal of time just trying to catch up. I know it is difficult to get everyone in a household up and running in the morning, but if you could please try to get here a little earlier, it will make a big difference for your child.

There are many other scenarios that offer the opportunity to model and support the mission of *learning is required* with parents and guardians, such as parent mathematics or reading nights, parent-teacher conferences, and opportunities to discuss why it is so important students work in class or at home on assignments to practice their learning.

Community members can also help to build a learning-centered culture. However, community members need a flow of positive information about the school. Consider the following questions.

- ▶ **What is good about your school or district?** For example, showcase the learning happening in the classroom with pictures and videos. Highlight the work of collaborative teams taking collective responsibility for student learning. Recognize the extracurricular activities students engage in.

- ▶ **What celebrations (large and small) can you share?** Think about where the school or district was a year ago and the improvements since then. Identify what to celebrate related to teacher, team, and student learning. Identify celebrations related to the school environment and behaviors students, teachers, and staff exhibit. Celebrate when community members engage in school activities.

- ▶ **What community groups can help you build this positive culture?** Make a list of community groups in your area. Consider which ones can provide students with the basic necessities so they can learn in school. Consider which ones can provide tutoring support or guest speakers to show students the options they have after graduation. Identify which ones might lend monetary support for field trips and other learning activities.

- ▶ **What businesses can you invite to see the good things happening in your school?** Identify the local businesses that contribute to the livelihood of the community. Consider how to invite their leaders or representatives in to view special projects, contribute as guest speakers, and celebrate student learning at assemblies or other events.

- ▶ **What role do real estate agents play in supporting schools?** Real estate agents interact with many new and potential community members. If these agents only know the end-of-year assessment data and school rating, then those are the only data they can share with clients. Tell your own story of success by making public other indicators that are true measures of your success, such as the number of students on the honor roll, obtaining industry certifications for future careers, enrolled in advanced placement (AP) classes, or engaged in community service.

Build a profile that highlights everything happening to ensure all students are learning. The few data points usually made public do not show community members a complete picture of a school or district, which they need to see if they are to support the school or district's mission. Show how students are growing in their learning and more students are learning grade- or course-level standards through intentional acceleration. Don't just tell a different version of the same story, tell and show a different story to anyone who will listen.

Symbols and Artifacts Show Learning Is Required

Symbols and artifacts in a school communicate meaning and define culture. Consider the meaning attached to a school logo. When anyone sees the logo on a letterhead, website, sweatshirt, or sign at the front of the building, what feelings or thoughts does it evoke? The emotions that symbols and artifacts elicit among community members contribute to the school's current and desired culture. A school's culture is reflected in what people see and hear throughout the school. Is there current grade-level student work on the walls? Are the learning spaces and hallways clean and inviting for learning? Are classroom walls supporting learning with anchor charts? Are book covers showcased to raise curiosity about reading? Are posters supporting learning? These are just a few artifacts to look for in a learning-focused culture.

Figure 2.4 (page 26) shows a template for a *symbol and artifact walk*. The intent of this activity is to raise staff's level of awareness of the messages the school sends to all who enter the building. Once teachers and administrators recognize these messages, they can be intentional about building the culture they desire. This activity is particularly effective if, before beginning the walk, participating teachers and administrators describe what they expect to see around the school. During the walk, participants should record the symbols and artifacts they see in various locations on campus in the chart under the first question (see figure 2.4, page 26). After the walk, the teachers and administrators address questions 2 and 3 to collectively acknowledge what messages are being communicated through the symbols and artifacts they observed and make a plan to communicate the message of a learning-centered culture.

At one school where we conducted the symbol and artifact walk, the teachers said they expected it would be obvious during the walk that the school culture revolved around students. They expected to see student work samples hanging up as evidence of this. As the teachers walked around the building, this focus was evident. However, the message the artifacts sent was not exactly what they had hoped; the student work samples were from September and it was now March. If the culture were truly about celebrating students and their work, the samples would reflect *current* accomplishments. This simple process gave way to a robust discussion about the symbols and artifacts needed to support a culture of *learning is required*.

At another school, a middle school, a television in the waiting room of the front office showed various images from the campus. The mission statement appeared followed by many pictures; a few pictures showed clubs and sports teams, but most of the pictures showed the learning process. There were pictures of students engaging in a science lab, working in groups on a mathematics task, reading books, helping other students in class, and drawing maps, to name a few. On the table were pamphlets sharing the mission of the school and the priority standards every student would learn by course. On the walls were student work samples and celebrations. The secretary happily greeted everyone who entered the office. These symbols and artifacts reflect a positive, learning-focused culture. Any parent, community member, or student would be excited and proud to attend such a school.

SMART Goals Are Audaciously Attainable

To create a learning-centered culture, schools and districts set goals that are meaningful for everyone and make action plans for how to achieve those goals. Schools and districts conduct this process every year as they review external assessment data, such as data from state tests. When learning is required, schools and districts continue to set schoolwide goals using external

Symbol and Artifact Walk

1. Walk around your school and observe the symbols and artifacts contributing to its story. Document your findings in the following section.

Location	What Do You See?	What Do You Hear?
School entryway		
Main office		
Hallways		
Traditional classrooms		
Library		
Cafeteria		
Bus drop-off area		
Computer lab		
Other: _____		
Other: _____		

2. What percentage of visual images supports or reflects the following items?

Academic Learning	Arts	Sports or Activities	Behavior Expectations

3. What contributes to your vision of culture and what needs to be changed?

What Positive Symbols and Artifacts Should Remain?	What Symbol and Artifact Modifications Do You Suggest?

Source: Kramer & Schuhl, 2017, pp. 35–36.

FIGURE 2.4: Symbol and artifact walk recording sheet.

Visit go.SolutionTree.com/priorityschools for a free reproducible version of this figure.

assessment data but challenge themselves to create stretch goals. Teams also set short-term goals to measure and celebrate progress throughout the school year. Monitoring progress toward goals the teachers, teams, schools, and districts create is an ongoing, integral part of creating a learning-centered culture.

To write meaningful goals related to student learning, the district, school, and teams write SMART goals. The *SMART* acronym describes the characteristics of an effective goal (Conzemius & O'Neill, 2014).

▶ **Strategic and specific:** The goal clearly names how and when educators will measure student learning, as well as the specific percentage of students proficient or higher educators expect in the current year compared to the previous year.

▶ **Measurable:** Teams can easily gather the data they need to determine whether or not they met their goals.

▶ **Attainable:** While every teacher wants 100 percent of students to be successful, teachers look at their current reality and set a goal they can reach if—*and only if*—they intentionally work as a collaborative team.

▶ **Results oriented:** The goal relates to student learning results.

▶ **Time bound:** For acceleration, the time frame for goal achievement is one school year or shorter.

Schools and teams may talk about two types of SMART goals: (1) program goals and (2) cohort goals. Use *program goals* to grow learning in a grade level or course from year to year. For example, a tenth-grade English language arts (ELA) team might set a program SMART goal for their current students' learning using the end-of-year state assessment data from the previous tenth graders. The program goal's focus is teachers building their collective teacher efficacy in a way that improves student learning in their grade level or course, regardless of the students who enter the program.

Cohort goals relate to specific groups of students and move through the grade levels with them. A cohort goal for a fifth-grade team would involve looking at data from the fourth-grade end-of-year state assessment and setting a goal for those same students in their fifth-grade year. There is less teacher accountability with cohort goals since the focus is on students. Acceleration uses program goals while referencing data for a cohort goal the previous year as part of the final determination of the program goal.

Once districts and schools create goals, teams of teachers look at proficiency and growth data from the previous year to create SMART goals for their programs. First, each team reviews results from the previous year to determine the effect of their instructional plan and consider the following questions.

▶ How well did students do on the priority standards taught the previous year?

▶ If students did not learn the priority standards, why?

The teacher team pores over the information to improve the results for the upcoming year by adjusting the curriculum, instructional practices, or pacing of the content. This review does not necessarily focus on individual students because these students have moved on to the next grade level or course.

Next, each team investigates the cohort data for their new students for the upcoming year or semester. During this time, teams answer two important questions: (1) Who are our learners? and (2) What are their needs? As teams work through this process, they set SMART goals for the upcoming year.

The traditional practice for districts, schools, and teacher teams has been to increase program goals by 5 to 10 percentage points each year. This is small incremental change. In a school of five hundred students, 5 percent is twenty-five students and 10 percent is fifty students. In a classroom of thirty students, a 5- to 10-percent increase amounts to only two or three students. In a school or district that has a significant number of students who are not yet proficient, such small goals do not work to ensure learning for all students.

An example of seventh-grade reading data teams use to create a typical safe goal looks like figure 2.5. Even if this seventh-grade team meets its goal of increasing students who are proficient or above by 10 percent, 62 percent (or nearly two-thirds of the seventh-grade class) will not be proficient with grade-level reading. At this rate, many students will need to remain in school beyond their expected graduation date or may never read proficiently. This attainable and safe goal usually amounts to some students learning, but not nearly enough.

Grade-Level Reading Data

Reading	Far Below Proficiency	Approaching Proficiency	Proficient	Exceeds Proficiency
Seventh Grade	42%	30%	24%	4%

Students scoring proficient or exceeds proficiency: 24% + 4% = 28%

10% increase: 28% + 10% = 38%

SMART goal: In the current school year, the number of seventh-grade students scoring proficient or exceeds proficiency on the state reading assessment will increase by 10%, from 28% to 38%.

FIGURE 2.5: Safe SMART goal example.

Acceleration requires that goals be audaciously attainable, not just safely attainable. How can schools and teams set SMART goals that reflect high expectations and still make them attainable? Teams, teachers, and students need to believe they can reach increased levels of achievement not just because they want it to happen but also because the data indicate it can happen. To accelerate learning, educators shift their mindset from how *far* students are from proficiency to how *close* they are. They shift from *deficit thinking* to *strengths-based thinking*. Deficit thinking instills a sense of failure. When this shift to strengths-based thinking happens, it is possible to create audaciously attainable goals, not just safe goals.

Most assessments report data in four categories similar to those in figure 2.5 (far below proficiency, approaching proficiency, proficient, and exceeds proficiency); *the approaching proficiency category is the zone of opportunity*. This category represents students who may have been just a skill or concept away from being proficient. These students could score in the proficient or exceeds proficiency categories in the following year. Consider the audaciously attainable goal for the same seventh-grade reading data in figure 2.6.

Grade-Level Reading Data

Reading	Far Below Proficiency	Approaching Proficiency	Proficient	Exceeds Proficiency
Seventh Grade	42%	30%	24%	4%

Approaching proficiency + proficient + exceeds proficiency = audacious goal

Students scoring proficient or exceeds proficiency: 24% + 4% = 28%

Moving students from approaching proficiency to proficiency or above: 28% + 30% = 58%

SMART Goal: In the current school year, the number of seventh-grade students scoring proficient or exceeds proficiency on the state reading assessment will increase by 30%, from 28% to 58%.

FIGURE 2.6: Audaciously attainable SMART goal example.

Audaciously attainable goals do not only focus on the students in the zone of opportunity. These goals raise the bar for *all* students as teams and teachers work to move all students to the next level up. Teams may also want to set a goal to reduce the percentage of students who are far below proficiency, meaning move them to approaching proficiency or higher. In essence, teams monitor growth across all levels.

In addition, teams should set goals and monitor progress for specific populations such as special education students, English learners, and high-proficiency students. Teams use the same process of using the percentage of students in the zone of opportunity (approaching proficiency category) for each student population to identify an audaciously attainable goal. In the example in figure 2.7 (page 30), the target for the special education students is 63 percent, for English learners it is 68 percent, and for high-proficiency learners it is 94 percent. Teams monitor the learning of all students (as well as diverse student populations) throughout the year on common assessments to ensure all students are growing in their learning to proficiency and to check on equitable practices.

As teams engage in this process of creating audaciously attainable goals, they identify which specific students fall into each category (far below proficiency, approaching proficiency, proficient, and exceeds proficiency). Teachers begin to name and claim the students who are far below proficiency and approaching proficiency. They understand who these students are and can describe their needs. This translates to big and small adjustments teachers make regularly to meet the diverse needs of their students. It can mean that teachers develop seating charts with preferential seating for students who need a little more support to understand a lesson. It can result in teachers checking in with certain students to ensure they understand an activity or assignment before they start the work. It can mean small-group minilessons for those students who need help with vocabulary to fully understand the learning target.

Schools and teams that adopt a learning-centered culture track progress on student learning throughout the school year. The example data tracker (or data board) in figure 2.8 (page 31) allows teams to monitor progress on audaciously attainable SMART goals as students take assessments over the course of the year. This example refers to external assessments such as annual state exams (the basis for the goal), ACT or SAT, AP exams, and interim assessments to measure progress at designated points throughout the year, which might be progress-monitoring tests

Ninth-Grade Mathematics			
	Special Education Learners	**English Learners**	**High-Proficiency Learners**
Exceeds Proficiency	7%	14%	64%
Proficient	14%	16%	18%
Approaching Proficiency	42%	38%	12%
Far Below Proficiency	37%	32%	6%
Proficient + Exceeds Proficiency	21%	30%	82%
Goal	63%	68%	94%

FIGURE 2.7: Audaciously attainable goals for diverse populations.

or district- or teacher-created assessments such as quarter, midterm, or semester exams. This is a check on the overall goal with an opportunity to adjust the goal as students grow. Classroom teachers can utilize a similar form to check in on each common formative and summative assessment to ensure students are learning and will reach the desired goal.

Teachers discuss and learn strategies to accelerate student learning and create an action plan to achieve their audaciously attainable SMART goals while learning about their students. They look for celebrations after each assessment throughout the year, as well as how to incorporate prior-knowledge skills into grade-level instruction (see chapter 3, page 33, and chapter 5, page 87). SMART goals allow celebrations to grow the cultural belief that all students can learn priority standards to grade level and support the mission that learning is required.

Conclusion

Acceleration is forward movement. Stepping forward into growth happens when the school culture is healthy and the focus is on learning. In such a culture, acceleration thrives. All stakeholders reflect on their purpose and take action to live out the learning-centered mission of the school and district and to show that learning is required.

Schools are learning communities in which everyone is a teacher, everyone is a learner, and everyone is a leader. A school that accelerates learning has structures in place to support the learning of students and teachers alike. The entire school community believes it is possible for all students to reach high levels of learning and sets audaciously attainable goals they can work together to accomplish. This creates a culture of learning and celebration—the foundation of acceleration. It is time to move forward into growth with confidence and determination.

Subject:

Grade	External Assessment	SMART Goal	Interim Assessment 1	Incremental Goal	Interim Assessment 2	Incremental Goal	Interim Assessment 3	External Assessment
Grade ___								
Grade ___								
Grade ___								
Grade ___								
Grade ___								
Grade ___								

FIGURE 2.8: SMART goal data board.

Visit go.SolutionTree.com/priorityschools for a free reproducible version of this figure.

Discussion Questions for Reflection and Action

As a team, discuss the following questions. Visit **go.SolutionTree.com/priorityschools** for a free reproducible version of these questions.

- ▶ What evidence indicates learning is required in your school and district?

- ▶ Do the school's current mission and vision statements communicate that *learning is required*? If not, what revisions are needed?

- ▶ What are the classroom norms, procedures, and routines to implement to support a learning-centered culture?

- ▶ What specific actions exemplify and support the mission of the school or district?

- ▶ Does your symbol and artifact walk show that learning is the focus? Discuss the evidence.

- ▶ Do all staff have high expectations for students and believe that they are the key to increased student learning? How do you know?

- ▶ How well do students, teachers, administrators, parents, and community members understand their role in promoting the mission?

- ▶ What characteristics make our SMART goals audaciously attainable? If they are too safe, what changes will make them audaciously attainable?

- ▶ How do teams establish SMART goals for different student populations to ensure every student learns?

CHAPTER 3

Priority Standards and Learning Cycles That Accelerate Learning

When Sarah first taught geometry, she quickly realized she needed to ask students which Algebra 1 teacher they had the previous school year. It mattered. Some students' learning stopped at systems of equations, others at quadratics, and still others at exponential functions. With every best intent, teachers made independent pacing and instructional decisions about what students could learn. As such, some students learned all the expected standards in Algebra 1 and others only partially learned Algebra 1—yet all earned course credit. Neither the students nor the geometry teachers the following year were set up for learning or teaching success at the start of the year. The Algebra 1 teachers had each worked hard individually instead of working collaboratively to collectively address student learning. The Algebra 1 teachers (at the time) did not provide equitable learning experiences for all students, nor did they ensure students learned course-level standards. They did not operate with a guaranteed and viable curriculum or a plan to teach priority standards to every student.

Accelerating student learning requires yearlong, unit-by-unit, and daily instructional plans. Without intentional plans, students may not even be given the opportunity to learn critical grade-level standards, which expands learning gaps and requires even more acceleration in later years. Time may be lost reviewing prerequisite skills at the start of the year that are not needed until much later, only to have to reteach them again later in the year. Opportunities for differentiation and small-group learning may be squandered during lessons. And some students in need of extension may never be challenged. Without a clear plan of what students will learn and when, teachers create inequities across a grade level or course.

Collaborative teams work backward from year-end expectations to craft a proficiency map that focuses on priority grade-level standards, unpack the priority standards to define grade-level expectations for proficiency, and design common assessments and effective lessons. With only about 180 school days in a school year, how should teachers pace and focus lessons?

For students to learn grade- or course-level standards, the teaching of those standards must begin on the first day of the school year. Yet, teaching grade- or course-level standards

> A goal without a plan is just a wish.
>
> —Antoine de Saint-Exupéry

can be difficult when most students (or even a few students) are demonstrating significant gaps in their learning. Daily classroom instruction is vital to students accelerating learning from prior-knowledge standards to grade- or course-level standards along a learning progression. If surprises are revealed during learning, changes are more navigable when there is a plan in place that teachers can adjust.

Collaborative teams learn more deeply about what students must know and be able to do as they plan for student learning unit by unit throughout the year (the subject of this chapter) and create common assessments to provide feedback to the team and students (see chapter 4, page 61). Teachers on the team then use their plans and evidence of learning to create daily lessons that include acceleration strategies designed to engage students in grade- or course-level standards every day (see chapter 5, page 87). Together, these chapters share a blueprint for creating the time and intentional lessons educators need to close student learning gaps through acceleration and ensure every student learns the identified grade- or course-level standards. This is equity in action and how teams contribute to a culture of learning.

The Shift to Focusing on Priority Standards and Learning Cycles

At the start of the school year, teachers and teams make decisions about what to teach and when—whether or not there is a district proficiency map. Within the first few days of school, teachers draw conclusions about how ready students are to learn grade-level standards and proceed accordingly. When gaps exist in student learning, too often the response is to go back and reteach earlier course- or grade-level content before addressing current grade-level content. This practice often puts students further and further behind. Additionally, valuable time for grade-level instruction is lost. As described in chapter 1 (page 5), the approach of slowing down until students are successful only leads to larger and larger learning gaps, which is why we advocate teaching grade-level standards using acceleration strategies to bring students up to the grade-level expectation. There is a need to have teachers work in collaborative teams to ensure every student learns grade-level priority standards so they can be successful from one year to the next.

Some curriculum-planning strategies are more productive than others when working to accelerate student learning to grade level or higher. Table 3.1 shows the key shifts in planning approaches teachers need to close achievement gaps. When remediation is the norm, teachers focus on everything students have *not* learned and it feels overwhelming. How can they ever hope to teach grade-level standards? Instead, teams can shift to focusing on what is most critical for students to learn in a grade level or course and accelerate learning to those standards using asset-based approaches that begin with recognizing what students have already learned.

Acceleration Strategies for Priority Standards and Learning Cycles

The pressure to teach every current grade-level standard to students in one school year when students have not mastered prior grade-level standards is daunting. The National Council of Teachers of Mathematics (NCTM) and National Council of Supervisors of Mathematics (NCSM, 2020) share:

> Educators should view students in terms of their strengths, not weaknesses, and avoid the urge to immediately reteach all the skills we think students should have learned before arriving at school this fall. It is more productive for teachers to think of learning opportunities that are most important for students in relation to the mathematics learning progressions. (p. 7)

TABLE 3.1: Shifts in Planning to Accelerate Student Learning

SHIFT FROM . . .	SHIFT TO . . .
Reteaching prior knowledge for several weeks at the beginning of the school year before teaching any grade-level standards	Embedding prior knowledge into relevant units and teaching prerequisite content *with* grade-level content
Following a district proficiency map (pacing guide) or textbook and teaching only at grade level, without addressing missing prior knowledge	Choosing lessons that match priority standards to provide time to teach prior knowledge according to student needs
Trying to teach every standard in a grade level or course and getting as far as possible each year based on student ability	Prioritizing standards so students have time to learn the most important content thoroughly
Slowing down to make sure all students learn without consideration for impacts on later units	Developing a proficiency map to teach each priority standard during a set time frame and determining as a team how to utilize classroom instruction and intervention time to support learning without falling behind pace

This is true across all content areas and means collaborative teams need to clarify what is most critical for students to learn and then devise strategies for having students learn those standards at grade level (see chapter 5, page 87), which will begin to close achievement gaps.

When teams plan for accelerating student learning with clear priority standards, an intentional proficiency map, and units with full learning cycles, they are answering the first critical PLC question, What do we want students to know and be able to do? (DuFour et al., 2016). To support acceleration, teams create plans that include opportunities to address the prior content knowledge students need to learn the priority grade-level standards to ensure every student learns at grade level or higher.

Identify Priority Standards

It is important for collaborative teams, with support from the district, to collectively define the priority standards that form a guaranteed and viable curriculum for students across a grade level or course. *Priority standards* are "the critical skills, knowledge, and dispositions each student must acquire as a result of each course, grade level, and unit of instruction" (Schuhl et al., 2021, p. 18) and may be called *essential standards*, *power standards*, or *promise standards*. In the absence of collectively agreed-on priority standards, teachers will select their own priority standards individually by nature of what they emphasize in their instruction and assessment, creating a lottery system for students as to what they will learn (DuFour et al., 2016). In *Taking Action*, RTI experts and coauthors Austin Buffum, Mike Mattos, and Janet Malone (2018) note:

> If the goal is to ensure that all students have access to essential curriculum as part of their core instruction, then a school must have absolute clarity on the skills, knowledge, and behaviors students must master in each grade and course and agree that every teacher is committed to teaching these standards aligned to the teacher's teaching assignment. (p. 129)

Many other education experts and researchers agree about the importance of ranking standards to clarify what is possible for students to learn in a given school year and place the most emphasis on what is most critical to learn (Ainsworth, 2004; Buffum et al., 2018; DuFour et al., 2016; Kramer & Schuhl, 2017; Reeves, 2002; Wiggins & McTighe, 2011).

To create the time needed for acceleration, we recommend teams prioritize eight to twelve standards as the most critical in a subject or course for the year. This does not mean all other standards are excluded. Rather, the remaining *supporting standards* fall into two categories: (1) important-to-know standards, which are also taught with priority standards, or (2) nice-to-know standards, which are not taught during the school year except as an extension or when students are already proficient with the more important standards (Schuhl et al., 2021). The eight to twelve priority standards are the standards teams design interventions for first when they see students are not learning. The priority standards are also the standards that will inform acceleration plans for student learning from prior knowledge to grade level. Figure 3.1 shows a diagram for standards acceleration.

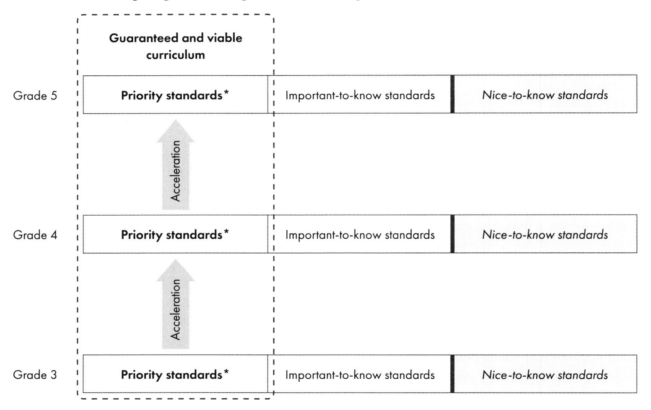

* Priority standards are the focus for acceleration to grade level.

FIGURE 3.1: Standards acceleration diagram.

In the book *School Improvement for All*, we share:

> How do we accelerate learning to minimize gaps? Answers will often flow from the determined priority standards. Teams will work to ensure each student learns the priority standards at high levels and provide additional time and support for both remediation of prerequisite skills needed to access the grade-level standards and intervention related to the grade-level priority standards themselves. (Kramer & Schuhl, 2017, p. 57)

The question then becomes, How do you determine the priority standards?

Ideally, teams unpack and make sense of all standards before selecting priority standards. However, when there is an urgent need for acceleration, the time may not be available to unpack standards first (Kramer & Schuhl, 2017). Instead, through the process we describe next, teams can identify initial priority standards they can adjust if needed as they unpack and make sense of what each means in terms of grade-level learning as the year progresses.

To strengthen the selection of priority standards, start with vertical conversations. The minimum standards a team works to ensure every student learns should provide a solid foundation for the next grade level or course. Does the fourth-grade team agree with the ELA standards the third-grade teachers chose? Do eighth-grade science teachers agree with the priority standards the seventh-grade teachers chose? Does the Algebra 2 team agree with the standards the Algebra 1 and geometry teams chose?

To initiate thinking at a district or school level, consider the protocol in figure 3.2. Teams have an initial discussion about the important knowledge and skills they feel students need to learn in their grade level or course and the knowledge and skills students should come to their grade level or course having learned. When teams have finished brainstorming the knowledge and skills needed in their own grade or course and those from the previous year, they can share their ideas

---

Subject: _____   Course or Grade Level: _____

1. What are the most critical knowledge and skills students need to learn in this grade level or course? Identify up to ten.

2. What are the most critical knowledge and skills students need to learn in the prior grade or course to be successful in this grade or course? Identify up to ten.

Source: Adapted from Kramer & Schuhl, 2017.

FIGURE 3.2: Critical knowledge and skills for acceleration.

*Visit **go.SolutionTree.com/priorityschools** for a free reproducible version of this figure.*

with one another to generate a stronger list of critical knowledge and skills. Each grade-level or course team talks with the grade-level or course team before and after theirs if applicable. Vertical conversations can start before selecting priority standards; it is not yet necessary to refer to specific standards during this brainstorming session.

Armed with the most critical knowledge and skills, teams can now analyze their list of standards. When selecting priority standards, best-selling author Douglas Reeves (2002) recommends beginning by identifying standards that (1) endure beyond the grade level or course (or a single test), (2) apply to other disciplines, and (3) are needed for learning in the next grade level or course. Teams may also want to consult a state testing blueprint (if applicable) to see which standards are most important on standardized exams. From the list of standards that meet these criteria, teams ask, "Which eight to twelve standards would we design interventions for *first* when students are not learning?" The answers produce the priority standards for acceleration and any remaining standards become important-to-know standards that will help develop the concepts students need to learn unit by unit.

Finally, the team documents the list of priority standards and identifies when in the school year teachers expect students to be proficient at grade level with each one. See figure 3.3 as an example of a list of priority standards for grade 4 ELA.

The time frames teams use when documenting priority standards vary. For example, teams might schedule learning by quarter, month, unit, or a specific date. If a standard spans more than a single time frame, teams should clarify which specific targets from the standard students should be proficient with by each date (that is, benchmark the progression of learning into smaller chunks of time). Eventually, the pacing of the priority standards will create a proficiency map to guide teams in planning their learning cycles for each unit. However, setting dates for specific targets may need to wait until the team unpacks the standard, which is the topic of the next section.

Share the list of priority standards and time frames with all adults who support student learning (grade-level teams, support specialists, counselors, and others), so everyone can coordinate acceleration for clearly defined standards and create corresponding learning progressions.

Unpack Priority Standards to Create Learning Progressions

Once teams choose priority standards and determine time frames for proficiency, teams begin to *unpack* each one (some educators also use terms like *unwrap* or *break apart*, among others). Without stopping to make sense of the standard together, three people on a team may interpret a priority standard three different ways, causing inequities in learning. Unpacking standards to generate learning targets and learning progressions ensures each teacher shares an understanding of what it means for students to learn the priority standard at grade level and how to accelerate learning as needed.

Rather than unpack every priority standard at once, teams work to unpack each one prior to the unit or time frame when they will teach and assess each throughout the year. Unpacking priority standards begins with clarifying what students need to know and be able to do to meet the grade-level expectations for proficiency. The team then discusses and documents their common understanding of the standard to strengthen their teaching in whole and small groups.

Priority Standards	Proficiency Time Frame
RL.4.2: Determine the theme of a story, drama, or poem from details in the text; summarize the text.	Quarter 2
RL.4.3: Describe in depth a character, setting, or event in a story or drama, drawing on specific details in the text (e.g., a character's thoughts, words, actions).	Quarter 2—Setting and event Quarter 3—Character
RL.4.5: Explain major differences between poems, drama, and prose, and refer to the structural elements of poems (e.g., verse, rhythm, meter) and drama (e.g., casts of characters, settings, descriptions, dialogue, stage directions) when writing or speaking about a text.	Quarter 4
RL.4.9: Compare and contrast the treatment of similar themes and topics (e.g., opposition of good and evil) and patterns of events in stories, myths, and traditional literature from different cultures.	Quarter 2
RI.4.1: Refer to details and examples in a text when explaining what the text says explicitly and when drawing inferences from the text.	Quarter 1—Explicit with text references Quarter 2—Inference with a supporting detail Quarter 3—Inference and support with details or examples
RI.4.2: Determine the main idea of a text and explain how it is supported by key details; summarize the text.	Quarter 1—Main idea Quarter 2—Main idea with key details Quarter 3—Summarize text to support the main idea
RI.4.5: Describe the overall structure (e.g., chronology, comparison, cause/effect, problem/solution) of events, ideas, concepts, or information in a text or part of a text.	Quarter 2
RI.4.7: Interpret information presented visually, orally, or quantitatively (e.g., in charts, graphs, diagrams, time lines, animations, or interactive elements on Web pages) and explain how the information contributes to an understanding of the text in which it appears.	Quarter 4
RI.4.9: Integrate information from two texts on the same topic in order to write or speak about the subject knowledgeably.	Quarter 3
W.4.4: Produce clear and coherent writing in which the development and organization are appropriate to task, purpose, and audience.	Quarter 1
RF.4.4: Read [grade-level text] with sufficient accuracy and fluency to support comprehension.	Quarter 1 Quarter 2 Quarter 3 Quarter 4 *See district guide for benchmark expectations each quarter.
RF.4.3: Know and apply grade-level phonics and word analysis skills in decoding words.	Quarter 1 Quarter 2 Quarter 3 Quarter 4 *See district guide for benchmark expectations each quarter.

Source for standards: National Governors Association Center for Best Practices (NGA) and Council of Chief State School Officers (CCSSO), 2010a.

FIGURE 3.3: Example of priority standards and time frames.

*Visit **go.SolutionTree.com/priorityschools** for a free reproducible version of this figure.*

We offer the following unpacking process (Kramer & Schuhl, 2017) adapted from the work of international educational consultant Larry Ainsworth (2003).

1. Identify the standard that most closely connects to the priority standard from the year prior (or earlier in the grade level, if needed) and the next year.

2. Circle or highlight the verbs and underline the nouns or noun phrases.

3. Write a list of the nouns or phrases to identify the content students must learn. This shows what students must know and begins to show the conceptual understanding of the standard. Clarify any as needed. (For example, if a team is discussing the causes of World War I, they would add in the actual causes to make sure everyone agrees.)

4. Write a list of the verbs with each noun or noun phrase to identify the skills students must demonstrate. These become the targets in the learning ladder and show what students must be able to do to be proficient with the standard. Clarify any as needed. (For example, if a team is discussing creating a model for photosynthesis, they might add in the key details needed for the model).

5. Create a learning ladder of targets from least complex to most complex at grade level and determine strategies to scaffold learning to grade level (Dimich, 2015). Identify prior-knowledge standards and skills that lead to the priority standard at the bottom of the ladder, showing the content needed to accelerate learning, and determine how to extend learning in the standard, if applicable, above the ladder.

6. Create the overarching student learning targets by bundling the targets from the standard (shown in the learning ladder) together for student reflection and assessment design.

7. Complete the discussion and document academic language and exemplars.

Figures 3.4 and 3.5 (page 42) each show an example of unpacking a priority standard to accelerate learning.

It might be tempting to identify prior-knowledge standards and skills several grade levels before the current one. For the purposes of the learning ladder, focus on standards in the progression that students learned one to three years prior. If students demonstrate their learning is at a lower grade level or course, adjust accordingly, but be mindful of the specific standards or skills needed for the priority standard instead of trying to account for all prior learning needed to access the learning of grade-level standards. This is when an innovative Tier 3 approach may be needed (see chapter 6, page 107).

Unpacked standards are not "done" when teachers have filled out templates like those in figures 3.4 and 3.5 (page 42). Rather, unpacking a standard initially and then revising it in future years ensures teachers on a team are working together to accelerate student learning with a common understanding of what it means to strengthen instructional practices and formative assessment in the classroom. The template merely prompts the important discussion and documents the resulting teacher learning.

As discussed with figure 3.3 (page 39), it is important to have a time frame for when teams expect proficiency with each priority standard so teams can unpack each standard in succession throughout the year for team planning and teams can ensure students learn each one. It is also important to understand the pacing of standards throughout the year to make sure teams have a guaranteed and viable curriculum and can accelerate learning by identifying the prior-knowledge standards to address within each unit.

Grade and Subject or Course: Grade 2 Reading	Proficiency Time Frame: Unit 3 (October 22)

Priority Standard

RL.2.2: (Recount) stories, including <u>fables and folktales from diverse cultures</u>, and (determine) their <u>central message</u>, <u>lesson</u>, or <u>moral</u>.

Prior-Year Standard Connection	Next-Year Standard Connection
RL.1.2: Retell stories, including key details, and demonstrate understanding of their central message or lesson.	**RL.3.2:** Recount stories, including fables, folktales, and myths from diverse cultures; determine the central message, lesson, or moral and explain how it is conveyed through key details in the text.

Content (Nouns) What Students Need to Know	Skills (Verbs With Nouns) What Students Need to Be Able to Do
• Fables from diverse cultures • Folktales from diverse cultures • Central message • Lesson • Moral	• Recount stories. • Recount fables from diverse cultures. • Recount folktales from diverse cultures. • Determine central message, lesson, or moral from text.

Academic Language

Retell	Folktale	Central message
Fable	Lesson	Moral

Learning Ladder		Scaffolding Strategies
Extensions	• Create a story or fable and identify its central message or moral. • Compare and contrast two fables with the same lesson or moral.	
Grade-Level Standard Most Complex ↑ Least Complex	• Determine central message, lesson, or moral from text. • Recount fables from diverse cultures in sequential order. • Recount folktales from diverse cultures in sequential order. • Recount stories in sequential order.	Tell students the central message, lesson, or moral and have students explain why. Read text aloud or have students read stories, fables, or folktales independently with first grade– or kindergarten-level text. Show pictures or videos of diverse cultures to build background knowledge.
Prior-knowledge standards	• Retell stories, including key details (RL.1.2). • Read grade-level text with purpose and understanding (RF.1.4a).	Read text aloud. Have students read familiar stories and retell the story with key details.

Grade-Level Student Learning Targets for Assessment and Reflection (Bundled Targets)

• I can retell stories.
• I can determine the central message, lesson, or moral of a story.

Exemplars at Grade Level

1. Read *The Ugly Duckling*.
   • What happens at the beginning, middle, and end of the story?
   • What is the moral of the story?
2. Read *The Tortoise and the Hare*.
   • Retell the fable.
   • What is the central message of the fable?

Source for standards: NGA & CCSSO, 2010a.   *Source: Adapted from Ainsworth, 2003; Dimich, 2015; Kramer & Schuhl, 2017.*

FIGURE 3.4: Example of an unpacked standard in reading.

Visit **go.SolutionTree.com/priorityschools** *for a free reproducible version of this figure.*

Grade and Subject or Course: Grade 7 Mathematics	Proficiency Time Frame: Unit 4 (November 18)

Priority Standard

7.RP.A.2a: Decide whether two quantities are in a proportional relationship, e.g., by testing for equivalent ratios in a table or graphing on a coordinate plane and observing whether the graph is a straight line through the origin.

Prior-Year Standard Connection	Next-Year Standard Connection
6.RP.A.3a: Make tables of equivalent ratios relating quantities with whole-number measurements, find missing values in the tables, and plot the pairs of values on the coordinate plane. Use tables to compare ratios.	**8.EE.B.5:** Graph proportional relationships, interpreting the unit rate as the slope of the graph. Compare two different proportional relationships represented in different ways. *For example, compare a distance-time graph to a distance-time equation to determine which of two moving objects has greater speed.*

Content (Nouns) What Students Need to Know	Skills (Verbs With Nouns) What Students Need to Be Able to Do

• Ratios
• Equivalent ratios
• Proportional relationships
• Ratio table
• Straight line through the origin on a coordinate plane
	• Decide whether two quantities are proportional using equivalent ratios.
	• Show if two quantities are proportional by
	   • Testing for equivalent ratios in a ratio table
	   • Graphing ratio pairs on a coordinate plane to see if they create a straight line through the origin

Academic Language

Ratio	Proportion	Equivalent ratios	Ratio table
Coordinate plane	Origin	Rate	Unit rate

Learning Ladder		Scaffolding Strategies
Extensions	• Write a context to match two proportional quantities. • Compare two proportional relationships. • Create a third quantity proportional to two others and show why.	
Grade-Level Standard Most Complex ↑ Least Complex	• Decide whether two quantities are in a proportional relationship and explain why. • Determine if ratios are equivalent using a ratio table. • Graph ratios to determine if they are proportional by creating a straight line through the origin.	Use colored cubes or pieces of paper to create equivalent ratios that match a ratio table. Draw a proportional graph and create a ratio table using the ordered pairs. Draw a story graph (for example, distance over time) to give context to a proportional relationship.
Prior-knowledge standards	• Generate equivalent ratios in a table or a graph (6.RP.3a). • Understand ratio and use ratio language (6.RP.A.1). • Generate equivalent fractions (4.NF.A.1).	Use colored cubes or pieces of colored paper to create equivalent ratios. Use objects and pictures to make sense of ratios. Use fraction tiles to generate equivalent fractions.

Grade-Level Student Learning Targets for Assessment and Reflection (Bundled Targets)
• I can decide if two quantities are proportional and explain why.
Exemplars at Grade Level

1. The ratio of red marbles to blue marbles in a bag is 24:32. The ratio of red marbles to blue marbles in a box is 15:20. Are the ratios of red to blue marbles in the bag and the box proportional? Explain why or why not.

2. Which table shows a proportional relationship between x and y? Explain why.

A.

x	12	18	24
y	9	15	18

B.

x	$\frac{2}{3}$	6	28
y	$\frac{1}{3}$	3	14

3. The graph shows the amount of money earned per hour of work. Does the graph show a proportional relationship? Explain why or why not.

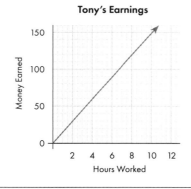

Tony's Earnings

Money Earned (vertical axis: 0, 50, 100, 150)

Hours Worked (horizontal axis: 2, 4, 6, 8, 10, 12)

Source for standards: NGA & CCSSO, 2010b.

Source: Adapted from Ainsworth, 2003; Dimich, 2015; Kramer & Schuhl, 2017.

FIGURE 3.5: Example of an unpacked standard in mathematics.

Embed Prior-Knowledge Standards Into Units

Teachers and teams need a plan for when to address standards and how to adjust along the way when needed. A proficiency map can serve as a pacing guide that provides direction to teams as they plan for accelerating student learning to grade level for each priority standard (Kramer & Schuhl, 2017). It outlines the guaranteed and viable curriculum teams promise to teach and ensure students learn. The proficiency map, which assigns standards to chunks of time—that is, units—is ideally crafted at the district level with input from teachers, especially if there is more than one school in the district for any grade level or course. In the absence of a district-level proficiency map, teams in schools can create one to effectively accelerate learning and guarantee the learning of the priority standards at grade level or higher for every student.

A *proficiency map* serves as a table of contents for more thorough unit plans and lists the priority standards and important-to-know standards in each unit, along with the length of time available to ensure students learn. Nice-to-know standards are also included in the proficiency map (accounting for every standard) and, if time permits for some or all students, teachers can include them in the grade-level learning as well or use them as extension opportunities (Schuhl et al., 2021).

When creating a plan for acceleration, a proficiency map also identifies the prior knowledge (that is, standards from previous grade levels or courses) that supports the grade-level learning. This allows teachers to deliver prior knowledge to students during the unit they will also be applying grade-level learning, rather than reviewing prior-knowledge standards at the start of the year and later teaching the corresponding grade-level standards.

See figures 3.6 (page 46) and 3.7 (page 48) for examples of proficiency maps for mathematics and ELA. The first row under the unit names and time frames lists the prior-knowledge standards students may need to learn in the unit as part of the team's acceleration plan. For example, in figure 3.7 (page 48), the third-grade ELA example, unit 2 shows the first- and second-grade standards that directly relate to theme and word meaning. In the examples, bold and underlined standards are priority standards, standards in regular text are important-to-know standards, and italicized standards are nice-to-know standards.

Both proficiency maps (see figures 3.6 and 3.7, pages 46 and 48) show the prior standards to teach within each unit, so teachers address them just in time with grade-level standards in the same unit to accelerate student learning most effectively (Hattie, 2017). Teams may want to use the priority standards from the previous grade level or course to determine which standards to place in each unit, leading to a more focused acceleration plan. They can also use their unpacked standards to identify the prior-knowledge standards students need in each unit.

The key components on a proficiency map include the following (Kramer & Schuhl, 2017).

- ► Names for units during the year
- ► Durations for each unit (in days or weeks), with a clear end date using a school calendar
- ► Every standard related to the unit, with indications for priority standards (for example, bold, underlined, or highlighted), important-to-know standards (regular text), and nice-to-know standards (italicized), as well as prior-knowledge standards for acceleration
- ► Time frames that place each standard within the unit according to when teachers expect students to be proficient with the standard, not each time they teach it
- ► An asterisk next to standards listed in more than one unit to let teachers know the standard is only partially addressed in each of the units it is listed, and identify which part students should be proficient with (which targets from the standard or what the benchmark is for the standard in the given unit)
- ► The number or code for each state standard and a brief description of the standard

Teams now have a strong yearlong plan with identified priority standards, unpacked priority standards, and proficiency maps. They know which standards are most critical for students to learn and when in the year students should learn each one. Teams have also clearly identified the prior-knowledge standards to address to accelerate learning to grade level within units of instruction. Next, it is time for teams to begin planning those units with acceleration in mind.

Focus Acceleration in Ten-Day Learning Cycles Within Units

When there is a need to accelerate learning, teams too often teach each priority standard (or each learning target within a priority standard) in discrete chunks of time without making connections or spiral-reviewing content. In such cases, acceleration is often not achieved because students ultimately forget what they learned earlier in the year. Instead, it is important to intentionally focus learning on smaller chunks connected to one another throughout a unit and help students make connections in learning from one unit to the next.

For each unit teams identify in the proficiency map, team members plan for learning with a focus on the priority standards, corresponding prior-knowledge standards, and any aligned important-to-know standards. Robert J. Marzano (2017), an acclaimed educational researcher and author, writes, "Teachers should plan from the perspective of the unit, which should provide an overarching framework for instruction" (p. 107). Within the framework the proficiency map provides, teams can design units that include common assessments, data analysis, intervention, and extension. Teachers can then work within the units to design lessons that accelerate learning. Note that there is flexibility within team-designed units. Coauthors Robert Eaker and Janel Keating (2015), in *Kid by Kid, Skill by Skill*, share:

> The team collaboratively agrees on a number of things that it will be tight about regarding each unit, but be loose regarding teacher methodology or instructional approaches. Teachers in a PLC are constantly reminded that teacher autonomy and creativity are not only allowed but, in fact, encouraged—within the set parameters of collaboratively developed units of instruction. (p. 55)

This all leads to intentional acceleration.

Notice that in the learning cycle in figure 3.8 (page 50), teachers identify the standards and the time frame for the unit on a calendar, unpack priority standards into targets, determine the proficiency expectations for each target, and create common assessments *before* the unit begins. Doing so provides individual teachers with the information they need to design effective lessons.

We advocate that teams never teach more than ten days without checking on student learning with an informal or formal common assessment created to targets generated from a priority standard or its progression (in fact, more frequency is even better). This means within each unit there are likely two or more ten-day learning cycles, culminating in an end-of-unit assessment. However, the cycle need not be exactly ten days. It might be six or eight days, depending on when it makes sense to check in on student learning of a target as a team.

Any team plan designed to accelerate learning includes a schedule for daily grade-level learning as well as when teachers address prior knowledge and skills. Depending on the time and capacity for the work from the start, teams may begin with a full unit plan (see figure 3.9, page 52, for an example) or generate individual ten-day learning cycles with each contained in a conceptual unit (see figure 3.10, page 56 for an example).

Grade 5 Mathematics	Unit 1 Multiplication and Division 25 days Ends October 11	Unit 2 Volume of Rectangular Prisms 15 days Ends November 2	Unit 3 Decimals and Conversions 35 days Ends January 5	Unit 4 Fractions: Addition and Subtraction 25 days Ends February 10	Unit 5 Fractions: Division and Multiplication 35 days Ends April 10	Unit 6 Graphing and Geometry 15 days Ends May 1
Prior-Knowledge Standards for Acceleration	3.OA.7: Fluently multiply and divide within 100. 3.OA.8: Solve word problems using four operations. 4.NBT.5: Multiply four-digit by one-digit and two-digit by two-digit numbers. 4.NBT.6: Divide up to four digits by one digit with remainders.	Continue to focus on addition, subtraction, multiplication, and division of whole numbers in preparation for the next unit.	3.NBT.3: Multiply a one-digit number by multiples of 10 4.NBT.2: Read and write whole numbers using base 10, numerals, and expanded form. Compare multidigit whole numbers. 4.NF.6: Write decimals for fractions with denominators of 10 or 100.	3.NF.2: Represent fractions on a number line. 4.NF.1: Create equivalent fractions. 4.NF.3c: Add and subtract mixed numbers with like denominators (includes fractions).	4.NF.4: Multiply a fraction by a whole number.	4.G.2: Classify two-dimensional shapes using angles and parallel or perpendicular lines. Spiral review priority standards from previous units.
Operations and Algebraic Thinking (OA)	* **5.OA.1: Evaluate expressions with parentheses (whole numbers).** * **5.OA.2: Write and interpret expressions (whole numbers).**		* **5.OA.1: Evaluate expressions with parentheses (with powers of 10).**		* **5.OA.1: Evaluate expressions with parentheses (with fractions).**	5.OA.3: Generate number patterns.
Number and Operations in Base Ten (NBT)	**5.NBT.5: Multiply using the standard algorithm.** 5.NBT.6: Divide up to four digits by two digits and show thinking.		5.NBT.1: Place value with 10s. **5.NBT.2: Multiply and divide by 10.** **5.NBT.3a: Read and write decimals.** 5.NBT.3b: Compare decimals. 5.NBT.4: Round decimals. **5.NBT.7: Add, subtract, multiply, and divide decimals.**			

Number and Operations—Fractions (NF)			5.NF.1: Add and subtract fractions. **5.NF.2: Add and subtract fraction word problems using models.**	5.NF.3: Interpret fractions as division. 5.NF.4a: Interpret fraction products. 5.NF.4b: Find the area of a rectangle. *5.NF.5ab: Explain and compare factors and products.* **5.NF.6: Solve real-world fraction multiplication problems.** 5.NF.7abc: Divide whole numbers and unit fractions.	
Measurement and Data (MD)	5.MD.3a: Recognize a cubic unit. 5.MD.3b: Identify volume as number of cubes. 5.MD.4: Find volume by counting cubes. 5.MD.5a: Discover the volume formula. **5.MD.5b: Apply the volume formula.** 5.MD.5c: Add volumes to find the total volume.	**5.MD.1: Convert measurements to solve problems (decimals).*		**5.MD.1: Convert measurements to solve problems (fractions).* *5.MD.2: Create a line plot with fractions and use it to solve problems.*	
Geometry (G)					*5.G.1: Understand a coordinate plane.* *5.G.2: Represent problems in first quadrant.* 5.G.3: Know attributes of two-dimensional shapes. **5.G.4: Classify two-dimensional shapes.**

Priority standards—bold and underlined; Important-to-know standards—regular text; Nice-to-know standards—italics; * Standard is addressed in two or more units.

Source for standards: Adapted from NGA & CCSSO, 2010b.

Source: Adapted from Kramer & Schuhl, 2017.

FIGURE 3.6: Example of proficiency map—Grade 5 mathematics.

Grade 3 ELA	Unit 1 Answer Text Questions 30 days Ends October 7	Unit 2 Theme and Word Meaning 30 days Ends November 23	Unit 3 Character Actions, Main Idea, and Produce Writing 30 days Ends January 20	Unit 4 View Points, Main Idea, and Narrative Writing 30 days Ends February 24	Unit 5 Folklore Theme, Author Point of View, and Explanatory Writing 30 days Ends April 14	Unit 6 Argument Writing and Read Grade-Level Texts 30 days Ends May 19
Prior-Knowledge Standards for Acceleration	RI.2.1: Ask and answer questions using who, what, where when, why, and how. RF.2.3a: Read long and short vowel sounds in one-syllable words. RF.2.3b: Know spelling-sound correspondence. RF.2.3c: Decode regularly spelled two-syllable words.	RL.1.2: Retell stories and central message or lesson. L.2.4a: Use context in a sentence for word meaning. RF.2.3d: Decode words with common prefixes and suffixes. RF.2.3e: Identify words with inconsistent but common spelling-sound correspondences.	RI.2.2: Identify main topic of text and focus of paragraphs. RF.2.3f: Recognize and read irregularly spelled words.	RL.2.6: Acknowledge different character points of view. W.2.3: Write narratives with a short sequence of events. RF.2.4c: Use context to confirm or self-correct when reading.	W.2.2: Write explanatory text with introduction, body, and conclusion. RI.2.6: Identify author's main purpose. L.2.5a: Identify real-life connections between words and their use.	W.2.1: Write opinion piece with introduction, opinion and evidence, and conclusion. RI.2.3: Describe connection between historical events, scientific ideas, or steps.
Reading: Literature (RL)	RL.3.1: Answer text questions using evidence. ***RL.3.3: Describe characters.**	***RL.3.2: Determine theme from stories using key details.**	***RL.3.3: Describe character actions applied to sequence of events.** RL.3.4: Distinguish literal and nonliteral word meaning. RL.3.5: Refer to chapter, scene, and stanza. RL.3.7: Explain how text illustration contribute to the text.	**RL.3.6: Distinguish own view from character point of view.**	***RL.3.2: Determine theme from folklore.** RL.3.9: Compare and contrast themes, settings, and plots (same author).	RL.3.10: Read grade-level text.
Reading: Informational Text (RI)	RI.3.1: Answer text questions using evidence.		**RI.3.2: Determine main idea with key details.**	*RI.3.4: Determine meaning of academic and grade-specific words.* RI.3.5: Use text features (headings) to locate information. *RI.3.8: Describe text structure.* **RI.3.9: Compare and contrast main idea and key details.**	**RI.3.6: Distinguish own view from author point of view.** RI.3.7: Use information gained from illustrations.	RI.3.10: Read grade-level informational text in different subject areas. **RI.3.3: Describe historical events, scientific ideas, steps, and sequence, and so on.**

Writing (W)		W.3.6: With guidance, use technology to publish writing and collaborate. **W.3.4: With guidance, produce writing with organization to task and purpose.** W.3.5: With guidance, revise editing.	**W.3.3abcd: Write narratives.** W.3.8: Recall and gather information from digital sources.	W.3.2abcd: Write informative/explanatory texts. W.3.7: Conduct short research project.	W.3.1abcd: Write arguments with valid reasoning and evidence. W.3.10: Write routinely over short and extended time frames.
Speaking and Listening (SL)	SL.3.1abcd: Discussions—prepare, use rules, ask questions, and explain ideas. SL.3.3: Ask and answer questions about information from a speaker, with details.	SL.3.2: Determine main idea and details of text read aloud. SL.3.4: Report on text, tell a story, or recount an experience. SL.3.5: Create audio recordings of stories or poems—add visual displays. SL.3.6 Speak in complete sentences.			
Language (L)	L.3.4d: Determine meaning using a glossary or dictionary.	L.3.4a: Use context clues in a sentence to determine word meaning. L.3.4b: Determine meaning of words with affixes.	L.3.1abcdef: Explain the function and form nouns and verbs. L.3.2abcdefgh: Use conventions when writing—capitalization, punctuation, and spelling. L.3.4c: Develop meaning of word using same roots (such as company and companion).	L.3.1ghi: Form and use adjectives, adverbs, subordinating conjunctions, and sentence types. L.3.6: Use grade-level conversational and academic words and phrases.	L.3.3abc: Choose words and phrases for effect and compare differences between spoken and written English. L.3.5abc: Identify word relationships and nuances in word meanings (literal, nonliteral, real-life connections, shades of meaning).
Foundational Skills (RF)		**RF.3.3a: Identify and know common prefixes and suffixes.** **RF.3.3c: Decode multisyllable words.**	**RF.3.3d: Read irregularly spelled words.**		**RF.3.3b: Decode words with Latin suffixes.** **RF.3.4abc: Read with fluency to support comprehension.**

Priority standards—bolded and underlined; Important-to-know standards—standards in regular text; Nice-to-know standards—italics; *Standard is addressed in two or more units.

Source for standards: Adapted from NGA & CCSSO, 2010a.   *Source: Adapted from Kramer & Schuh, 2017.*

FIGURE 3.7: Example of proficiency map—Grade 3 ELA.

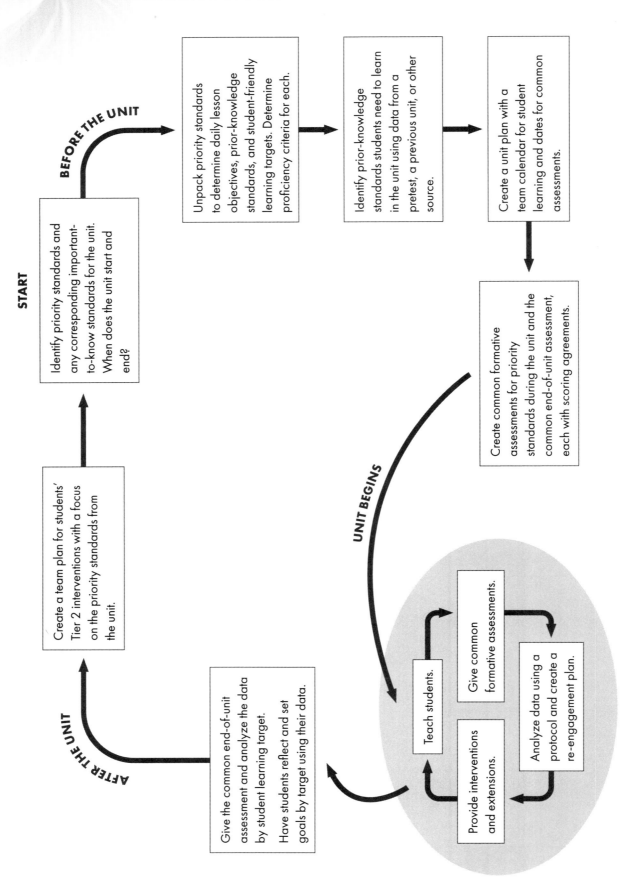

START

BEFORE THE UNIT

Identify priority standards and any corresponding important-to-know standards for the unit. When does the unit start and end?

Unpack priority standards to determine daily lesson objectives, prior-knowledge standards, and student-friendly learning targets. Determine proficiency criteria for each.

Identify prior-knowledge standards students need to learn in the unit using data from a pretest, a previous unit, or other source.

Create a unit plan with a team calendar for student learning and dates for common assessments.

Create common formative assessments for priority standards during the unit and the common end-of-unit assessment, each with scoring agreements.

UNIT BEGINS

Teach students.

Give common formative assessments.

Provide interventions and extensions.

Analyze data using a protocol and create a re-engagement plan.

AFTER THE UNIT

Give the common end-of-unit assessment and analyze the data by student learning target. Have students reflect and set goals by target using their data.

Create a team plan for students' Tier 2 interventions with a focus on the priority standards from the unit.

Source: Adapted from Buffum et al., 2018; DuFour et al., 2016; Kanold & Larson, 2015; Kramer, 2021b; Putnam City School District, Oklahoma City, Oklahoma.

FIGURE 3.8: learning cycle.

*Visit **go.SolutionTree.com/priorityschools** for a free reproducible version of this figure.*

In the calendar in figure 3.9 (page 52), the common formative assessments happen within a ten-day window, although each cycle's duration is less than ten days. The first common formative assessment happens on January 11, which is the seventh day of the unit; the second occurs on January 21, seven instructional days later; and the third occurs on February 1, also after seven more instructional days. Notice there is time between the last common formative assessment and the unit assessment, which provides teachers another opportunity to differentiate and ensure students learn the standards in the unit before the end-of-unit assessment. The calendar also shows *flex days*, which allow time for the team to intervene and extend immediately during core instruction using the data from the assessments to form small groups or regroup students by specific targeted need. The team plans for intervention to accelerate learning to grade level instead of always responding by adding days to the end of a unit.

The overall concept of the second-grade mathematics unit in figure 3.9 (page 52) is adding and subtracting. To accelerate learning, teachers teach the unit with a focus on conceptual understanding with connections made to students' prior learning from kindergarten and first grade. Teachers focus on what it means to add and subtract, using word problems for context and talking about whether a larger or smaller answer makes sense to any problem, every day. They build an understanding using the concept of place value. They also strategically address the prior-knowledge and grade-level standards the calendar shows (see figure 3.9, page 52). The focus is not on any one algorithm or set of steps students might quickly mimic without fully understanding.

Figure 3.10 (page 56) shows a ten-day learning cycle template that guides teams to unpack a priority standard and then plan their instruction and student learning calendar to include no more than ten days before a common formative assessment. The unpacking protocol matches that in figures 3.4 (page 41) and 3.5 (page 42), so teams are identifying targets students need to learn and the prior knowledge students may need to reach grade-level understanding. The calendar in figure 3.10 (page 56) is similar to the calendar in figure 3.9 (page 52), but only shows one chunk of learning leading to a common formative assessment and time to intervene or extend learning, rather than the entire unit. Teams are planning for acceleration by addressing prior knowledge and grade-level learning every day. The ten-day learning cycle template ends with a data-analysis protocol the team uses to analyze student work from common formative assessments and make a re-engagement plan for a flex day or small-group learning to further accelerate learning. Teams often start with the ten-day cycle in figure 3.10 (page 56) when first enacting acceleration and eventually create full unit plans (see figure 3.9, page 52).

Planning for student learning together as a team (by making sense of priority standards and any corresponding important-to-know standards) and determining the resources to use is critical for providing equitable learning experiences for students across a grade level or course and grows teacher learning as well. When designing units to include acceleration strategies, teams are intentional and proactive in their planning. The focus is on conceptual understanding that connects the skills and knowledge of prerequisite skills with the current grade-level or course standards each day during core instruction.

Course: Grade 2	Mathematics Unit Plan
Time: January 6–February 22 (22 days)	**Unit:** Addition and Subtraction within 100

Big Ideas:

- There are many strategies for adding and subtracting.
- Algebraic thinking involves choosing, combining, and applying effective strategies for answering real-world problems.
- Understanding place value can lead to number sense and efficient strategies for adding and subtracting.

Essential Questions:

- In what ways can operations affect numbers?
- How can different strategies be helpful when solving a problem?
- How does a digit's position affect its value?

Standards for Mathematical Practice:

1. Make sense of problems and persevere in solving them.
2. Reason abstractly and quantitatively.
3. Construct viable arguments and critique the reasoning of others.
4. Model with mathematics.
5. Use appropriate tools strategically.
6. Attend to precision.
7. Look for and make use of structure.
8. Look for and express regularity in repeated reasoning.

Student Learning Targets:

1. I can add two-digit numbers and show my thinking. (2.NBT.5 and 2.NBT.9)
2. I can subtract two-digit numbers and show my thinking. (2.NBT.5 and 2.NBT.9)
3. I can solve word problems using addition and subtraction. (2.OA.1)

Prior Knowledge

- Add and subtract single-digit numbers within 20. (Grade 1)
- Add and subtract two-digit and one-digit numbers. (Grade 2, earlier in the year)
- Solve one-step word problems with addition and subtraction. (Grade 1)

Standards	Vocabulary	Skills	Activities (Resources)	Assessment

Priority Standard
2.NBT.5: Fluently add and subtract within 100 using strategies based on place value, properties of operations and/or the relationship between addition and subtraction.
	Add
	Subtract
	Place Value
	• Ones
	• Tens
	• Hundreds
		• Add and subtract numbers within 100 with ease by applying strategies:
		  • Decomposing numbers into tens and ones
		  • Using commutative and associative properties
		  • Using mental strategies based on the numbers being added or subtracted
		  • Using an open number line
		  • Using a place value chart
			Chapter 5, lessons 1–10
			Exploration: p. 235 (Add and subtract with base 10 pieces)
				• Common formative assessment—learning target 1
				• Common formative assessment—learning target 2
				• Common formative assessment—learning target 3
				• Unit Test—learning targets 1, 2, and 3

Priority Standard	Addition	• Choose when to use addition or subtraction to solve a word problem.	Chapter 5, lessons 12–14
2.OA.1: Use addition and subtraction within 100 to solve one- and two-step word problems involving situations of adding to, taking from, putting together, taking apart, and comparing, with unknowns in all positions, e.g., by using drawings and equations with a symbol for the unknown number to represent the problem.	Add Subtraction Subtract Equation Unknown	• Represent addition and subtraction word problems using objects, drawings, and equations with unknowns in all positions. • Solve addition and subtraction word problems that involve one step. • Solve addition and subtraction word problems that involve two steps. • Solve word problems with unknown numbers in different positions (for example, $5 + \_\_\_ = 13$, $\_\_\_ + 8 = 13$, $5 + 8 = \_\_\_$).	Team word-problem bank Illustrative mathematics tasks
Important-to-Know Standard		• Explain addition and subtraction using place value.	Chapter 5, Lessons 1–10
2.NBT.9: Explain why addition and subtraction strategies work, using place value and the properties of operations.		• Explain addition and subtraction using the properties of operations (commutative, associative, identity).	

Notes and Reflection:

- Use base 10 blocks to explore addition and subtraction within 100 before using written strategies.
- Show addition and subtraction on an open number line to show how to think in terms of 10s and 1s when adding and subtracting.
- Students do not need to know the term *commutative property*, but can hear it and need to know it means two numbers can be added in any order, $2 + 3$ is the same as $3 + 2$. The commutative property does not work for subtraction (order matters).
- Students do not need to know the term *associative property*, but it means any two numbers in a list of three numbers can be added together first before adding the third number (for example, $3 + 2 + 4$ means a student can find $(3 + 2) + 4 = 5 + 4 = 9$ or $3 + (2 + 4) = 3 + 6 = 9$).
- Students do not need to know the term *identity property* but it means a number added to 0 always equals the original number ($3 + 0 = 3$).
- *Note—students do not need to know how to add and subtract using the standard algorithm until fourth grade—show it to students who understand addition and subtraction using place value only.

FIGURE 3.9: Example of unit plan and calendar—Grade 2 mathematics.

continued ▸▸

Calendar

Monday	Tuesday	Wednesday	Thursday	Friday
January 3 Students work in pairs at stations throughout the classroom to review adding and subtracting one-digit numbers and one-digit and two-digit numbers. At the end of class, students add two-digit numbers based on their learning from the review.	**January 4** I can add two-digit numbers and explain my thinking. *Prior knowledge:* Number talks—add single-digit numbers. *Grade-level focus:* Add two-digit numbers without regrouping using base 10 pieces and open number lines. (Lesson 1)	**January 5** I can add two-digit numbers and explain my thinking. *Prior knowledge:* Number talks—add single-digit numbers. *Grade-level focus:* Add two-digit numbers with regrouping using base 10 pieces and open number lines. (Lesson 2–3)	**January 6** I can add two-digit numbers and explain my thinking. *Prior knowledge:* Number talks—Add single-digit numbers. *Grade-level focus:* Add two-digit numbers with regrouping using base 10 pieces and open number lines. (Lesson 2–3)	**January 7** I can add two-digit numbers and explain my thinking. *Prior knowledge:* Add two-digit and one-digit numbers using place value and open number lines. *Grade-level focus:* Add two-digit numbers with regrouping using open number lines and place value charts. (Lessons 4–5)
January 10 I can add two-digit numbers and explain my thinking. *Prior knowledge:* Number talks—Add two-digit and one-digit numbers. *Grade-level focus:* Add two-digit numbers with regrouping using open number lines and place value charts. (Lessons 4–5)	**January 11** ***Common formative assessment: I can add two-digit numbers and explain my thinking.** Review subtraction using two digits and one digit with regrouping.	**January 12** **Team flex day: Re-engage students in learning addition using common formative assessment data and small groups.**	**January 13** I can subtract two-digit numbers and explain my thinking. *Prior knowledge:* Number talks—Subtract single-digit numbers. *Grade-level focus:* Subtract two-digit numbers without regrouping using base 10 pieces and open number lines. (Lesson 6)	**January 14** I can subtract two-digit numbers and explain my thinking. *Prior knowledge:* Number talks—Subtract single-digit numbers. *Grade-level focus:* Subtract two-digit numbers with regrouping using base 10 pieces and open number lines. (Lessons 7–8)
January 17 Holiday	**January 18** I can subtract two-digit numbers and explain my thinking. *Prior knowledge:* Number talks—Subtract single-digit numbers. *Grade-level focus:* Subtract two-digit numbers with regrouping using base 10 pieces and open number lines. (Lessons 7–8)	**January 19** I can subtract two-digit numbers and explain my thinking. *Prior knowledge:* Subtract two-digit and one-digit numbers using place value and open number lines. *Grade-level focus:* Subtract two-digit numbers with regrouping using open number lines and place value charts. (Lessons 9–10)	**January 20** I can subtract two-digit numbers and explain my thinking. *Prior knowledge:* Number talks—Subtract two-digit and one-digit numbers. *Grade-level focus:* Subtract two-digit numbers with regrouping using open number lines and place value charts. (Lessons 9–10)	**January 21** ***Common formative assessment: I can subtract two-digit numbers and explain my thinking.** Review solving one-step word problems—draw a picture and write an equation with a question mark for the unknown.

January 24	January 25	January 26	January 27	January 28
Team flex day: Re-engage students in learning addition or subtraction using common formative assessment data and small groups.	I can solve word problems using addition and subtraction. Prior knowledge: Addition and subtraction word problems using single-digit numbers and finding the total. Grade-level focus: Solve one-step word problems with the unknown as the total or the second number in the equation. (Lesson 12)	I can solve word problems using addition and subtraction. Prior knowledge: Addition and subtraction word problems using single-digit numbers and finding the total. Grade-level focus: Solve one-step word problems with the unknown as the first number in the equation. (Lesson 12)	I can solve word problems using addition and subtraction. Prior knowledge: Addition and subtraction two-step word problems using single-digit numbers and finding the total. Grade-level focus: Solve two-step equations that involve adding twice or subtracting twice. (Lesson 13)	I can solve word problems using addition and subtraction. Prior knowledge: Addition and subtraction two-step word problems using single-digit numbers and finding the total. Grade-level focus: Solve two-step equations (Lesson 14)
January 31	**February 1**	**February 2**	**February 3**	**February 4**
I can solve word problems using addition and subtraction. Prior knowledge: Addition and subtraction two-step word problems using single-digit numbers and finding the total. Grade-level focus: Solve two-step equations. (Lesson 14)	***Common formative assessment: I can solve word problems using addition and subtraction.** Review adding and subtracting within 100.	**Team flex day: Re-engage students in solving one- and two-step word problems using common formative assessment data and small groups.**	Review for unit test • Add within 100. • Subtract within 100. • Solve one- and Two-step word problems. *Use station rotations.	***Unit assessment** • I can add two-digit numbers and show my thinking. • I can subtract two-digit numbers and show my thinking. • I can solve word problems using addition and subtraction.

Source for standards: NGA & CCSSO, 2010b.

Source: Adapted from Kramer & Schuhl, 2017.

Visit go.SolutionTree.com/priorityschools for a free reproducible version of this figure.

Priority Standard Unpacking for Ten-Day Cycle

Grade and Subject or Course:	Time When Teachers Expect Proficiency:
Priority Standard	
Prior-Year Standard Connection	**Next-Year Standard Connection**
Content (Nouns) **What Students Need to Know**	**Skills (Verbs With Nouns)** **What Students Need to Be Able to Do**
Academic Language	

Learning Ladder		Scaffolding Strategies
Extensions		
Grade-Level Standard Most Complex ↑ Least Complex		
Prior Knowledge		

Grade-Level Student Learning Targets for Assessment and Reflection (Bundled Targets)
Exemplars at Grade Level

Ten-Day Cycle Calendar

Monday	Tuesday	Wednesday	Thursday	Friday

FIGURE 3.10: Ten-day cycle planning template.

continued ▸▸

Common Formative Assessment Team-Data Analysis

1. Identify the priority standard or learning target assessed.

2. Identify the students who demonstrated learning at levels of advanced, proficient, close to proficient, or far from proficient. Total the number of students in each level for the team.

Advanced	Proficient	Close to Proficient	Far From Proficient

3. Look at samples of student work. What are the trends in thinking or reasoning unique to the advanced students? What are the trends unique to the proficient students? Continue with each level and write down the trends in student work for each.

Advanced	Proficient	Close to Proficient	Far From Proficient

4. Determine a collective plan to target interventions or extensions for each group of students. Which teacher will be responsible for the learning of each group? When will you re-evaluate the close-to-proficient and far-from-proficient groups to see if learning occurred?

Advanced	Proficient	Close to Proficient	Far From Proficient
Teacher:	Teacher:	Teacher:	Teacher:
		Date for re-evaluation:	Date for re-evaluation:

Source: Adapted from Ainsworth, 2003; Kramer & Schuhl, 2017.

*Visit **go.SolutionTree.com/priorityschools** for a free reproducible version of this figure.*

Conclusion

Accelerating student learning begins with a plan—one that guarantees students experience grade-level standards every day and ensures students learn priority standards to grade level (or beyond). Teachers incorporate prior-knowledge standards and skills along the learning progression to the priority standard within designated units. With a strong outline, teachers and teams can develop unit plans, assessments, and lessons that accelerate student learning. A clear and doable curriculum is the first step to ensuring students learn grade-level standards every year.

Discussion Questions for Reflection and Action

As a team, discuss the following questions. Visit **go.SolutionTree.com/priorityschools** for a free reproducible version of these questions.

- ▶ How clear are your team's priority standards, important-to-know standards, and nice-to-know standards?

- ▶ How does your proficiency map ensure a guaranteed and viable curriculum centered on priority standards?

- ▶ How does your team collectively make sense of the priority standards students must learn and document your discussions (unpack standards)?

- ▶ How does your team determine the prior-knowledge standards students need to learn each unit?

- ▶ How does your team plan units or ten-day learning cycles?

- ▶ How does your team determine the learning targets to use with students during a unit?

- ▶ What are next steps for your team related to planning for student learning?

CHAPTER FOUR

An Assessment System That Accelerates Learning

When Sarah first started teaching high school mathematics, she dutifully followed the pattern of assessment she had experienced as a student. Halfway through each unit, she gave a quiz and then ended each unit with a review day and a large chapter test. These tests were designed to show students whether they had learned the content or not and to put a score in the gradebook to justify final grades. She didn't use the tests for teacher analysis of learning or student reflection and ongoing learning.

Sarah went over each assessment with students and expected every student to understand any mistakes they had made in preparation for the next unit. She found it frustrating when students stared back blankly and did not learn from the quiz and perform better on the end-of-unit assessment. She also focused on an overall score for each quiz and test instead of analyzing student learning on each target, and she seldom re-engaged students in learning even if they hadn't mastered the content. Often, the day after each test, she taught the next lesson in the book and kept moving forward.

When Sarah later worked at a school that functioned as a PLC, her collaborative team gave common assessments aligned to specific targets and analyzed data with colleagues to best structure interventions and extensions. Common assessments were an opportunity for students to gather evidence of their learning and for her team to analyze effective instructional practices and plan for continued learning. Students had opportunities to show they had learned later too if needed—an important part of acceleration. In addition to common assessments, teachers used classroom formative assessments (such as exit tickets, whiteboard activities, pair shares, journaling, and other strategies that gather evidence of student learning) during every lesson to gauge students' progress and adjust the lesson accordingly or give feedback to students to learn from any misconceptions. To help students see assessments as part of their learning experience, teams started calling assessment days *"show what you know" days*, emphasizing that an assessment is an opportunity for students to show what they know so they can use that information to continue learning. Assessments became part of her students', her team's, and her own learning story each year. Assessments provided continuous opportunities for Sarah and her colleagues to identify the students' learning needs and accelerate learning to grade level or higher.

> Of all the influences on student learning, feedback is among the top-ranked—and this is also the case for teacher learning.
>
> —JOHN HATTIE

Every minute spent administering an assessment is a valuable minute of instructional time. Therefore, assessments must serve as an instructional strategy to accelerate student learning. *Assessments* are a tool to gather evidence that students are progressing toward grade-level learning, give students the confidence to persevere in learning, and generate data that inform next steps in the learning process for teachers and students. In a learning-centered school, teachers and students view assessments as part of the learning story, not as a final grade or judgment. When used as part of a learning story, assessments provide meaningful feedback to both the student and teacher. Use them to determine next instructional and learning steps.

As described in chapter 3 (page 33), accelerating student learning starts with a yearlong plan (proficiency map) for learning with clearly identified priority standards and units. Teams develop the units and create ten-day learning cycles with dates for common assessments so they can collectively determine what students have learned or not learned yet and plan for continued learning. Next, teams also create the common assessments that will be part of the learning cycle before the unit begins. This advance work on assessments informs how teachers design lessons and give students more effective and equitable feedback every day.

The Shift to Learning From Assessments

It can be challenging for educators to shift their traditional conceptions of assessment as an event instead of a process. Too often, the full-day standardized exams and end-of-year testing windows dominate what teachers think of as assessment. In reality, teachers give many assessments to students every year, including progress-monitoring assessments, diagnostic assessments, benchmark assessments, common formative assessments in the middle of a unit, and common end-of-unit assessments (and yes, annual standardized tests). However, when educators use assessments as events, those assessments can heighten frustration if teachers ignore the test results or do not use them to affect practices to grow and accelerate student learning. Constant assessments quickly frustrate teachers and students, especially if the assessments seem random, disconnected from instruction, or a waste of valuable time.

Guiding coalitions or learning teams and grade- or course-level teams may need to clarify the purpose of each assessment and discuss how to analyze the resulting data from each. Hattie (2012) explains, "Of course, the assessment is about the student, but the power of interpretation and the consequences of assessment are more in the hands of teachers" (p. 163). It is teachers' responsibility to use assessment results to improve their own practices as well as accelerate the learning of students. Assessment experts and coauthors Jan Chappuis and Rick Stiggins (2020) define *assessment* as "*the act of gathering information*" (p. 3). To borrow an analogy from W. James Popham (2011), emeritus professor in the UCLA Graduate School of Education and Information Studies, an individual assessment instrument is like a surfboard—a tool one must use for it to have meaning. The formative assessment process is the entire surfing experience. The assessment provides the data teachers need to focus instructional decisions. The question is what teachers and students are doing with this information and how they can use it to accelerate learning. All Things Assessment (https://allthingsassessment.info) and The Assessment Center (https://solutiontree.com/assessment-center) creators Cassandra Erkens, Tom Schimmer, and Nicole Dimich (2017) recommend six research-based tenets for assessment that benefit teachers and students: "(1) assessment purpose, (2) communication of results, (3) accurate interpretation, (4) assessment architecture, (5) instructional agility, and (6) student investment" (p. 5). Design an assessment to learn about student thinking, so teams can share results with one another and students. Then, respond to those results in real time and have students reflect and learn in the process.

Table 4.1 shares some common yet unproductive beliefs related to assessments and how teachers' practices should shift to accelerate learning. Shifting assessment practices in this way supports teachers accelerating student learning. Importantly, assessments are not about generating grades; students should view assessments as opportunities to show themselves what they know and as feedback to confidently make plans for continued learning. Daily formative assessments and team

TABLE 4.1: Shifts in Assessment to Accelerate Student Learning

SHIFT FROM . . .	SHIFT TO . . .
Only administering diagnostic and district benchmark assessments	Integrating diagnostic and benchmark assessments with frequent team common assessments and classroom formative assessments
Solely relying on computer programs to assess students for intervention and design individual student-intervention plans	Using multiple measures to assess students and design acceleration plans that include small groups, minilessons, and strategic use of teacher-selected computer modules
Using the assessments provided with the textbook or curriculum for team common assessments	Reviewing and modifying textbook assessments to align with learning targets and creating original assessments as needed
Only administering multiple-choice or computerized assessments	Balancing multiple-choice or computer assessments with constructed response, one-to-one assessments, and performance assessments
Giving team common assessments on the same day every week (for example, on Fridays)	Assessing students when it makes sense instructionally to do so within ten-day learning cycles
Scoring every assessment for the purpose of recording a grade in the gradebook	Viewing assessments as a source of feedback to students and teachers about instructional practices, who has or has not learned, and how to design meaningful interventions
Giving different assessments or failing to use common administration and scoring practices with common assessments	Giving the same assessments at the same time in the same way across a collaborative team and scoring and analyzing the assessment together
Focusing all instruction and assessment on the state assessment	Emphasizing learning of priority standards and using state assessment results as one indicator of that learning
Giving infrequent common assessments (for example, once per quarter)	Giving common formative and end-of-unit assessments every ten days or less to respond to student learning in real time
Giving pretests that mirror the common end-of-unit assessment to measure growth	Giving short pretests (if needed) that measure relevant prior knowledge and skills to immediately inform instruction on the priority standard for the unit

common assessments provide the key to effective acceleration. As teams design assessments, they clarify the standards and level of performance required to deem students proficient (or higher) with each. They plan for differentiation and small-group learning in core instruction. Teams then use data on specific learning targets to design meaningful interventions and extensions, as well as to engage students in goal setting and reflection. The following section explores several assessment strategies teachers and teams can employ to accelerate learning this way.

Acceleration Strategies Through Assessments

Every assessment provides information related to student learning on priority standards or prior-knowledge standards. Teachers and teams utilize that information to better differentiate core instruction and plan for interventions that bring students up to grade level or higher:

> Using assessment well means capitalizing on the information collected and using those insights to facilitate learning and foster hope for students. When students see their work in terms of their strengths and what they understand, and see deficits as opportunities to grow, assessment provides more information about how to get better. (Dimich, 2015, p. 2)

The strategies in this section guide teachers and teams to use assessment well. If they do so, students will see their evidence of learning on any assessment as meaningful and use the information to self-assess their progress, as well as engage in additional learning opportunities their teachers provide based on the results. Students will see purpose in learning prior-knowledge standards because there is a connection from that learning to the grade-level learning, which involves students in the acceleration process.

Audit Current Assessment Practices

The first step to ensuring purposeful assessment practices is to conduct an assessment audit at the school or team level to determine the number, frequency, and purpose of classroom assessments and larger-scale assessments. Consider the following questions.

- ▸ When do teachers administer each assessment?
- ▸ When do teachers collect and analyze assessment results?
- ▸ What do teachers do with the assessment results and when?
- ▸ How do teachers learn from the results?
- ▸ How do students learn from the results?
- ▸ Which assessments are designed to provide the information critical to acceleration?

Figure 4.1 shows a template a guiding coalition or collaborative team might use for assessment audits. Some common examples of assessments teachers give to students appear in the template but readers should add, change, and remove entries as appropriate for their school or district.

Sometimes an audit reveals not every assessment is needed. Sometimes an audit reveals teachers are all giving common assessments on the same day every week, but teachers should stagger them for more accurate results. Students who are testing all day on Fridays, for example, may have test fatigue later in the day, which can create inaccurate results. Sometimes the audit reveals another assessment is needed, and sometimes it shows a grade level or course not getting enough

Assessments	Purpose and Use of Each Assessment	Grade Level, Frequency, and Timing
National Standardized Assessments • AP exams • SAT or ACT • National Assessment of Educational Progress (NAEP)		
State Assessments • ELA—Reading • ELA—Writing • Mathematics • Science		
District Assessments • Progress-monitoring assessments • Early literacy • Diagnostic • Benchmark or interim		
Common End-of-Unit Assessments • Unit test • Performance • Essay		
Common Formative Assessments (Mid-Unit) • Quiz • Observations • Exit ticket		

Classroom Formative Assessments (During Lessons)
• Checks for understanding
• Observations
• Students sharing thinking
• Examples include:
  • Whiteboard activities
  • Journal writing
  • Group discussions
  • Think-pair-share
  • Games		

Other		

FIGURE 4.1: Assessment audit template.

Visit go.SolutionTree.com/priorityschools for a free reproducible version of this figure.

data from assessments. When analyzing assessment practices to reconsider, an audit is a first step to clarify which assessments teachers are giving and why.

When the audit is complete, the guiding coalition or learning team, or all staff can discuss any shifts they need to make to assessment practices in terms of quantity, frequency, and purpose, and how to maximize teacher and student learning from each assessment.

Create a Balanced Assessment System

Each assessment teachers give gathers evidence of student learning. However, if assessments are not balanced and intentional throughout the school year, assessments will frustrate teachers and students alike because there will not be enough time to adequately analyze and respond to the gathered data before it is time to administer the next test. For acceleration to be successful, assessments must work in concert with one another instead of being random and contrary to the process of teaching and learning.

Balancing assessments means considering how much instructional time an assessment consumes, how long it takes to score the test and analyze the data, and how closely tied the assessment is to current learning targets. In a balanced assessment system, team common assessments and classroom formative assessments should be frequent and form the majority of the assessments students take. These assessments are "lightweight" or quick for students to take, efficient for teachers to score, and immediately relevant to instruction. Large-scale external assessments, by contrast, are "heavy"; teachers should keep these assessments to a minimum because they are time-consuming (and often stressful) for students, return results slowly, and usually cover a broad range of standards or topics. Educational coauthors Robert Eaker and Janel Keating (2015) summarize:

> The assessment that's the most important is the one closest to the student—the kind of assessment good teachers do daily to check on the learning from the lesson that day or that week. They can very quickly answer the questions, Are the kids learning, and how do we know? (p. 172)

There should be many more classroom formative assessments and common end-of-unit assessments than national, state, district, or progress-monitoring assessments because they provide focused information to grow students and teachers.

It is not uncommon for schools to give too many external assessments (interim assessments, progress-monitoring assessments in multiple subjects, district benchmark assessments, multiple early literacy assessments, and so on). When this happens, teachers do not have time to diagnostically analyze the data to inform classroom instruction and intervention, nor do they have time to give their own team-created common assessments. National or state assessments, which teachers use to monitor program strengths and weaknesses over the long term, should occur once per year. Progress-monitoring assessments, which allow teachers to see strengths and weaknesses of their instruction and group students for intervention about previously taught priority standards, should happen only about three to four times a year. Teachers should use other diagnostic or benchmark assessments selectively and with a defined benefit in terms of responding to student learning—for example, for forming intervention groups, validating common assessment data, or checking alignment with state expectations for a grade level or course. A balance with more team common assessments and daily classroom formative assessments is key to student learning.

Written well, common assessments provide a wealth of real-time information related to student learning and any targeted interventions that teachers need to immediately employ. Teams learn which instructional practices are most effective and collectively brainstorm additional strategies to use for intervention if needed. Formative assessment during lessons should occur every day, so teachers and students can adjust teaching and learning as needed. In real time, teachers can use the results to learn about their practices and student thinking to create small groups, differentiate activities, and design collective interventions to grow learning to grade level. Teams can celebrate growth in learning and students gain confidence as they see their learning improve. Chappuis and Stiggins (2020) state, "Tracking and self-reflection can have positive motivational effects simply because improvement can become its own reward" (p. 363).

Figure 4.2 shows a balanced assessment system. Larger circles mean the assessments happen with more frequency and make up a larger portion of the assessment system because they are more critical to accelerating student learning. Most of teachers' and teams' energy should be spent on classroom and team common assessments to accelerate learning for priority standards, thus they have the largest circles.

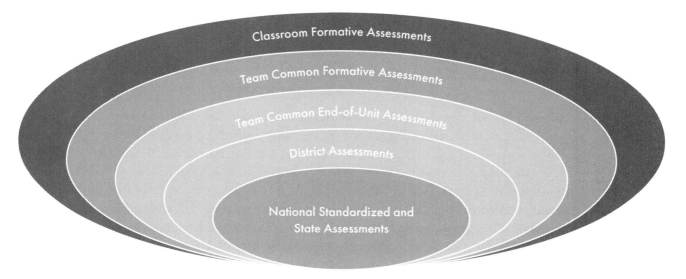

FIGURE 4.2: Balanced assessment system.

With a balanced assessment system in mind, review your assessment audit from figure 4.1 (page 65) to consider the overall system and how each assessment supports the others. Consider the following questions.

- ▶ How much time do you spend administering the different types of assessments in a grade level or course? Do you spend more time with team common assessments and daily formative assessment during instruction?

- ▶ How aligned are the various assessments you give to students? Do you have similar expectations for proficiency with grade- or course-level standards with each type of assessment?

- ▶ How accurate is your feedback to the team and the student from each assessment?

- ▶ Do you give assessments that could be eliminated because they provide the same learning information as another assessment? Are there any additional assessments that you need to give to understand student learning more fully?

At a high school in California, for example, an assessment audit revealed why mathematics teachers were frustrated with assessments and felt they did not have time for common formative assessments during a unit, only end-of-unit assessments. The current expectations in the district were that the mathematics teachers give the state assessment as well as five strand-specific practice state exams, the iReady progress-monitoring tool three times a year, and an additional diagnostic exam, in addition to any AP exams students might take. Teachers were using about fifteen instructional days (three weeks) each year to administer larger-scale exams. The state assessment was required, but the other three exams gave similar information, so the district considered eliminating redundancies. The district wanted to keep the iReady progress-monitoring assessments since teachers used them throughout the K–12 span. The mathematics teachers chose which strand-practice exams to give based on the courses they were teaching and spread the exams over three years. The district stopped using the additional diagnostic exam. After the audit, teams spent about five to seven days on larger-scale assessments throughout the year, giving more time to accelerate learning and utilize team common assessments to drive instructional decisions in real time. Although this example comes from a high school, elementary schools tend to administer many primary-grade assessments teachers should examine to see if any can be reduced to provide more time for team common assessments and teaching with acceleration in mind.

Create Common Assessments Unit by Unit

When teams engage in the learning cycle (see figure 3.8, page 50) to teach the priority standards and respond to student learning, they learn together, strengthen practices, and collectively grow the learning of more students. Common assessments students take during and at the end of the unit are an essential part of that process; they are also at the heart of the PLC process (DuFour et al., 2016). Teacher teams must clarify what students must know and be able to do (PLC critical question one) to create quality common assessments to gather evidence of that learning (PLC critical question two) so they can design effective interventions (PLC critical question three) and extensions (PLC critical question four; DuFour et al., 2016). It is from these common assessments that teachers across a team can determine what students have learned as a starting point for accelerating learning. The majority of teacher and student learning is a result of common assessments and classroom formative assessments during lessons.

As mentioned in chapter 3 (page 33), the learning cycle—from one common assessment through the next—should never exceed ten days. Teacher teams develop any common formative or common end-of-unit assessments *before* the unit begins to strengthen instruction. Teams may also need to give a pretest; for accelerating learning, pretests are short and assess students' strengths and needs on prerequisite standards for the upcoming priority standards in the next unit, not grade-level priority standards. Teachers determine who may need review or reteaching on prior content from the very start of the unit, whether through small-group instruction or a separate intervention time. If the teachers already know who has or does not have the prior knowledge and skills (perhaps from learning evidence gathered in a previous unit), then no pretest is necessary. The goal of any assessment is to inform next instructional steps and include students in the rationale.

When designing common assessments, there are several factors for teachers and teams to keep in mind. First, creating common assessments for a particular target or standard does not mean teachers need to write the assessment items from scratch. Rather, they can use assessments in their curriculum resources, assessments they have written previously, or questions gathered from other sources if they ensure the questions align to the target or standard. Second, the team will want to format the assessment to gather data by student and by target for a strategic and specific team response that accelerates learning. The formatting should allow students to determine which learning targets they have learned and which they have not learned *yet*.

Figure 4.3 shows a checklist for teams creating common assessments for each unit. The formatting of this checklist gives teachers and students the information they need about learning for each priority standard or target. When teachers and teams build assessments using this checklist, the common assessments provide the information they need to analyze instructional practices and design quality interventions and extensions. Each assessment allows for acceleration of learning in a targeted and specific way. Teams can determine how many students are in need of supports and accelerate learning to grade level one target at a time for each group of students.

Common Assessment Criteria	Check If Addressed
1. The targets or standards being assessed are written on the assessment.	
2. Questions on the assessment align to the targets or standards being assessed.	
3. There are enough questions per target or standard for teachers to know whether students learned the target or standard (for example, more than one question and, if multiple choice, four to five questions per target or standard).	
4. The questions on the assessment are a balance of lower- and higher-level questions and match grade-level proficiency expectations.	
5. The team has agreed how to score the assessment and what students must show in their work and reasoning to demonstrate proficiency.	
6. Directions are clear and easy to read. If the assessment is oral, teachers have a common script to read, common manipulatives or text, and a common checklist to record student learning data during the assessment.	
7. If the assessment is on paper, the font size is large enough and there is space for students to write answers if needed.	
8. There are team agreements for how to administer the assessment and the resources students can use, if any.	
9. The team has agreed how to modify or accommodate any assessments for students who require it.	

Source: Adapted from Kanold, Schuhl, et al., 2018; Kramer & Schuhl, 2017.

FIGURE 4.3: Creating common assessments checklist.

Visit **go.SolutionTree.com/priorityschools** *for a free reproducible version of this figure.*

Teacher teams can use the assessment rubric in figure 4.4 to analyze and grow assessment practices for learning. Teams analyzing their practices with the rubric reflect on how they create and also how they use their common assessments for teacher and student learning. To reach level 3, teams consistently analyze student learning data together and create a collective targeted and specific response. To reach level 4, students reflect on the learning they showed on the common assessment using a reflection tool designed to clarify what each student learned or still needs to learn (sometimes with a plan for any additional learning).

	Level 1 Beginning	Level 2 Attempting	Level 3 Practicing	Level 4 Embracing
Common Formative Assessment (During Unit)	Assessment is too long—uses too many instructional minutes to get data for students and teachers. The assessment is at a lower level of rigor than the intent of the standard or the items on the unit assessment. Each teacher on a team makes his or her own assessment.	Assessment is appropriately short in length. Assessment is common; however, teachers may not score it together or may not determine proficiency in advance. Teams write the assessment without considering the final expectations as determined on the summative assessment.	Teams determine proficiency before giving the assessment, and scoring agreements are clear. The rigor matches the intent of the standards and matches the summative assessment. Teachers reflect on the data to make instructional decisions.	Teams analyze trends in student work to determine what students who exceed, meet, nearly meet, and do not meet expectations demonstrate in terms of their understanding and application. Teams take differentiated instructional actions. Students analyze their results and set goals.
Common Summative Assessment (End of Unit)	Teams create the assessment at the end of the unit just before the assessment day. Teams use a publisher test or other assessment as is without making sure every test item aligns to a standard in the unit. Directions or questions are unclear. Scoring details are unclear or not specified. Assessment includes only multiple choice or only constructed response. Teachers may give assessment at the same time. Teachers may modify the assessment.	Teams create the assessment before the unit begins. The assessment contains clear directions and questions. Teams make scoring agreements in advance of giving the assessment. Assessment may only be one format (multiple choice or constructed response). All the teachers on a team give the assessment at roughly the same time. Teachers may modify the assessment or administer it differently from the rest of the team. Teams look at data and then move on.	Teams create the assessment before the unit begins. Items are clearly aligned to the learning targets and standards. Teams determine proficiency by learning target or standard in advance of giving the assessment. Scoring agreements are clear to teachers and students and teams calibrate their scoring. The assessment has a variety of formats. The assessment matches the rigor of the standards. Teams analyze data and teachers determine next instructional steps.	Teams create the assessment before the unit, align items, and emphasize priority standards. There are enough items to determine proficiency on the standards assessed. There is a balance of rigor on the assessment. Teachers analyze the data by standard and by student to determine what students learned and have not learned yet and which students learned and have not learned yet. The team makes a targeted plan. Students analyze and reflect on their assessment data and make learning goals.

Source: Kramer & Schuhl, 2017, p. 109.

FIGURE 4.4: Common assessment rubric.

*Visit **go.SolutionTree.com/priorityschools** for a free reproducible version of this figure.*

With common assessments in place, teachers can give more effective feedback to students during class because the teachers understand the final expectation and how students must demonstrate their learning. Teachers can also better differentiate lessons knowing the clear expectations for proficiency with a grade-level standard. And, by giving common assessments throughout a unit, the teachers on the team will expand their toolkits of effective instructional practices while accelerating learning.

Within the framework of common end-of-unit and common formative assessments (mid-unit), teachers can craft lessons that provide opportunities to check for student learning throughout the lesson and give students immediate feedback. The diagram in figure 4.5 shows how teams might think about the connection between their common end-of-unit assessments, common formative assessments, and their checks for understanding (noted with check marks) during each lesson that result in possibly altering lesson plans as well as their plan for formative feedback (noted with *F*) to students (teacher to student or student to student).

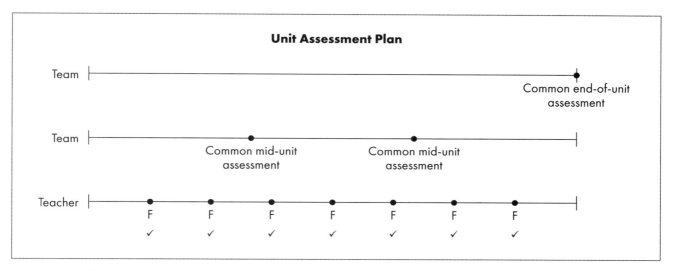

Source: Adapted from Kramer, 2021b; Schuhl, 2016.

FIGURE 4.5: Common assessment and daily formative assessment connection in each unit.

Implement Common Formative Assessment Strategies

As we stated in chapter 1 (page 5) and reiterate throughout this book, common assessments teachers use formatively and formative assessment during daily instruction are integral to learning, and particularly to acceleration. The foundational work on the power of formative assessments is Paul Black and Dylan Wiliam's (1998) article, *Inside the Black Box*. They researched students in grades K–12 and entry-level college in multiple disciplines across several countries. Black and Wiliam (1998) find formative assessment processes have an effect size of 0.4 to 0.7 and can increase the learning of lower-performing students to near grade level. The largest gains in learning come when teachers use their assessments diagnostically, students receive descriptive feedback, and students are involved in continued learning from the assessment.

After several more studies also revealed the importance of formative assessments, in 2010, Marzano wrote *Formative Assessment and Standards-Based Grading*, in which he describes research showing that over a fifteen-week period (most semesters are eighteen weeks), the number of formative assessments positively correlates with student learning increases. For example, one formative assessment has an effect size of 0.34 (13.5 percentile-point gain in learning) and thirty formative assessments have an effect size of 0.82 (29 percentile-point gain).

More recently, Hattie (2017) finds providing students with formative evaluation has an effect size of 0.48 and other components of formative assessments have even higher effect sizes. For example, students self-reporting grades has an effect size of 1.33; response to intervention (responding to student learning and accelerating it to grade level), 1.27; and instructional strategies that include feedback, 0.7. Common formative assessments are more than just tests. What teachers and students do with the results is what truly makes them formative. Formative strategies teachers use during instruction include feedback and continued student learning from that feedback to accelerate learning.

In the most basic sense, formative assessments are about generating information related to student learning for teachers and students, which allows these assessments to take many forms—both formal experiences like team common assessments and informal experiences within the classroom during daily lessons. Here, we describe several strategies for formative assessment, starting with building student self-efficacy through the use of assessments.

Student Self-Efficacy

Assessments are an opportunity for students to show not only teachers but also themselves what they have learned. Each assessment provides an opportunity for students to clarify what they have learned and what they have not learned *yet*. For example, students knowing they need to learn a model for photosynthesis is quite different and much more empowering than students feeling defeated by a broad unlearned topic like *science* or *unit 5*, which both fail to give direction. In *Principles to Action*, NCTM (2014) explains:

> At the center of the assessment process is the student . . . An important goal of assessment should be to make students self-assessors, teaching them how to recognize the strengths and weaknesses of past performance and use them to improve their future work. (p. 95)

It is important students develop a growth mindset if they are to believe that, with effort, they can learn content in various subject areas (Dweck, 2016). *Developing a growth mindset* means students will fail along the way and learn from their mistakes and misconceptions. Students and teachers should embrace such moments as experiences vital to learning through productive struggle. Educational author and mathematics professor Jo Boaler (2016) states, "When we teach students that mistakes are positive, it has an incredibly liberating effect on them" (p. 15). In fact, real learning takes place in the moment students identify mistakes and learn from them. If students do not productively struggle, they do not learn.

Having a growth mindset leads to students developing *self-efficacy*, the belief one can succeed and the confidence to persevere toward that success. *Student self-efficacy*, which has an effect size of 0.92 (Hattie, 2017), means students know they can learn when they apply identified strategies. They have determined ways to learn and believe they can learn to grade level because they have seen their growth and successes over time. Self-efficacy is an important part of acceleration and students believing they can learn to grade level or higher.

Albert Bandura (1995), professor emeritus at Stanford University and renowned social cognitive psychologist, studied self-efficacy and determined four influential factors to develop a strong sense of self-efficacy; here is that list, in the order of impact.

1. **Engage in mastery experiences:** Help students see and celebrate their growth in learning through perseverance.

2. **Observe vicarious experiences:** Show students other similar students who have learned and succeeded.

3. **Social persuasion:** Verbally encourage and share with students a belief they can succeed.

4. **Awareness of psychological and emotional states:** Help students understand the impact their feelings and stress levels may have on their self-efficacy and their work.

Consider how assessment practices can develop self-efficacy in students. Marzano's (2010) research concludes that having students track their progress visually (for example, using a graph) has an effect size of as much as 0.70 (26 percentile-point gain). Seeing such growth supports Bandura's (1995) first influential factor of mastery experiences. Additionally, Hattie (2017) reports an effect size of 1.33 (41 percentile-point gain) when students self-report their grades and understand the expectations associated with learning standards.

There are a variety of tools teachers can use to have students track and reflect on their progress on specific learning targets. Figure 4.6 (page 74) shares one reflection tool students can use throughout a unit to monitor progress and celebrate learning. The teacher gives the reflection tool to students at the start of the unit and then prompts them to reflect on their learning each day using evidence from classwork, homework, exit tickets, or common assessments. Where are the students now relative to learning each target? Each assignment or check ties back to the learning targets for the unit and students see connections to any assessment they take.

Figure 4.7 (page 75) shares a reflection tool to use after the end-of-unit common assessment. Students look at their feedback and determine which learning targets they learned and which they still need to learn. In upper elementary, middle, and high school, students can also make a learning plan for any standards they have not yet learned as part of the reflection.

Figure 4.8 (page 76) shares a student-reflection tool for a priority standard teachers teach several times throughout a quarter, semester, or year. Each time teachers give an assessment related to the standard, students track their progress, ideally seeing growth over time, which increases student confidence and self-efficacy.

When students can see their learning progress throughout a unit and after each common assessment, they develop self-efficacy. They see how their learning is accelerating to grade level or higher which, in turn, further accelerates learning. Chappuis and Stiggins (2020) share, "Engaging students regularly in noticing and reflecting on their own progress helps them develop an inner dialogue of self-monitoring necessary to becoming self-regulated learners" (p. 363). Students who are aware of their learning and the learning they still need can accelerate their learning with understanding and purpose.

Pretests

As mentioned previously, when teachers use pretests simply to measure growth from the beginning of a unit to the end, pretests are not the best use of instructional time, especially if students have never interacted with the content before and should show great growth gains. Acceleration requires teachers to integrate prerequisite knowledge into instruction *just in time* for students to use it to access grade-level priority standards. As such, teams give a short pretest on

Unit 2: Ratios and Rates

Learning Targets:

1. I can write and describe ratio relationships. | Starting . . .   Getting There . . .   Got It! |
2. I can use ratios to convert measurements. | Starting . . .   Getting There . . .   Got It! |
3. I can write and explain unit rates. | Starting . . .   Getting There . . .   Got It! |
4. I can solve ratio and rate problems. | Starting . . .   Getting There . . .   Got It! |

Vocabulary:

ratio	
rate	
unit rate	

Schedule		Homework Complete?
Day 1 *September 13*	Learning target 1: I can write and describe ratio relationships. (2.1) *Focus—Write ratios three ways (a to b, a:b, $\frac{a}{b}$).* **Homework**—p. 42: 1, 5, 9, 12	
Day 2 *September 14*	Learning target 1: I can write and describe ratio relationships. (2.1) *Focus—Use ratios to explain situations in word problems.* **Homework**—p. 42: 15, 20, 25	
Day 3 *September 15*	Learning target 2: I can use ratios to convert measurements. (2.3) *Focus—Convert metric measurements.* **Homework**—p. 51: 4–10	
Day 4 *September 16*	Learning target 2: I can use ratios to convert measurements. (2.4) *Focus—Convert customary measurements.* **Homework**—p. 58: 5–12	
Day 5 *September 17*	Learning target 1: I can write and describe ratio relationships. Learning target 2: I can use ratios to convert measurements. *Focus—Ratio math lab* **Homework**—Finish ratio math lab.	
Day 6 *September 20*	★ **Check for Understanding** • Learning target 1: I can write and describe ratio relationships. • Learning target 2: I can use ratios to convert measurements. **Homework (review) worksheet:** Rewrite fractions as decimals and decimals as fractions.	
Day 7 *September 21*	Learning target 3: I can write and explain unit rates. (2.7) *Focus—Rewrite rates as unit rates.* **Homework**—p. 75: 3, 11, 19, 21, 22	
Day 8 *September 22*	**Flex Day**—Stations to practice learning targets 1, 2, and 3 **Homework:** p. 75: 5, 17, 23, 25	
Day 9 *September 23*	Learning target 4: I can solve ratio and rate problems. (2.8) *Focus—Write equivalent ratios and rates using ratio tables.* **Homework**—p. 83: 1, 3, 6, 10	
Day 10 *September 24*	★ **Check for Understanding** • Learning target 3: I can write and explain unit rates. **Homework worksheet:** Write ratios and rates for real-life situations.	
Day 11 *September 27*	Learning target 4: I can solve ratio and rate problems. (2.8) *Focus—Solve word problems involving ratios and rates.* **Homework**—p. 83: 11–16	
Day 12 *September 28*	Learning target 4: I can solve ratio and rate problems. (2.8) *Focus—Solve word problems involving ratios and rates.* **Homework**—p. 84: 21–25	
Day 13 *September 29*	**Review Day** **Homework (review) worksheet**	
Day 14 *September 30*	★ **Unit Test** • Learning target 1: I can write and describe ratio relationships. • Learning target 2: I can use ratios to convert measurements. • Learning target 3: I can write and explain unit rates. • Learning target 4: I can solve ratio and rate problems.	

Source: © 2004 by Sarah Schuhl.

FIGURE 4.6: During-the-unit student-reflection tool.

Student Name: _____

Unit 2: Potential and Kinetic Energy

Write your score for each learning target and identify if you have learned the standard or not learned it yet.

Learning Target	Questions	Score	Circle Level of Understanding	
I can compare potential and kinetic energy.	#1–5		I got it!	Still learning it
I can graph and interpret the relationship between kinetic energy and the mass and speed of an object.	#6–12		I got it!	Still learning it
I can model how distance changes the amount of potential energy stored.	#13–14		I got it!	Still learning it

This test showed I have learned . . .

This test shows I still need to learn . . .

I _____ with my test scores because . . .
    (agree or disagree)

My plan to learn the targets I still need to learn is . . .

Source: Adapted from Kanold, Schuhl, et al., 2018; Kramer & Schuhl, 2017.

FIGURE 4.7: End-of-unit student-reflection tool.

Student Name: _____

Learning Target: I can summarize.

This means I can . . .

- Retell the text in order using my own words
- State the main idea of the text
- Share a few important and specific details from the text
- Write a short and focused summary

	Proficiency Rubric: I can summarize.
4	Summary includes the main idea and most important details to support it. Summary is short, focused, non-biased and written in the student's own words.
3	Summary includes the main idea and important details to support it. Summary is short, focused, in sequential order, and written in the student's own words.
2	Summary includes a main idea and many details, in sequential order, some of which do not support the main idea, which also extends the length of the summary. Summary may include some copied part of the text.
1	Summary describes the text without a main idea. Summary may include copied parts of text or be quite long. Summary may retell the story out of sequential order.

For each assessment, record your learning by writing the date and coloring the bar graph to show your score.

4									
3									
2									
1									
Date									

FIGURE 4.8: Student-reflection tool for standards over time.

prior-knowledge standards *if* teachers are unsure where to start leveling up to grade level during instruction. If teachers know from previous learning experiences, common assessments, or progress-monitoring assessments whether students have learned the prior knowledge they need to learn the upcoming grade-level standards, no pretest is necessary. The data generated from any pretest show the team how to maximize learning during Tier 1 core instruction (differentiation, small groups, and so on) or Tier 2 interventions throughout the unit so students can learn the priority standard at grade level.

A pretest may take the form of an *obtrusive test*, meaning core learning stops for a formal assessment, such as a pencil-and-paper quiz. Such a pretest should be short (lasting about twenty minutes), so learning can still occur during core instructional time. Pretests may also be *unobtrusive*, such as observations in class or conversations with a small group of students while other students are applying learning. Figure 4.9 shows an obtrusive pretest and figure 4.10 (page 78) shows an unobtrusive pretest, demonstrating two different ways a team might assess a third grader's understanding of addition and subtraction.

Name: _____

Look What I Can Do!

I can show what I have learned about addition and subtraction.

1. Write the answer to each addition or subtraction problem in the box.

   $2 + 4 = \boxed{}$ $6 + 7 = \boxed{}$ $\boxed{} = 10 + 2$ $5 + 4 = \boxed{}$

   $10 - 6 = \boxed{}$ $14 - 8 = \boxed{}$ $\boxed{} = 5 - 1$ $8 - 3 = \boxed{}$

2. Add or subtract. Show your thinking.

   $\begin{array}{r} 25 \\ +\ 31 \\ \hline \end{array}$ $\begin{array}{r} 46 \\ -\ 23 \\ \hline \end{array}$ $\begin{array}{r} 38 \\ +\ 15 \\ \hline \end{array}$ $\begin{array}{r} 32 \\ -\ 14 \\ \hline \end{array}$

3. Jeremy has 35 pieces of candy. He eats 15 pieces. How many pieces of candy are left? Use words, pictures, or numbers to show your thinking.

FIGURE 4.9: Grade 3 pretest—addition and subtraction (obtrusive).

Addition and Subtraction Pretest

For each skill, determine if a student is at a level 1, 2, or 3 of understanding. Use NE if there is no evidence the student can do the skill.

- 3—Student is proficient (may make a minor mistake—no reteaching needed).
- 2—Student is close to proficiency (needs to be retaught part of the skill).
- 1—Student has a minimal understanding of the skill and needs support to answer.

Student	Single-Digit Addition and Subtraction Facts	Add and Subtract Without Regrouping	Add and Subtract With Regrouping	Word Problems

FIGURE 4.10: Grade 3 pretest—addition and subtraction (unobtrusive).

As a team, determine the learning you are trying to assess in a pretest. The pretest in figure 4.9 (page 77) is checking on (1) single-digit addition and subtraction facts, (2) adding and subtracting with and without regrouping, and (3) reading and solving a one-step word problem using addition or subtraction. The team might also have decided to create a different pretest that utilizes stations around the room with problems or games like the pretest in figure 4.10 shows; teachers observe students working in pairs to solve the problems or games. Using a checklist like the one in figure 4.10, teachers gather data about the prior-knowledge skills students need for larger-digit addition and subtraction and an understanding of multiplication and division as repeated addition or subtraction. Teachers often use such a pretest at the start of the school year to accelerate learning by having students remember (together) how to solve problems while learning the routines in the classroom.

Pretests take many forms. They can be like those figures 4.9 (page 77) and 4.10 or they may be as short as an exit ticket (obtrusive), a five-minute quick write to a prompt (obtrusive), or filling in the *Know* and *Want to Know* columns of a KWL chart as part of instruction (unobtrusive; students would add to the KWL chart throughout the unit).

The data gathered from any pretest should inform teachers' next steps in instruction. Depending on the results, a teacher might implement a lesson focused on prior knowledge at the start of the unit if the majority of students are in need of such learning; use minilessons or small-group work during core instruction; design flex days, bell ringers, or homework; or guide students to intervention and extension time at a different time during the school day. The time spent administering a pretest is valuable when both teachers and students learn from the results at the beginning of and throughout the unit.

Rolling Assessments

By definition, *grade-level standards* define the expectations students must meet by the end of the school year. However, teachers and teams cannot wait until the end of the year to assess broad skills such as reading a grade-level text, using reading strategies to determine the meaning of unknown vocabulary words, or speaking and listening in a world language. Districts, schools, or teams must determine benchmarks students should reach at specific intervals to be on track for proficiency by the end of the school year. For example, which letters and sounds should kindergarten students know by the end of quarter 1, quarter 2, or quarter 3 to master the alphabet by the end of the year? What level text should a student be able to read in each grade level by the end of each quarter? To what level of proficiency should students be speaking and listening each quarter in a world language course?

Students will master skills at different speeds, and it can be very time intensive to assess skills for every student one to one in a single sitting. As such, teams can create *rolling assessments*. Each rolling assessment matches a benchmark that will give teachers and students information about whether students are on track to be proficient with the priority standard by the end of the school year.

Teachers can give rolling assessments at any time before the designated date. Once teachers feel a student has demonstrated proficiency with letter names, counting, or another identified skill, they can pull the student aside during small groups or while other students are applying learning to assess the benchmark skill. Teachers can assess students who are not yet proficient on multiple occasions during a team-determined time period to see what focused acceleration is needed for them to reach proficiency by the designated date. With this approach, teachers will not need to suddenly test all students in a short window of time. Teachers design the rolling assessment to gather evidence of student learning relative to a benchmark without interrupting instruction and to strategically respond with a focus on acceleration.

Typically, a *rolling assessment* is a checklist assessment for data or a printed assessment on which the teacher or students can circle correct or incorrect responses; teachers most often use a rolling assessment in the primary grades. Figure 4.11 (page 80) shows an example of a rolling assessment that tracks students' letter recognition. It is divided into sections for quarterly benchmarks to ensure students meet the standard by the end of the school year.

Opportunities for Reassessment

Students may not demonstrate proficiency *yet* on a common formative (or even end-of-unit) assessment. While the teacher may have wanted students to be proficient by the date of the assessment, the ultimate goal is for students to be proficient with the priority standard in time for the next grade level or course. The teacher and team have a choice: give the student a low grade for not yet demonstrating proficiency by a certain date or work with the student to learn and give the student another opportunity to show the student has learned the standard. Ideally, the consequence for not learning *yet* is to keep learning and practicing until the student is proficient with the skill in the standard. Once the student achieves growth or full proficiency, the student receives feedback and a grade that reflects the student's current level of understanding, not one that penalizes the student for not meeting the deadline. DuFour (2015) adds, "The best way to teach

Check each letter the student recognizes from the letter flash cards. Teachers can assess the student at any time prior to the benchmark date.

Quarter 1

Student	a	m	t	s	i	f	d	r	o	g	l	h	u	c	b	n	k	v

Quarter 2

Student	e	w	j	p	y	n	k	v	e	w	j	p	y	T	L	M	F	D	I	N	A	R

Quarter 3

Student	H	G	B	x	q	z	J	E	Q

Source: Adapted from University of Oregon Center on Teaching and Learning, n.d.

FIGURE 4.11: Kindergarten rolling assessment for letter recognition.

students responsibility is to insist that students do what responsible people do. Responsible people do the work. Responsible people seek assistance when they are struggling to succeed" (p. 184). In other words, penalizing a student for not having learned by the team's deadline expands learning gaps and misses an opportunity to teach students how to be responsible and take ownership for learning in a way that will accelerate their learning to grade level.

Accelerating learning means students know they can continue to learn and reach grade-level proficiency throughout a unit or even after it is completed. Ideally, students will be proficient in the window of time set for the unit; it will be less work for students if they are proficient by the common end-of-unit assessment. If not, however, students need more learning and must reflect on their current learning, understand their misconceptions, and learn the standard through team-designed acceleration strategies that include minilessons or interventions. A *reassessment* is a new assessment covering the same targets or standards as the original assessment but with new questions, contexts, or passages so students are showing true growth. Researchers and educators including Buffum and colleagues (2018); DuFour (2015); Thomas R. Guskey (2015); Kanold, Schuhl, and colleagues (2018); Marzano (2010); Reeves (2016); and Tom Schimmer (2016) all report the rationale for reassessments.

Schimmer (2016) says, "The process of reassessment is about learning from mistakes and reassessing once students have reached new levels" (p. 68). He advocates having students analyze their original assessment to determine which standards or targets they learned, which they need more practice with, and where more learning is necessary (Schimmer, 2016). Students then make a learning plan.

Some key criteria for a reassessment include the following.

- ▸ Students do additional work with immediate feedback to learn the standards or targets.

- ▸ Students analyze and learn from their original assessment. Which standards or targets did they learn? What were any trends in misconceptions on those standards or targets not learned *yet*? Students revise their work from the original assessment to apply their learning of the skills.

- ▸ The reassessment must be novel and new, meaning it is not the same assessment as the original. Students may reassess on only the standards or targets missed or the full assessment to show they have retained proficiency. In either case, students read new passages, get word problems with new contexts, or solve mathematics computations with new numbers, for example. How will students demonstrate they have *learned* the skills in the standards or targets and are not simply repeating answers from memory? The reassessment often has similar formatting to the original common assessment.

Reassessment does not mean instruction in the next unit should stop until all students are proficient. Rather, as we explain in chapter 6 (page 107), teams will use small groups, minilessons, and additional intervention time for the additional learning. Furthermore, the purpose of the reassessment is not to give students a pass for not taking an original assessment seriously. Students are reflecting on learning throughout the unit and engaging in activities to learn. For those who still have not learned, it is an opportunity to do additional work to learn, to be held accountable to learning the priority standards, and then to demonstrate that learning. Most importantly, teachers accelerate learning to grade level, which is crucial for future student success. Reassessment is a specific example of bringing the mission of *learning is required* to life.

Test Talks

Students do not always know how to address assessment items in a metacognitive sense. Even if they understand the content, they might not know how to answer the test question or demonstrate their learning in the context of the test question. Many students tend to skim questions and answer quickly. Some students have not learned that multiple-choice items have one correct answer (or a couple of correct answers), and the remaining choices are *plausible distractors*, meaning they are the common misconceptions students might have. Students might not read directions carefully or may not understand what *show your work* means on a mathematics assessment versus a science or social studies assessment. Similarly, students may not have learned to reread passages for the purpose of answering the questions posed after the text.

Students cannot demonstrate proficiency with grade-level or prior-knowledge standards if they do not understand how to answer assessment questions. In addition to accelerating learning to grade level for priority standards, learning is accelerated when teachers use assessments accessible to students and students can truly demonstrate learning to give teachers and themselves accurate feedback for continued learning.

In the Glendale Elementary School District in Arizona, teachers engage students in test talks. *Test talks* are a strategy to teach students how to think about the structure of various assessment items in addition to the content. Throughout a unit, teachers create assessment-like items (or find released items), have students read the question and answer it, and lead a discussion with students about the intent of the person who wrote the question.

- ▶ Why did the test maker create this question?
- ▶ What is the test maker trying to learn about student thinking?
- ▶ (For multiple-choice questions) How is the test maker trying to "trick" students with each wrong answer (distractor)? How do they know what the right answer is?
- ▶ What do the test maker's directions mean? What does the test maker want students to do?
- ▶ What does the test maker want students to do after reading a passage and seeing the first question?
- ▶ Why does the test maker say students can use scratch paper to answer the question?

Have students answer the questions in pairs first and then randomly call on students to share responses with the whole group. It is important to use test talks as a fun and engaging activity without a focus on any state or progress-monitoring assessment. Ideally, teachers use them as a warm-up activity or during lessons throughout the year. Confident students are more likely to try any assessment because they see the assessment as a true "show what you know" experience. Design test talks to grow confidence in students and lessen their fear of taking assessments.

Learning Passports

A *learning passport* mimics a passport for international travel, but rather than students earning stamps for visiting countries, they earn stamps for showing proficiency with priority standards learned throughout the year. The learning passport contains the standards and targets for the grade level or course so the teacher can stamp each. Figure 4.12 shows an example of a learning passport from Glendale Elementary School District in Arizona.

As a review strategy, learning passports can be an engaging and fun way to have students prepare for end-of-unit and end-of-year assessments. Also use learning passports at the end of the year for students to share with their next grade-level teachers to show proficiency with priority standards.

There are a variety of ways students might demonstrate proficiency to earn a stamp. Consider how students can work in pairs or groups to actively show learning instead of independently practicing assessment-like questions. While the items students use in a review will be like those on the test, the focus does not need to be on the test itself, rather on students' demonstrating their knowledge. Some options for activities to use for stamps (or for review in general) include the following.

- ▶ **Stations:** Create stations in the classroom (at desks or using poster paper on the wall). Each station represents a standard or target clearly labeled at the station. Students answer questions at the station in pairs and check their answers. They revise any incorrect answers and move to the next station. The teacher monitors the stations and stamps learning passports at the station or has students show their answers (on paper, worksheet, whiteboard, and so on) to stamp the passport.

PASSPORT TO AzMERIT

Name: _____

Homeroom: _____

Goal Statement: _____

_____

_____

Third-Grade Mathematics

Standard	Benchmark 1	Benchmark 2	Benchmark 3	I can teach someone else.	I got it!	I am getting closer!	I am still working at this.
3.OA.1							
I can describe a situation using a multiplication equation and solve the equation.	■	■					
3.OA.2							
I can describe a situation using a division equation and solve the equation.	■	■					
3.OA.3							
I can solve word problems using arrays and equations involving multiplication and division.	■	■					
I can solve multiplication and division problems in which the unknown is in any of the three possible positions.	■	■					
3.OA.5							
I can apply the break apart strategy to solve a multiplication equation.	■	■					
3.OA.4							
I can use fact families to determine the unknown number in division equations.	■	■					
3.OA.7							
I can multiply and divide using the relationship between multiplication and division.	■	■					

FIGURE 4.12: Student learning passport example.

continued ▶▶

3.OA.8						
I can solve two-step word problems using equations in the four operations and pictures to represent the problem.						
I can solve two-step word problems using equations in the four operations and a tape diagram to represent the problem.						
I can solve two-step word problems using equations in the four operations with a letter standing for the unknown number.						
3.NBT.2						
I can solve addition problems using the partial sums method.						
I can solve addition problems using open number lines.						
I can solve subtraction problems using open number lines.						
I can solve subtraction problems using open number lines and the relationship between addition and subtraction.						
I can solve a subtraction problem and use addition to check my work.						
Overall						

Reflection Statement: How well did you do during small-group instruction for mathematics?

_____

_____

_____

How do you feel about AzMERIT?

I am so ready!	I think I'm ready.	I am almost ready.	I am still working on being ready.

Source for standards: NGA & CCSSO, 2010b.

Source: © 2021 by Glendale Elementary School District. Adapted with permission.

▶ **Bingo:** Teachers use bingo for a specific standard or target, which students should write at the top of the bingo board, so it aligns to their passport. For concepts like grammar, mathematical computations, or solving equations, share about thirty possible answers with students. In pairs, students generate a bingo board by randomly placing twenty-four of the answers on their board (free space in the middle). The teacher gives the prompts (written on slides or on note cards put under a document camera). Students work in their pairs to answer the question, mark the square if the answer is on their board, and shout "Bingo!" when they have five answers in a row. Then the game starts again.

▶ **Gallery walks:** Place poster paper around the room with a different standard or target at the top of each. In pairs or groups, have students write what they have learned related to the standard or target and generate one question the test might ask for that standard or target. Each pair or group of students uses a different-colored pen. They move around the room clockwise and continue to add to the posters. When finished, the students do a gallery walk and reflect on the standards and targets they have learned and those they have not learned yet. The next day, this can become a station activity, with stations near each poster (see first bullet).

▶ **Games:** Consider how to specify the standard or target that is the focus of the game and how to have students make their thinking visible (written) while working in pairs or groups so the teacher can give stamps when students show proficiency. For example, a teacher team creates a game board with squares from start to finish and when students land on a square after using a spinner or die, they draw a card that asks a question related to the standard or target and answer the question in order to stay on the square.

▶ **Relay race:** For a given standard or target, the teacher holds slips of paper with written test items. Students work in pairs and each pair has one pencil (the "baton"). The student holding the pencil walks to the teacher to get a question and returns. Together, the two students answer the question. The second student takes the pencil and the work to the teacher and explains the answer if needed. Then the teacher gives a new question to the student, who returns and now oversees writing the answer (and explanation if needed). The second student hands the pencil to the first student and the relay race continues with students answering as many questions as they can.

▶ **Find the mistake:** Students often find it interesting to discover or explain mistakes. For a given standard or target (or different ones at different stations), have students find the mistake. The teacher might give a mathematics problem and have students identify the error and fix it, or give a multiple-choice item, identify a wrong answer, and ask students to explain the mistake a student made to arrive at that wrong answer. Similarly, teachers could give students a passage with a certain number of grammatical errors and students then find or fix the mistakes.

Students who are not yet proficient might get stamps by working with a partner or group—this is OK and will increase students' confidence. Teachers can add accountability to activities by randomly calling on individual students to share the thinking of the pair or group. When using reading passages, consider having students read the passage independently, discuss it with a partner, and then answer any questions together.

Together, student reflection on assessments and teams' intentional creation and use of common assessment practices grows student self-efficacy and accelerates learning. Students see assessments as "show what you know" opportunities to learn about their own thinking and focus future learning. They become part of the assessment process and stronger learners as a result.

Conclusion

Assessments provide the feedback teachers and students need to determine next instructional or learning steps—the real-time diagnostic information they need to accelerate learning. As such, assessments are an integral part of the learning cycle. It is important that assessments work in concert, from national or state assessments to district assessments and team and classroom assessments. Teams create mid-unit and end-of-unit common assessments for priority standards in advance of learning cycles and then incorporate formative assessments into daily instruction.

To ensure teachers and students have sufficient data about learning without wasting instructional time, schools audit their current assessment practices and shift the balance toward brief, common formative classroom assessments, rather than time-consuming external exams. These common formative assessments can take a variety of formats. Common assessments provide opportunities to strategically accelerate learning to grade level for the priority standards and include students in the process to grow their self-efficacy. Teachers gather evidence of what students have learned and create learning experiences to guide students from their current level to grade level or higher. Students, in turn, see what they have learned and still need to learn, and can be part of accelerating their own learning, while gaining confidence in their abilities.

Discussion Questions for Reflection and Action

As a team, discuss the following questions. Visit **go.SolutionTree.com/priorityschools** for a free reproducible version of these questions.

▸ How do teachers advance instruction and learning *because* of the instructional minutes spent giving an assessment?

▸ Does your school or district's assessment audit indicate a need for any adjustments in the assessments that teachers currently give to students? What might you change?

▸ How do state and progress-monitoring assessments connect to team common assessments and classroom formative assessments?

▸ How often are teams giving common assessments (common formative assessments and common end-of-unit assessments)?

▸ What is a current strength in your team common assessments? What is an area to strengthen?

▸ What are students, teachers, and teams doing with the results of common assessments?

▸ What are different ways teachers on your team or in your school check for student understanding using classroom formative assessments?

▸ What strategies related to assessment might you try to accelerate learning?

CHAPTER 5

Daily Grade-Level Instruction That Accelerates Learning

When Sarah's boys were in the third and fifth grades, her husband, Jon, decided to coach their community soccer team, having been a strong soccer player himself throughout grade school and recreationally as an adult. Quickly Jon learned the players on his team had little or no soccer experience. With their first game two weeks away, Jon and his assistant coach had to make some quick decisions about what to teach the players. The coaches realized even though players were unable to dribble a soccer ball, spending the entire practice solely on dribbling would not get the players where they needed to be for game time. Instead, Jon and his assistant coach divided initial practices into three parts: (1) individual foundational skills (dribbling and shooting), (2) team skill development (passing), and (3) a scrimmage to simulate future games. During each part, players learned through practice and feedback.

As the year progressed, the players' foundational and team skills during practice grew to include defensive strategies and coordinated plays, while also including previously learned skills to strengthen muscle memory and ensure skills became routine. And every practice continued to include a scrimmage to incorporate skills players learned, show the purpose for the learned skills, and strengthen the team for game days.

Did the season end with first-place trophies? No. But it did end with students eager to play soccer; they signed up to play again in future years and continued to learn the game, many with a great deal of success. Players who initially grouped together around the ball and looked at their feet when dribbling, spread out on the field and looked up to make strong passes or shots on goal. The season ended with players who learned the fundamentals of soccer as well as the nuances of the game to a level where they were ready for the next season and believed they could be great soccer players. If Jon had focused all coaching sessions on dribbling until each player perfected the skill, the games would not have gone well. The scrimmages were critical to the success of players; they knew what to do during games. Similarly, students interacting with grade-level content every day in lessons is critical to closing achievement gaps and accelerating learning to grade level or beyond.

As we discuss throughout this book and as the analogy of the soccer team demonstrates, the only way to close achievement gaps is to integrate foundational skills with game-day performance—or prerequisite content with grade-level learning. The only way

> If a student's core instruction is focused on below-grade-level standards, then he or she will learn well below grade level.
>
> —AUSTIN BUFFUM, MIKE MATTOS, AND JANET MALONE

students will have an opportunity to learn grade-level standards is if teachers teach grade-level standards every day during core instruction (Buffum et al., 2018). *Accelerating learning* means growing students to grade-level skills, with an emphasis on strategically merging grade-level and prior-knowledge standards into lessons.

If students are still learning to read independently but need to identify key details and the theme using grade-level text, a teacher might read the text aloud and then ask students to share key details or the theme. Later in the lesson, the teacher might use small groups to teach foundational reading skills or strategies. Similarly, in mathematics, if students are struggling with computations but need to solve word problems, the teacher may allow students to use a calculator for computations once they have generated a strategy to solve the problem by drawing a picture or writing an equation. Later in the lesson, the teacher might work with students in small groups to continue building fluency with computational or procedural skills.

The only way students will be college and career ready is if they are grade-level ready from one year to the next—starting in preK or kindergarten. Determine the students' grade-level or course readiness for learning on each priority standard and work together to plan learning cycles and units that grow student learning with a focus on the instructional strategies necessary to teach grade-level standards every day.

The Shift to Grade-Level Learning Every Day

Teachers want students to learn and plan lessons for that purpose. Yet, too often, frustrations grow when students are not as prepared as hoped or do not grasp all the standards the teacher is rapid-fire teaching. In a quest to teach everything to students not yet grade-level ready, teachers try to teach *all* of the grade-level standards *in addition to* every prior-grade-level standard. Even with all the instructional strategies and technology tools available, students do not have the time to digest all that learning and apply it. As we discussed in chapter 3 (page 33), it is impossible to teach every grade-level or course standard in a single school year and have students learn them, let alone additional standards—thus, the importance of prioritizing standards, designing team common assessments, and teaching strategically.

With best intentions to grow learning, teachers have tried various approaches to instruction. Traditionally, teachers might instruct using one-size-fits-all lessons, or teaching to the whole group every day without any differentiation or targeted small-group learning. Alternately, teachers may level students into small groups within a classroom or across a grade level or course, and teach students core instruction in leveled groups, which means some students do learn grade-level standards and others do not. Frustration at the sheer quantity of standards to teach and students' lack of preparedness may lead to lowered teacher expectations, memorization tactics, or a focus on teaching over learning. Despite teachers' efforts, these instructional approaches cannot overcome learning gaps.

Just as there are shifts in thinking about culture, planning units, and using assessment, there are shifts needed in instruction if students are to learn grade-level or course priority standards in a school year. Table 5.1 shows the instructional shifts teachers need to teach to grade level or beyond with corresponding student learning.

The focus of this chapter is establishing high expectations for all students and then utilizing instructional strategies to reach those expectations. Students need to grow in their learning if they are to learn priority standards at grade level when they are not there yet. And educators must

TABLE 5.1: Shifts in Instruction to Accelerate Student Learning

SHIFT FROM . . .	SHIFT TO . . .
Teaching skill by skill in isolated and discrete chunks of time	Teaching through a lens of conceptual understanding to build retention through connections and understanding of content
Focusing only on lower-level, foundational, or basic skills in lessons	Teaching foundational skills in small chunks and engaging students in higher-order reasoning and sense-making when teaching content
Using an abundance of direct instruction and lectures to fill gaps in learning and get to grade-level standards	Using minimal direct instruction and guiding students to apply and practice content with feedback from the teacher and peers
Creating tracked classes or leveled groups for core instruction	Teaching all students core instruction in mixed-ability classrooms to guarantee grade-level and prior learning
Instructing primarily through whole-group lessons	Engaging students to learn in pairs or small groups through discourse throughout a lesson
Following the textbook lesson by lesson and reading from the script	Selecting the most important parts of resources to use that best match the priority standards and adapting any scripts as needed
Predetermining a student's learning ability or giving excuses (such as past performance or socioeconomic status) for why students are not learning	Believing all students can and will learn grade-level priority standards and working in collaborative teams to ensure students meet these high expectations

look beyond growth for its own sake. Growing a student from a first-grade understanding to a second-grade understanding is phenomenal when the student is in second grade, but not enough if the student is in fifth grade. Is there a celebration? Yes! But it is not until the student achieves fifth-grade proficiency on the priority standards that it is time to celebrate a true win.

The only way to close these gaps is to accelerate learning—grow students *more* than a year's worth of growth if they are to learn at grade level—through meaningful instruction and systematic intervention (see chapter 6, page 107). In a learning-centered culture, teachers work together to ensure every student accelerates learning to the grade-level priority standards. They work within units and learning cycles to incorporate instructional strategies for accelerating learning every day in the classroom.

Acceleration Strategies as Part of Instruction

Accelerating student learning to grade level happens when teachers include grade-level standards in every lesson using high-quality instructional strategies. This *first-best instruction* grows student learning and is designed to prevent students later needing time- and resource-intensive interventions (Buffum et al., 2018; see chapter 6, page 107). The strategies we share in this chapter are not all-inclusive but are effective instructional strategies to accelerate learning and require a mindset of high expectations for all students. Students can learn grade-level standards, but only if teachers teach at grade level every day. Student learning happens every day in the classroom. Each time students get feedback from the teacher or their peers that affirms or alters their understanding as they work to learn grade- or course-level targets, learning happens. The goal is to grow student learning along a learning progression so they can simultaneously learn grade-level content.

Despite the impact poverty and social-emotional challenges have on learning, all students can learn no matter their circumstances (Hattie, 2009, 2012, 2017; Hattie & Yates, 2014; Marzano, 2017; Marzano & Pickering, 2011; Payne, 2005). Hattie's (2012, 2017) research suggests the impact of a student's socioeconomic status has an effect size of 0.52, which is larger than the expected learning of a student aging one year with an average teacher (effect size of 0.4). However, there are numerous influences on achievement with a larger effect size than socioeconomic status, some of which we discuss in other chapters of this book. Additional key influences that relate to instruction for acceleration include the following (Hattie, 2017).

- ▸ Self-reported grades and student expectations (1.33)
- ▸ Response to intervention (1.29)
- ▸ Classroom discussion (0.82)
- ▸ Teacher clarity (0.75)
- ▸ Feedback (0.70)
- ▸ Vocabulary programs (0.62)
- ▸ Spaced and massed practice (0.60)
- ▸ Metacognitive strategies (0.60)
- ▸ Not labeling students (0.61)
- ▸ Cooperative versus individualistic learning (0.55)
- ▸ Teacher-student relationships (0.52)

It is also essential that teachers adopt a mindset that focuses on student learning over teaching (DuFour et al., 2016; Hattie, 2012; Marzano, Warrick, Rains, & DuFour, 2018). Teachers and collaborative teams "work together to evaluate the impact of their planning on student outcomes" (Hattie, 2012, p. 37) and analyze the effectiveness of their instructional strategies using evidence of student learning. DuFour (2015) states, "Ensuring that all students succeed requires a school to embrace the following mantra: good teaching is not what *I* do *for* my students but instead what *we* do *with* our students" (p. 206). Armed with these important mindsets, instructional strategies for acceleration lead to high-quality core instruction. Use the following strategies for any additional instruction students receive from their assigned teacher or any teacher on the collaborative team.

Design Quality Lessons Tied to Grade-Level Learning Every Day

Just as it is important to plan for a guaranteed and viable curriculum and units of learning that produce equity in student learning across a grade level or course, so it is important to plan daily lessons within each unit. Teachers implement any instructional acceleration strategies more effectively through a quality lesson design. The ability to grow student learning to grade level starts with intentional lessons that focus on grade-level standards every day. To accelerate learning, teachers and teams also integrate just-in-time foundational knowledge and design learning experiences that include differentiation in lessons. The following questions can guide this process.

- ▶ What is the grade-level priority standard focus for the lesson?

- ▶ What is the prior-knowledge standard that leads to the priority standard in the lesson?

- ▶ What standard (if any) should you spiral review during the lesson?

- ▶ How will you address each standard during the lesson to generate feedback about student learning?

While collaborative teams discuss the instructional practices that most effectively grow student learning, each teacher does not need to teach every aspect of every lesson the same way. DuFour (2015) shares, "Effective instruction requires both an expectation that all teachers use practices proven to have the greatest impact on student learning while simultaneously enabling teachers to infuse their own style and differentiate instruction for individual student needs" (p. 206). There are unique student needs to address in each classroom and teachers use distinct styles to implement the effective strategies.

There is not one lesson structure to implement every day. In fact, while classroom routines are important for social-emotional learning and expected structures, the order teachers implement the parts of the lesson can vary. For example, a teacher might start with an exploration to see what students already know or can learn together at the start of the lesson, and then include some direct instruction with time for application and learning. Another day, some direct instruction and whole-group learning might start the lesson, with practice and application afterward. These are just two examples of how teachers might design a lesson.

Rather than focusing on constructing the order of a lesson, consider instead the overall framework and elements to include. Every lesson plan starts with a *lesson goal*—an understanding of what students must learn by the end of the lesson related to a grade-level standard. When accelerating learning, the lesson also includes the scaffolded supports or prior knowledge that teachers need to also address for students to be able to engage in learning the grade-level standard. Defining the objective of the lesson and each of its parts addresses the factor of teacher clarity, which has an effect size of 0.75 (Hattie, 2017).

Another element to strong instruction is student reflection. Students are active participants in the learning process. How do students tie their learning to the lesson goal each day? How do they monitor and reflect on their progress toward learning the grade-level standard in each lesson? Teacher clarity grows student clarity and gives purpose to each lesson and assignment. Giving students time to reflect and own their learning is an important part of accelerating learning because students see their growth and can articulate the learning they still need.

When accelerating learning, teachers include prior-knowledge standards and grade-level standards in each lesson. How will students connect the prior knowledge to the grade-level learning? This is another lesson-design element. Connecting new learning to prior knowledge has an effect size of 0.93 (Hattie, 2017). Have students share connections in the warm-up to the lesson so they understand where the learning is headed, or pose a grade-level task and have students apply their learning *so far* to see how they might tackle the task in the middle or at the end of the lesson. What is important is that students are the ones making the connections, rather than the teacher telling students the connections.

When creating a lesson, consider how students *actively engage*, meaning how they apply or explore learning in an observable way. This lesson-design element provides opportunities for formative assessment during a lesson. When planning each part of a lesson, teachers ask, "What am I doing during this part of the lesson? What are students doing?" The goal is for students to do more of the learning work than the teacher in each lesson. In fact, even in a guided release model, *we do* and *you do* are two-thirds of the lesson, and *I do* is only one-third at most.

Feedback is another important element of a quality lesson design—feedback from the teacher to students, students to students, and students to the teacher. In their book *Instructional Agility*, Erkens and colleagues (2018) emphasize the importance of responding in real time to the formative assessments teachers use throughout each lesson (part of the balanced assessment system we shared in chapter 4, page 61). Teachers gather evidence of student learning through engaging conversations, questioning, observations, and the practice of skills they assign students during the lesson. Each strategy allows an opportunity for providing feedback to students and changing the lesson plan as needed. The teacher's ability to pivot in a lesson for the purpose of addressing learning needs (while still meeting the outcome of the lesson) depends on having a clear lesson goal.

The remaining elements of strong lesson design are student discourse, task selection, differentiation, and closure. Students learn through student-to-student discourse, which has an effect size of 0.82 (Hattie, 2017). How will students talk to and learn from one another? Provide question and sentence stems and think about roles students might have in group settings to teach students how to learn from one another.

The tasks teachers choose to use during lessons inform the opportunities they give to students to learn. Grade-level and prior-knowledge tasks leading to the priority standard that meets grade-level reasoning expectations are critical for students to learn grade-level content.

When teachers select higher-order reasoning tasks, opportunities arise for differentiation. Teachers can plan for scaffolding, ask extension questions when students or groups finish early, and so on. Differentiation may also happen when teachers organize students into small groups for part of the lesson or alter the task in some way for students to learn using the revised version.

Finally, *student-led closure* means students leave the lesson knowing what they learned and what questions they still have related to the lesson goal. This could happen in a pair share, through journaling, or even on an exit ticket that includes student reflection about the lesson goal (Kanold, Kanold-McIntyre et al., 2018).

Figure 5.1 summarizes the important lesson elements. How a teacher answers the questions in this chart leads to an understanding of lesson design that engages students and grows learning.

Having a lesson plan that focuses on student learning with time for that learning to occur with feedback and differentiation is a critical first step to accelerating student learning to grade level every day. Internationally known educational author Jeffrey Benson (2021) discusses the need for students to trust the teacher and one another to show not only what students do know and can do but also what they have tried, which may not be accurate. He describes the importance of social-emotional learning considerations with formative assessment during lessons by stating:

> If your question stumps and confuses the students, you probably assumed they were further along in their understanding. . . . Ask another question; find the prompt that sends them into action, or helps them confirm and deepen their understanding, or confirms your assessment of their academic development. (Benson, 2021, p. 117)

Individual strategies to implement during lessons and as part of classroom routines follow.

Lesson Element	Questions to Address in the Lesson Plan
Lesson goal	• Which grade-level targets from a priority standard will students learn because of this lesson? • How will students make sense of the grade-level standard and learn? • Is there a process standard students will learn with the content in the lesson? If so, which one is the focus?
Student reflection	• How will students name and understand the lesson targets for the day? How will they answer the questions, What I am learning? Why I am learning this? and How I will show I learned it? • How will students reflect on their learning throughout and at the end of the lesson?
Connections	• What prior-knowledge standards does the teacher need to address in the lesson? • How will students engage in applying or learning the needed prior knowledge?
Student engagement	• During each part of the lesson, what are teachers doing? What are students doing? • How do students actively engage throughout the lesson?
Feedback	• How will students learn from feedback the teacher and peers give during the lesson? • At what moments in the lesson is time built in for the teacher to observe student learning and give meaningful feedback?
Student discourse	• How will students communicate with one another throughout the lesson to learn? How will students make their thinking apparent? • What will student discourse look like in whole-group or small-group structures?
Task selection	• What grade-level tasks will students engage in learning during the lesson? • What is the balance of higher-order and lower-order reasoning during the lesson?
Differentiation and small groups	• How will the teacher differentiate tasks if needed? • How can the teacher utilize small groups in the lesson for targeted instruction?
Closure	• How do students know if they learned the lesson targets by the end of the lesson?

Source: Adapted from Kanold, Kanold-McIntyre, et al., 2018; Kramer & Schuhl, 2017.

FIGURE 5.1: Questions to guide lesson design.

*Visit **go.SolutionTree.com/priorityschools** for a free reproducible version of this figure.*

Plan for Massed and Spaced Practice

When students learn new skills, they need to practice them. Two types of practice help students initially learn and then fix a skill in their memory: (1) massed practice and (2) spaced practice.

Massed practice means spending a concentrated lesson on a skill with repeated applications in a short time. Typically, teachers use massed practice with the grade-level standard they address in the lesson because it is new learning. When it is new content for students, teachers chunk instruction into manageable segments, with time built in for application and massed practice between chunks to make sense of each new piece of content (Marzano, 2017).

Spaced practice is "having multiple exposures to an idea over several days to attain learning and spacing the practice of skills over a long period of time" (Hattie, Fisher, & Frey, 2017, p. 129). Spaced practice is sometimes also referred to as *spiral review*.

If the focus of the lesson is a priority grade-level standard, spaced practice occurs at the start of the lesson with an activity (warm-up, do now, bell ringer, and so on) that asks students to apply prior knowledge related to the lesson priority standard. Ask students to tackle the task independently or in groups and gather feedback about their readiness for the day's lesson.

If the focus of the lesson is a prior-knowledge standard leading to a priority standard, consider how to also explore the grade-level priority standard. The teacher might address the grade-level standard in the warm-up to the lesson so students understand where their learning is headed, or perhaps in the middle or end of the lesson when the teacher poses a grade-level task and has students apply their learning to see how they might tackle the task. Observing students while they work on the grade-level task gives a teacher feedback about readiness for the grade-level standard and insights into how to accelerate learning further toward that grade-level standard. In this case, the spaced practice is both the prior-knowledge standard the teacher previously addressed and the grade-level standard the teacher is introducing. There will also be massed practice of the prior-knowledge standard during the lesson.

Figure 5.2 shares examples of how a teacher might balance massed and spaced practice during a lesson that includes prior knowledge and grade-level learning.

As a reminder, accelerating learning does *not* mean students should spend several days re-learning foundational skills before learning grade-level standards. Such an approach counters grade-level

Grade	Lesson Focus	Connection Standard in Lesson	Plan
Grade 4 Reading	Priority grade-level standard: Determine the main idea of a story.	Prior knowledge: Determine the main idea of a story when read to or with a text that is at a lower grade level (grade 2 or 3).	*Spaced practice:* Warm-up—Listen to a story or read a third-grade-level passage and determine the main idea. Students share ideas with one another and discuss the textual evidence that justifies their main idea. *Massed practice:* Lesson—Students read a grade-level passage and determine the main idea or read a grade-level passage and have students follow along before determining the main idea of the passage with supporting details.
Grade 7 Mathematics	Priority grade-level standard: Solve two-step equations.	Prior knowledge: Solve one-step equations (grade 6).	*Spaced practice:* Warm-up—Give students three one-step equations to solve. Have students share their strategies for solving each equation in groups. *Massed practice:* Lesson—Share a situational word problem that requires two steps to solve. Have students reason to a solution and share the matching equation. Give students two-step equations and see if students can work in groups to find the missing values. Choose which student strategies to share with the class. Classwork or homework—Practice additional application problems related to solving two-step equations.

FIGURE 5.2: Example of spaced and massed practice to balance grade-level and prior-knowledge standards.

learning every day. Instead, space out the foundational skills (phonics, basic mathematics facts, and so on) over time into five- to fifteen-minute portions of daily lessons, with the remaining time spent addressing prior-knowledge standards and scaffolding grade-level learning. Brief reviews of foundational skills with grade-level learning over time is a more effective way to accelerate learning than many days focusing on foundational prerequisites in the absence of grade-level learning.

Utilize Whole-Group and Small-Group Learning

Throughout a lesson, students learn in both whole- and small-group settings. Teachers ask themselves when each grouping is appropriate, keeping in mind a focus on grade-level learning and differentiation. For example, "When in the lesson does it make sense to provide instruction to the whole group? When in the lesson might some students need a minilesson or small-group learning activity? How will students engage with one another in small-group settings for richer feedback and learning? And how will students engage with one another during shorter whole-group learning experiences?" Teachers also consider how they can best gather real-time feedback related to student learning during the lesson.

Generally, whole-group learning involves the entire class and provides an opportunity for the teacher to introduce a new concept or skill, summarize learning from an exploration or activity, or model strategies. Unfortunately, during whole-group learning, "student attention deteriorates over the course of a lesson" (Hattie & Yates, 2014, p. 39). Teachers should use whole-group learning strategically; it should not be the sole learning mode. Feedback during whole-group learning can be a challenge, but the teacher can create ways to quickly check on student learning (for example, students write their thoughts on individual whiteboards and hold them for the teacher to see). This allows the teacher to check for understanding and make adjustments in the lesson, but is not generally an opportunity for students to make corrections in their learning.

When constructing whole-group portions of a lesson, the teachers ask themselves, "How will every student engage in the learning?" Whole-group learning requires pauses for students to digest information. For example, the teacher might have students show their thinking on whiteboards, engage in a partner or group discussion, read independently and answer the question with at least one other student, or use digital resources to see and hear student thinking. Teachers might also provide time for students to write what they have learned so far (that is, summarize) or ask a question they have about the learning so far in the lesson. These are all engaging formative assessment strategies when teachers use them to gather information about student learning.

For example, before reading a novel, a teacher might have students look at the cover and ask, "What do you notice? What do you wonder?" Students might share their ideas with one another before the teacher randomly calls on students to share their thoughts with the entire class. Think-pair-share allows students to safely share ideas and validate their thinking or learn from a peer, so students are then more comfortable sharing with the class. This *partner sharing* also means every student engages in answering and is learning through discourse. Coauthors John Hattie and Gregory Yates (2014) find that student-to-student discourse has a large effect size (0.82) when students see one another as valuable resources and can safely share their thinking. The teacher no longer needs to call on each student to generate feedback but can gather feedback by listening to partner discussions and randomly hearing ideas from a few partner groups.

Teachers often need to train students on how to communicate with one another. In a pair share, the teacher may need to give explicit directions like, "Partner A, tell partner B what you wonder," and then follow-up with, "Partner B, tell partner A what you notice." When calling on a student, the teacher asks, "What did you and your partner discuss?" to build relationships and safety in a whole-group setting.

Small-group learning allows teachers to gain even more information related to student learning and provides an opportunity for students to learn from one another and from the teacher. When students are working in small groups, teachers can walk around the room, observe and listen to students making sense of their learning, and provide meaningful and timely feedback. Students also have an opportunity to provide feedback to one another.

Sometimes small groups should be *heterogeneous* (groups of students with varying levels of knowledge or skill on a topic) and other times they may be *homogeneous* (groups of students with similar learning needs) for minilessons and differentiation (NCTM & NCSM, 2020). For example, students might sit in heterogeneous groups of four throughout class and learn together through discourse as part of whole-group instruction (Kanold, Kanold-McIntyre, et al., 2018). Sometimes that same group may work as a small group with a higher-level task as the teacher gathers information about how students are thinking and answering questions. Other times, the teacher might regroup students and, while some groups are engaging in a higher-level task, pull other students aside for a small-group learning experience related to an intervention skill.

Teachers can use small groups to differentiate after a whole-group lesson. The teacher places students in groups based on ability with a targeted skill and designs a minilesson for strategic groups that need additional instruction or support while others are practicing skills at self-directed stations. Even though they are in leveled groups, all students are working along the learning progression that leads to understanding the grade-level priority standard and engaging in grade-level learning during the whole-group part of the lesson.

When students work in whole- or small-group settings, consider roles for students and classroom expectations to minimize transition time from one structure to the other and clarify student actions. In heterogeneous small-group learning, one student might be responsible for making sense of the task, another for gathering questions to ask the teacher or another group, another for recording the group's thinking, and another for keeping the group on task and making sure students each share their thinking during the activity. (Teachers provide direct instruction and question or sentence prompts to guide students in these roles.) These roles shift among group members over time and members are each held accountable to possibly share their team's thoughts or work, perhaps by the teacher randomly calling on a member (for example, teacher rolls a die and it lands on 3, so student 3 in each group shares with another group or with the whole class). Accountability to learning is a critical aspect of both whole- and small-group learning (Kanold, Kanold-McIntyre et al., 2018).

Teach Conceptually

Imagine that you are a student, and every day throughout each school year, teachers tell you a different series of steps to follow in your mathematics class and hand you a different graphic organizer to make sense of and complete in ELA class. When students "learn" through rules and memorized steps, they receive hundreds or even thousands of disconnected sets of directions over the course of their school experience. Without learning to make decisions about which strategies to use and building connections between concepts, students may feel lost and frustrated (Which set of steps should I use for this problem or assignment?). Students wait for a teacher's direction and if they don't receive an answer, they may feel stuck and give up without trying. As an alternative, we recommend teaching for *conceptual understanding* to support students' independently generating strategies to apply in each learning experience and, therefore, grow student retention.

Too often in mathematics, teachers try to accelerate learning by quickly sharing a series of steps for solving a problem, leaving students wondering why the algorithm works. Students miss an opportunity to make connections to prior knowledge and instead learn there is *one way* to solve each problem, when there are often many strategies with varying entry points if students understand the *concept* they are learning. Boaler (2019) notes, "It is challenging for students to develop a growth mindset when subjects are presented in a fixed way—as a series of questions with one answer and one method to get to it" (p. 102).

In *Adding It Up*, the National Research Council's foundational text in mathematics research and education, coauthors Jeremy Kilpatrick, Jane Swafford, and Bradford Findell (2001) describe conceptual understanding for mathematics this way:

> *Conceptual understanding* refers to an integrated and functional grasp of mathematical ideas. Students with conceptual understanding know more than isolated facts and methods. They understand why a mathematical idea is important and the kinds of contexts in which it is useful. They have organized their knowledge into a coherent whole, which enables them to learn new ideas by connecting those ideas to what they already know. (pp. 118–119)

Similarly, for ELA, students too often receive a set structure or acronym for writing an essay or teachers tell them to use one specific graphic organizer for each writing prompt. In social studies, students might learn a series of steps for writing a response to a document-based question. While these prescribed steps can be strong instructional supports, some students miss the nuances of writing, and teachers need to remind them each year of the steps for each type of writing (narrative, expository, or argumentative, for example) without seeing the connections between each. The Council of the Great City Schools' (2020) report *Addressing Unfinished Learning After COVID-19 School Closures* discusses conceptual understanding for ELA:

> In English language arts, instruction is often organized around strategy-based instruction. That is, teachers provide direct instruction on comprehension strategies and have students practice and focus on them in isolation instead of teaching students how to use these strategies in service of gaining meaning, developing vocabulary, and building knowledge from the text. Instead of taking students through a litany of practice activities and thematic units, teachers should focus on topic texts that build knowledge and employ text-dependent questions that engage students deeply with the text and build understanding. Ultimately, the learning goal across all grade levels is to cultivate every student's ability to read with understanding and to gain knowledge and skills through the careful study of grade-level texts not only in English language arts, but across all content areas. Moreover, students should develop the ability to consolidate and evaluate what they have heard or read, and to clearly express this understanding orally and in writing. (p. 9)

Teachers can apply descriptions for conceptual understanding in mathematics and ELA to other subjects as well. Teachers ask themselves, "How are students learning and reasoning before working to fluency with a skill? What are the concepts and applications of solving mole equations in chemistry and how do they connect to previous learning? What are the concepts and applications related to world wars in social studies and how do they connect to previous learning? What are the concepts and applications related to understanding poetry and how do they connect to previous learning?"

How, then, can students learn to make connections themselves and develop fluency with skills and concepts to readily apply to future learning? The answer does not involve showing students one way to solve tasks or answer questions. When teaching through a lens of conceptual understanding, teachers determine what students are learning in the learning cycle and identify its connections to learned prior skills. They ask themselves, "What are the key aspects of the content learned? How will it apply to future learning?" Consider the connections and concepts, apply the learning using a variety of strategies, and end with strategies to build fluency with skills. Some examples appear in figure 5.3.

Priority Skill	Concept	Connections
Add fractions.	*Add* means to join together.	Adding fractions on a number line is like adding whole numbers on a number line.
Write an argumentative essay.	Identify a personal claim or an author's claim and back it with evidence.	Essays have a thesis and are well organized, with clear body paragraphs, an introduction, and a conclusion. Claims connect to opinions and must be backed with evidence and reasoning.
Create a model for a weather cycle of rain.	Water and temperature affect weather in a continuous cycle of water evaporation and rain.	Some days are sunny, others cloudy or rainy. Once the rain stops, the clouds disappear. Some days are humid. These life experiences connect to the water cycle and how water evaporates and forms clouds, which produce rain.
Explain how Italy's geography impacts the country's economy.	Land and waterways impact the trade of goods, which is part of a country's economy.	Oceans, rivers, and other large bodies of water allow boats to carry goods from one place to another, while plains allow trains to do the same. Mountains can slow down travel. Connect this thinking to Italy's geographical features and location.

FIGURE 5.3: Example of clarifying concepts students are learning.

Clarifying the overall concept students are learning and how the priority standard fits into previous and future learning strengthens students' conceptual understanding. Additionally, it builds a growth mindset and student self-efficacy as students make choices for solving tasks based on the conceptual understanding they develop over time.

This balance of conceptual understanding and skills creates a toolkit of strategies for students to use when learning new concepts or reviewing previously learned concepts—without a focus on steps. For some students, being stuck because they can't think of the one set of steps to use is a reason to give up. Instead, to show students there are many strategies they might try, teachers may want to create a poster titled, *I'm stuck! Now I'm going to try . . .* or similar. This visual supports students in independently selecting strategies and reminds them that opting out of trying is not the solution. Additionally, when students realize they can select from many strategies in their learning toolkit, they further develop self-efficacy. Figure 5.4 shows two examples of these kinds of posters.

It is tempting for teachers to accelerate learning by rushing to give students hints and rules to reach an answer. However, to truly accelerate learning, students do not need to know the answer; they need

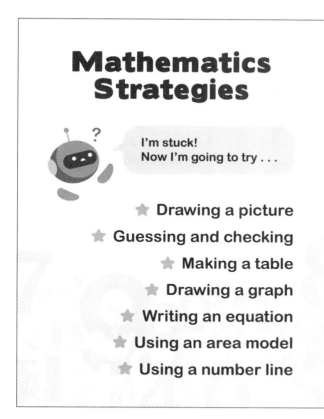

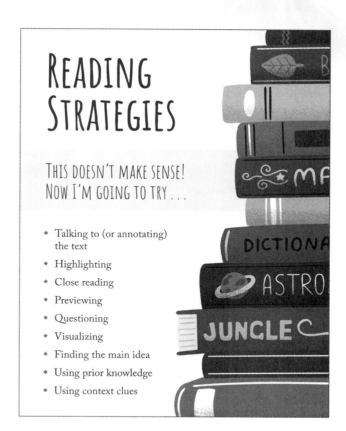

FIGURE 5.4: Examples of posters for students to reference when they get stuck.

to master the thinking and reasoning required to reach the answer. Conceptual understanding teaches students in a way they can remember and apply to new situations. Conceptual understanding represents the transfer of knowledge that accelerates learning in every aspect of life.

Incorporate Reading and Writing Every Day

When students need accelerated learning, they also often need supports with reading and writing. Sometimes, teachers may be tempted to read or write for students with the intent to help them access the content of the lesson (or simply to save time). However, students will not learn to read and write independently unless given the opportunity to do so every day in every subject area. This does not mean writing full essays or reading entire novels; rather, as an acceleration strategy, students interact with the content they need to learn through some form of reading and writing. They learn from literary or informational text and they share their thinking and reasoning through writing (or drawing in the primary grades). In addition, if students need supports with reading or writing to reach grade level, teams can utilize Tier 2 or Tier 3 interventions (see chapter 6, page 107).

Professor and writing expert Steve Graham and colleagues (2016) share three recommendations from research related to reading and writing at the secondary level:

1. Explicitly teach appropriate writing strategies using a Model-Practice-Reflect instructional cycle.

2. Integrate writing and reading to emphasize key writing features.

3. Use assessments of student writing to inform instruction and feedback. (p. 4)

Students learn through writing, and teachers can see student thinking for more effective feedback. Additionally, when students read and write frequently in all disciplines, they begin to make connections between how authors in different subject areas structure their writing, which provides examples for how students can utilize structure when they write.

Figure 5.5 shares some of the reading and writing experiences students engage with during lessons. It is easy for teachers to take learning experiences away from students by reading to them or accepting verbal responses instead of written responses. While there is a time and place for such supports, we have observed too many classrooms where, nearly every time teachers require reading or writing, the teacher (or an appointed student) does the reading and writing for the full group of students—especially when most students are below grade level in reading and writing. The strategies in figure 5.5 are small ways students might read and write independently every day in every subject.

Independent Reading Experiences	Independent Writing Experiences
• Story	• Write an essay or story.
• Current event article	• Answer a prompt.
• Directions	• Summarize a story.
• Questions to answer in a book or on a worksheet	• Summarize the learning for the day.
• Word problems	• Ask a question.
• Science labs	• Record work when solving a mathematics problem.
• Student work presented as error analysis	• Show thinking on a whiteboard.
• Textbook	• Complete an exit ticket.
• Charts and graphs	• Explain thinking or reasoning.
• Information in a graphic organizer	• Document science lab results.
• Anchor charts	• Set goals and reflect.
• Computer work	• Work on a computer (typing).

FIGURE 5.5: Examples of independent reading and writing experiences during lessons.

Schoolwide agreement on the names for reading strategies and common writing rubrics strengthen students' reading and writing within a grade level and from one grade level to the next. If one teacher calls a reading strategy *annotate the text* and another, *talk to the text*, students may get confused and think the strategies are different. When teachers refer to *close reading*, do they all use the same language for the three steps? When strategies have the same names, teachers in any subject at any level can reference the strategy and students will understand how to use it to access or communicate information. When there is a consistent writing rubric (whether every assignment utilizes every element or not), students learn more quickly what they need for quality writing and can better give feedback to one another and themselves.

Reading and writing every day does not mean students must do all their work without support. The following are some strategies teachers can use to scaffold the process without doing the work for students.

▶ After students read independently, the teacher asks students to share their understanding of the text with a partner. Then the teacher randomly calls on a student to share with the class what the student and the partner discussed.

- After students read independently, the teacher reads the information aloud and asks students how well it matched or did not match their initial read.

- The teacher employs *three reads* (a strategy in which students read a text three times with a different focus each time), with partner shares after each round.

- Before students independently read a story or piece of informational text, the teacher provides background knowledge (through pictures or video), so students can better make sense of the text.

- When introducing a writing task, the teacher asks students to write their thinking without worrying about grammar and conventions. Later, students strengthen and polish their responses through peer or teacher feedback.

All grades and subject areas require students to read and write. Students not yet learning at grade level often need support with both reading and writing. Therefore, it is important to reinforce the skills and make them a routine part of instruction in every class, every day. Reading and writing are lifelong skills students need to grow learning and reasoning.

Engage Students Actively

Engaging students during lessons is critical to accelerating learning. There are many ways to engage students in their learning. Students might read text, discuss learning with a partner or group, write their thinking on a whiteboard or poster, or solve a mathematics problem, to name a few. Hattie (2017) puts engagement, concentration, and perseverance in learning at an effect size of 0.56. Additionally, coach and school leadership specialist Kathy Dyer (2015) states:

> Research has historically indicated strong correlations between student engagement (typically defined as attention to the area of focus, active participation in learning, and time on task) and student achievement. These correlations remain strong for all levels of instruction, across all subject areas, and for varying instructional activities.

When planning for engagement in lessons, consider ways students can do more of the work and thinking than the teacher during a lesson.

Student engagement in the classroom is either passive or active. *Passive engagement* is difficult to discern in the moment. Are students really listening to the direct instruction? Are students truly reading the assigned passage? Are students watching the video to compare it to a recently read novel? Are they processing what they are writing as they fill in guided notes? While each activity requires engagement, the engagement is passive in nature. An observer cannot tell how much reasoning or learning is happening since the engagement is solely in the student's mind and thus difficult to measure.

Active engagement is observable through student action, whether it be discourse, written work, group projects or activities, participation in a science experiment, or effort in a mile run, to name a few. Active engagement provides time for the teacher to circle the room and give feedback, and for students to give feedback to one another, and then act on that feedback for continued learning. Active engagement during lessons is key to accelerating learning.

As Marzano (2017) states, engagement requires the teacher to recognize when students are disengaged and quickly respond. Active engagement provides an opportunity to re-engage students when they are not showing the learning teachers expect; this is because active engagement makes student learning observable. Teachers have time to identify which students need supports (based on their observations) and can scaffold learning accordingly in real time. Students each are held accountable to learning through active engagement since they share their thinking or learning evidence with other students, the teacher, or both. Additionally, active engagement grows student perseverance as students tackle tasks and work toward completion.

Think about your lessons and consider the following questions.

- How often are students actively engaged?
- How often are students passively engaged?
- How might the time students spend actively engaged increase?

When Sharon observed student engagement with a principal at a school in Oklahoma, they charted the percentage of time students were passively and actively engaged in lessons and shared the overall percentages with the school (without teacher names or subject areas). The percentage of active engagement was exceptionally low. Teachers brainstormed strategies to increase active engagement for every student. They committed to arranging desks in groups of three or four to increase learning through small-group discourse; using pair share and calling on random students to answer questions during whole-group instruction; having students work in groups at chart paper or whiteboards around the room to show their thinking; having students make their thinking visible for quick feedback; and using more wait time and scaffolds instead of telling students the answers if no one is quick to share. The teachers agreed the classroom would be a bit noisier and more chaotic at times and then discussed how to build a classroom culture for students to learn the routines and procedures they need to actively engage in learning (see chapter 2, page 17).

Active engagement requires a classroom culture steeped in respect, a belief from students they can learn from one another, and a supportive environment where students can learn from mistakes without the fear of being ridiculed. Clear classroom expectations (see chapter 2, page 17) and small-group learning experiences contribute to students learning actively in class.

Utilize Error Analysis

Error analysis is a skill that engages students in analyzing another student's work and determining the misconception it shows or the accuracy of the student's thinking. The ability to analyze errors leads to students better analyzing and revising their own work (Marzano, 2017). Analyzing errors in others' work (and in one's own) grows conceptual understanding and develops higher-order reasoning skills. Additionally, when students engage in error analysis, teachers see how they are understanding concepts and then adjust the lesson accordingly (Erkens et al., 2018).

Sarah observed a seventh-grade mathematics classroom where the teacher used error analysis to celebrate student learning and deepen understanding. As part of the lesson, students used clickers to answer questions involving the order of operations. For one question, most students correctly answered *12* and a handful of students incorrectly answered *5*. The teacher explained that arriving at *5* indicated a common error and challenged students to work in small groups to find the mistake that led to that answer. Sarah observed students leaning in, very curious about the error, much more than they may have been had they explained the correct solution to one another in the group. She even heard one student say, "Hey, take a look at this!" while waving his paper. "I got 5. We can look at my work and figure it out!" His group celebrated the student for an incorrect response! He and the group learned from the common mistake evidenced in his work and could apply the learning to future problems.

As another example, teachers might give students a multiple-choice question and ask them why one of the distractors (wrong answers) is incorrect. Teachers may use student work for groups to analyze and revise as a learning tool before students analyze and revise their own work. They may use anchor papers and have students determine how to revise them to make them stronger. There are many ways for students to analyze and learn from errors in a culture of learning. In such a culture, students learn to embrace their own errors as learning opportunities too.

Give Meaningful Feedback

Every acceleration strategy involves quality formative feedback to students from peers or the teacher. Due to its importance in student learning, feedback is also an acceleration strategy on its own. When planning lessons, ask, "How are students learning from feedback? How are students acting on any feedback they receive?" The feedback may come from the teacher circling the room or through small-group discourse that ensues from group learning conversations. Feedback to students can help them learn from mistakes or misconceptions or validate and affirm student thinking and work. In a safe classroom with a culture of learning (see chapter 2, page 17), feedback is seen as positive and a focused way to accelerate learning.

Reeves (2019) recommends teachers use *FAST* feedback.

- ▸ **Fair:** The feedback is consistent from one student to the next and from one teacher to the next.

- ▸ **Accurate:** The feedback is accurate to the target the teacher taught or assessed.

- ▸ **Specific:** The feedback is not general but gives a specific indication of what students need to work on and have already learned.

- ▸ **Timely:** The feedback is immediate, and students act on the feedback to continue learning.

FAST feedback means feedback is about the work, not the student. Rather than making broad, person-focused statements like "You're doing great!" focus on the work to discuss what students show they have learned or not learned yet. If a student has a unique approach to answering a question or solving a problem, be sure to check if the approach can lead to the answer before telling the student the approach is wrong. The student does not always have to solve a problem as the teacher modeled in class. Telling students they are making progress does not let them know specifically which part of their work is accurate and which needs revision. Being specific to give students direction is important. Finally, feedback is timely when given during lessons in class; for common formative assessments, consider how to quickly return feedback to students.

As an example, Sarah observed a teacher circling the room while students were working in small groups and making their thinking visible on poster paper. The teacher had many opportunities to quickly analyze student thinking by looking at the work on the posters. The teacher then gave feedback to students about the work they displayed and connected the feedback to the expectations for proficiency. When one group showed divergent thinking, the teacher stepped back, asked questions, and determined with the students that their thinking would, in fact, work and lead to an accurate conclusion. If students had an error in thinking, the teacher would talk to the group using questioning strategies so they uncovered the error, or the teacher would point out the error so students would know everything prior showed correct reasoning and where to focus their efforts. The feedback was given in real time so the teacher affirmed students' thinking before continuing or they had the time to revise work if needed.

Reeves (2019) also reminds teachers that not all feedback needs to be a grade in a gradebook, but rather, teachers can give feedback *during learning experiences* so students can grow their learning. Teachers create time to give FAST feedback during a lesson when students are actively engaged in learning, whether in small groups or independently, and then check on the action students take. Teachers might give feedback through anchor papers and have students sort the work using a rubric to then transfer the learning to their own writing. Students might give feedback to one another using a student-friendly rubric. Teachers might also grade papers and circle an error for specificity, and then let students revise their work to learn from the error. There are many ways to give feedback. However, effective feedback must tie to student work and specific learning targets to develop a growth mindset; when teachers give feedback in a culture of respect, learners honor and use it.

Empower Student Learning Through Reflection and Goal Setting

It is difficult to accelerate student learning without empowering students—those doing the learning. Making students equal partners in their learning empowers them and builds a growth mindset and self-efficacy (Kramer & Schuhl, 2017). As students learn concepts and apply strategies to tasks, they can reflect on which strategies work better than others and begin to understand that with focused effort, they can successfully learn. Students reflecting on their learning using learning targets and setting goals are two ways for students to see their progress and develop a growth mindset.

In *School Improvement for All*, we offer the following strategies that focus on student-directed learning and ensure students will own their learning (Kramer & Schuhl, 2017). This is not an exhaustive list; however, each item on the list engages students in their learning from the beginning of the unit, not just when it is time to take a test. Students and teachers become partners in the learning process:

- Students name their learning targets.
- Students manage their materials and data and track their progress.
- Students set goals and learning plans or activities for themselves.
- Students self-assess their work.
- Students reflect on what they have learned and make connections to new learning.
- Students generate possible test items at appropriate rigor levels.
- Students participate in rubric development.
- Students engage in meaningful dialogue about their learning.
- Students support each other in addressing learning gaps. (Kramer & Schuhl, 2017, p. 52)

Students need to be able to name their learning to understand the purpose of classwork, homework, and any assessments. Teachers or students can write the targets on the assignments. What does each learning activity show students about what they have learned or not learned yet? For example, ask, "How did the activity today show learning related to the target, *I can find the theme of a story?*" As a team, consider how to create a meaningful reflection tool for students to use throughout a unit and after each common assessment. Chapter 4 (page 61) shares some examples.

Teachers can also create activities in ways that help students more clearly understand what they expect in student work. Teachers might share anchor papers or exemplars showing proficient, below-proficient, and above-proficient responses to questions. They can ask small groups to sort the three samples and discuss why they ranked each sample as they did. Then, as a class, students and the teacher discuss characteristics of proficient work and codevelop a rubric for evaluating responses. Students each then get their individual responses back and make their answers stronger based on the class discussion. In the future, the teacher displays the anchor papers and rubric, and students use the rubric to self-assess their work and give feedback to one another.

Teams may want to create student folders to collect reflection tools. Here, students chart their learning throughout the unit and after common assessments. Students can use these tools to reflect on learning at the end of each semester or year, and share them at parent conferences to show what they have learned, what goals they have met, and what they are still learning. Veteran educators and speakers Tim Brown and William M. Ferriter (2021) write, "Teams that design regular opportunities for self-assessment activate their students as full partners in the assessment process" (p. 53). This is true for all preK–12 students. In the lower grades, students might chart growth using pictures or stamps; in the upper grades, students writing reflections and using graphs are appropriate.

Coauthors John Hattie, Douglas Fisher, and Nancy Frey (2017) write, "In addition to knowing what they're supposed to learn, students should know how they will know they've learned it, and how they can assess themselves along the way" (p. 56). Data trackers and student-reflection tools allow students to compare their learning evidence to success criteria to better understand where they are on their learning journey. They can track their learning both by current score and growth over time to see their learning successes and celebrate. When students have not learned *yet*, the tracker helps students each articulate what they need to learn, thus making the learning feel more doable. Students owning their learning helps them better understand and welcome small-group placements for accelerated learning. Student goal setting and reflection is a key to developing the self-efficacy students need to try in class and learn more confidently.

Conclusion

A key component to acceleration is students learning grade-level standards every day. To fully accelerate learning, teachers also plan ways to incorporate prior knowledge and skills to support students along the learning progression to the priority standard in each daily lesson. Then, teachers and teams can develop lessons that accelerate student learning through conceptual understanding, massed and spaced practice, reading and writing, whole- and small-group instruction, and active engagement to empower learners to see they can learn at grade level through student reflection and goal setting.

The intentional design of each lesson is critical to improving student learning results. Clarify the grade-level learning and plan for scaffolding and differentiating to accelerate student learning to grade level or beyond. Consider how students will learn from one another and how they will act on the feedback they receive throughout each active learning experience. Instruction happens every day and is where the greatest opportunity to learn takes place. It is in the classroom, every day, that learning grows and students develop the self-efficacy to succeed.

Discussion Questions for Reflection and Action

As a team, discuss the following questions. Visit **go.SolutionTree.com/priorityschools** for a free reproducible version of these questions.

- ▶ How do you plan for a daily lesson focused on a priority standard? What are the teacher and the students doing during each part of the lesson?

- ▶ How does your team utilize massed and spaced practice of priority standards?

- ▶ Which strategies are teachers on your team using for effective whole- and small-group learning?

- ▶ Identify priority standards students are learning. How can they be taught for conceptual understanding? What connections do the priority standards have to prior learning?

- ▶ How can you incorporate student reading and writing into daily lessons?

- ▶ What strategies can you use during lessons to increase active engagement?

- ▶ How do students receive and act on feedback during lessons?

- ▶ What are tools your team can use for student reflection and goal setting?

CHAPTER 6

An Intervention System That Accelerates Learning

At Sarah's high school, many students were earning *Ds* and *Fs*, especially in mathematics and ELA classes. This, coupled with low state-assessment scores showing students learning below grade level, prompted the principal to create a schoolwide intervention program for students. At first, students with a *D* or *F* in ELA or mathematics went to a homeroom teacher during the half-hour intervention time before lunch. Students with higher grades had one hour for lunch. Teachers had thirty to forty students for intervention, each needing different supports because students had low grades for a variety of reasons. Many of these homeroom teachers were not mathematics or ELA teachers and did not know how to intervene. The intervention system did not produce more learning for students.

Eventually, after several more iterations, the school created reading and mathematics success courses for freshmen whose learning was below grade level. The school also enrolled students in these intervention courses into heterogeneously mixed freshman English and Algebra 1 classes (where teachers utilized acceleration strategies). Collaborative teams started giving common assessments tied to priority learning targets so the intervention time during the school day could be targeted and specific and teachers could share students as needed. No longer did all teachers intervene on mathematics and reading, but rather, in their own subject areas. These and other supports began to show students the learning teachers expected, and student learning began to improve.

It can be a daunting task to ensure all students learn priority standards to grade level when there are so many students in need of support. Yet, students learn at different rates and at different speeds. Priority schools may have as many as 90 percent of the students below grade level in reading, number sense, or writing. There is a tendency on such campuses for teachers to lower expectations of learning due to misplaced love for the students and a desire for students to succeed. However, students know they are cared for and can succeed when teams work collaboratively to ensure students learn the priority standards (and more) at grade level. DuFour (2015) reminds, "Any school dedicated to ensuring all students learn at high levels must stop debating what they *think* students can or can't do and instead change the question to this: *How will we get every learner there?*" (p. 205). Acceleration is one part of the answer to that question, but when students need additional support, educators utilize a schoolwide intervention system.

> Interventions must be provided in addition to effective, grade-level core instruction. Not in place of it.
> —RICHARD DUFOUR

Tiered intervention systems like multitiered systems of supports (MTSS) and response to intervention (RTI) are founded on the premise that *all* students have an opportunity to learn grade-level priority standards during Tier 1 (core) instruction. The Tier 1 instruction focuses on the priority grade-level standards and includes differentiation (see chapter 5, page 87). However, some students need additional time and support beyond core instruction to learn priority standards—this is Tier 2. Traditionally, the focus of Tier 2 is *intervention on targeted priority standards*, meaning a need for additional learning at grade level or on the prior knowledge and skills from the previous grade level. Some students also need Tier 3 supports *in addition to* Tier 1 and Tier 2 instruction. Tier 3 addresses foundational skills well below grade level in some key areas. These most often include such universal skills as reading, writing, number sense, communication in the school's predominant language, and appropriate behavior (Buffum et al., 2018). Buffum and colleagues (2018) add, "the school must have a plan to provide [Tier 3] assistance *without denying these students access to essential grade-level curriculum*" (p. 22).

In MTSS and RTI, the Tier 1, Tier 2, and Tier 3 designations focus on both students' academic learning and their behavior. Tier 1 includes the behavior expectations for all students and the need to clarify, define, and explicitly teach behaviors to students at each location on campus so they can be successful learners in a safe environment. In Tier 2, students in need of additional learning supports related to behavior engage in behavior intervention. Tier 3 then addresses foundational skills related to behavior for individual students in need of significant supports.

Figure 6.1 shows an inverted pyramid of interventions to illustrate a focus on Tier 1 instruction for all students and then Tier 2 and Tier 3 supports for students based on individual academic or behavior needs. The pyramid shows how teams drill down to the need of every student (Buffum et al., 2018). The intervention pyramid was originally designed under the assumption that no more than 20 percent of students would need Tier 2 interventions at any given time and only 5 to 8 percent would need Tier 3 (Buffum et al., 2018). Unfortunately, this is not the reality when a school has many students in need of accelerating learning to grade level or beyond. Most priority schools have many students needing both Tier 2 and Tier 3 supports, so the pyramid is bloated in Tier 2 and Tier 3 when the work of acceleration begins.

TIER 1

For *all* students—a focus on core instruction (with differentiation) and behavior expectations.

TIER 2

For some students in need of additional time and support—focused on interventions based on academic or behavior learning in Tier 1.

TIER 3

For a few students in need of remediation—focused on foundational skills and behaviors.

Source: Adapted from Buffum et al., 2018.
FIGURE 6.1: RTI pyramid of interventions.

There is a common misconception about special education when discussing a pyramid of interventions. The MTSS or RTI framework is not built with a focus on students who have such an educational designation, nor as a checklist to have students enter the special education program, but rather for every student, regardless of educational label (special education, English learner, and so on). In fact, the intervention pyramid provides systemic interventions that, when teams intentionally implement them, can address some students' learning needs with accompanying supports to negate the need for a special education designation. There will always be students in need of learning supports guaranteed through a 504 Plan or Individualized Education Program (IEP). However, any educational learning plan will be stronger if teachers have data from the student's learning in all three tiers to create and implement the learning plan. *All students* can learn when staff (grade-level or subject-area teams in partnership with special education teachers) take collective responsibility and intentionally design instruction, interventions, and extensions for student growth and learning (Frizielle, Schmidt, & Spiller, 2016). Equitable practices demand that educators eliminate any labels and teach all students. We sometimes hear this phrased as, "Rip the labels, and teach the kids."

Addressing student learning and behavior is not always as clear when most students need all three tiers to learn. When the intervention pyramid is bloated in Tier 2 and Tier 3, determining when during the day students receive intervention, remediation, or extension may vary from a traditional model of core instruction, additional time in the day for Tier 2, and then an additional pull-out for Tier 3. However, working together to accelerate learning to grade level or beyond is non-negotiable.

The Shift to Multitiered Systems of Support

Teachers, in general, want every student to learn and be successful. To that end, many educators spend a lot of time and energy on their own, relentlessly addressing the needs of students but coming up short, feeling frustrated, and teetering on the edge of burnout and exhaustion. Sadly, the COVID-19 pandemic and the resulting stressors in schools exacerbated such teacher workloads and feelings.

The idea of interventions and extensions is very appealing, especially when teachers understand that it requires a collective effort and is not on any one teacher's shoulders. However, sharing the workload does not mean sending students to another educator to be "fixed" and then returned. Rather, collaborative teams analyze data from multiple sources—state assessments, progress-monitoring assessments, and team common formative and end-of-unit assessments—and together plan meaningful learning experiences designed to accelerate learning to grade level or beyond. Student learning is not on any one teacher's shoulders; it is on the shoulders of every teacher and staff member. Therefore, at various times teachers will share students, co-teach, collectively design or share plans for small-group instruction, or determine how to utilize technology most effectively, to name a few strategies. Collaboratively creating purposeful learning experiences in each tier of an intervention system using data and trends in student work contributes to large gains in student learning—an effect size of as much as 1.29 (Hattie, 2017).

In too many schools, however, individual teachers determine which interventions or extensions students will engage in. We have seen educators try many strategies for intervention or as part of MTSS. Some are highly effective, and others do not accelerate learning as much as is possible. To successfully implement MTSS, schools may need to shift current practices. Table 6.1 (page 110) describes these shifts.

TABLE 6.1: Shifts in Multitiered Systems of Supports to Accelerate Learning

SHIFT FROM . . .	SHIFT TO . . .
Using only one assessment (or a few very spaced out during the year) to place students into long-term intervention groups	Using frequent team common assessments and daily classroom formative assessments to determine targeted and specific intervention groups
Teaching Tier 1 core instruction using leveled groups	Teaching Tier 1 core instruction using heterogeneous groups and then creating small, flexible intervention groups based on data
Keeping all students with their core teacher for interventions and extensions	Sharing students among teachers so each can address a targeted and specific skill with a group of students
Using only computer programs for intervention	Combining live experiences and assigned computer modules as part of a learning progression toward the priority standard
Sending students to an interventionist or another teacher to be "fixed"	Analyzing student work and instructional strategies as a team to share students with an agreed-on targeted and specific intervention plan
Assuming students in special education are all in need of Tier 3 supports or that Tier 3 intervention should be left for special education teachers	Understanding that intervention tiers are for *any* student in need of additional learning supports, regardless of any educational label, and are not a checklist for special education
Assigning teachers at random to act as interventionists	Determining teachers who are highly qualified to provide additional learning supports for any subject or grade level
Replacing the grade- or course-level learning with below-grade-level content or causing students to miss Tier 1 core instruction to attend Tier 2 or Tier 3 interventions	Ensuring all students receive grade-level Tier 1 core instruction in inclusive classrooms
Placing students in intervention or extension groups each week without analyzing data or monitoring the effectiveness of any intervention	Analyzing data as a team and using the data to place students in interventions and monitor their effectiveness
Using letter grades on a report card to determine interventions	Using common assessment data tied to learning targets with student work to determine specific and targeted interventions
Assuming students know how to behave and punishing them when they do not	Teaching expected behaviors with plans for intervention if needed, and recognizing students' social-emotional needs

The task of effectively using MTSS to accelerate student learning to grade level or beyond takes a systemic, coordinated, intentional, and thoughtful approach immersed in *quantitative* (numeric) and *qualitative* (descriptive) data. Effectively creating and utilizing MTSS may seem a bit overwhelming and it might be easier to simply task teachers each with designing and implementing any interventions or extensions themselves in their own classroom or purchase a third-party computer program to handle the responsibility. However, neither will work effectively as part of a system to accelerate learning. The strategies in this chapter emphasize a collaborative and student-centered approach to intervention.

Acceleration Strategies for Intervention

Acceleration can only be successful in closing achievement gaps if all students who require additional time and support to learn actually receive it. How does a school offer learning support to every student in need? And how does the school offer support if most students need the additional time during the day required for Tier 2 and Tier 3 supports? It starts with a focus on strong core instruction. For that reason, Tier 1 is sometimes referred to as *prevention* (Buffum et al., 2018).

DuFour (2015) states, "A successful system of interventions is grounded in highly effective initial teaching. Thus, the key to effective intervention is to have more good teaching in more classrooms more of the time" (p. 205). Good teaching in core instruction includes small groups, differentiation, formative assessment with feedback, and time spent on grade-level standards every day—all the aspects of acceleration we discussed in previous chapters. So, how can strong core instruction *prevent* students from needing an abundance of additional learning supports? *Accelerating learning to grade level or higher in core instruction* means students learn what they need, so they no longer need Tier 2 or Tier 3 supports as frequently.

Drilling down to each student's needs starts in Tier 1. Teams plan for student learning using the learning cycle we shared in chapter 3 (page 33), with any flex or intervention days as part of Tier 1 or Tier 2. Daily formative assessment checks throughout lessons drive Tier 1, which requires that teachers work with students in small groups every day during first-best instruction. Responses to common formative assessments might also happen in Tier 1. When students have not learned the content yet after core instruction, they receive Tier 2 intervention. Results of the common end-of-unit assessments and sometimes common formative assessments drive Tier 2 and offer an opportunity for teachers to share their students to specifically target any identified misconceptions. When students need even more supports, Tier 3 provides them, using small-group or individualized sessions that do not interfere with students' learning priority standards.

A school cannot eliminate the achievement gap without a working three-tier system of interventions in which all the tiers are functioning and align to support student learning. And, in schools with a pyramid bloated with Tier 2 and Tier 3 needs, schools also need some creativity to meet the needs of students so they can be successful in future grades and courses. Recognizing what targeted support students need is vital to creating acceleration strategies that are effective and grow student learning. Learning starts with strong core instruction that includes acceleration, and Tier 2 and Tier 3 provide opportunities for *teams* and specialists to increase student learning by skill. Creating MTSS requires looking at the school day structure to create the time needed and determining the content to target for the learning in each tier.

Repurpose Time in the Master Schedule for Intervention

To create meaningful interventions, schools must allot time for the additional instruction. A school utilizing MTSS may designate a block of time for core instruction and then allocate about thirty minutes in the master schedule for grade-level teams or the entire school staff to orchestrate Tier 2 interventions, with the option to share students (as identified on team common assessments) for targeted and specific skills support. Schools can create time for Tier 3 in the schedule via individual student pull-outs when teachers are not teaching priority standards or with a designated reading or mathematics support class for students to attend in addition to their grade-level course.

Students are not eager to go to a class called *intervention*. Consider naming the time designated for Tier 2 interventions after the school mascot—for example, *Bobcat Time* or *Tiger Time*. Many schools use the acronym *WIN* (What I Need) for this time. For students who do not need interventions, schools and teacher teams create meaningful learning experiences for extension during that designated time of day.

In many elementary schools we visit, there are intervention times for students allocated during the school day, but at different times of day for each grade level, often to utilize paraprofessionals or other additional adult supports for each grade-level intervention. Consider instead scheduling intervention at the same time for the entire school (or at least by grade bands such as K–2 and 3–5), so teachers and other adult supports can share students across grade levels by targeted foundational skill (often reading first for greatest acceleration). Counselors, elective teachers, and administrators can then all support small groups of learners needing help with a targeted skill.

Secondary schools are more inclined to have the same time of day allocated for interventions due to the division of the school day into periods. Intervention time (whether a full period or a partial period) is best in the middle of the school day, rather than at the start or end. For example, a middle school might have periods 1 and 2, then an intervention time, then the remaining periods of the day. Administrators can add an intervention period to an existing schedule by taking about five minutes from each class period. When intervention is at the same time for everyone, subject-area department members can identify foundational skills and share students who need the same prerequisite skills in that subject area regardless of current course. For example, a mathematics department at a high school might create and assign students to intervention groups for number sense and ratios, graphing, and solving one- or two-step equations. Similarly, the English department might establish intervention groups for reading fluency, comprehension development with lower-grade-level texts, or summarizing. For foundational skills such as reading and number sense, the most qualified teachers for the specific skill lead the intervention.

When most students in a school need acceleration in their learning from several grade levels prior, further alterations to the master schedule may be necessary. Specifically, schools can create a system that uses intervention time to move students through a set of prerequisite skills and concepts (which teachers would normally address in Tier 3) in one- or two-week intervals. In other words, teachers utilize the thirty-minute intervention time scheduled in the day for Tier 2 to address Tier 3–level needs with respect to prior knowledge or foundational skills. (Note that individual sessions for students with other Tier 3 needs would still occur as well.) We call this the *vitamin approach* because students get a learning vitamin to supplement and strengthen their core instruction. During that designated intervention time, all students are placed in small groups with like needs based on a diagnostic assessment. Teachers share students across grade levels and departments to provide instruction to students who need to work on closing vast achievement gaps. This all-hands-on-deck approach to filling these gaps for students occurs daily. At the end of a learning cycle, teams might interrupt this daily attention to the most basic skills to provide Tier 2 interventions for current learning (based on common formative assessments) and then return to Tier 3 interventions a few days later (Kramer & Maeker, 2022). Figure 6.2 shows an example of a ten-day learning cycle for Tier 1, with intervention time for both Tier 2 and Tier 3.

	Monday	**Tuesday**	**Wednesday**	**Thursday**	**Friday**
Week 1					
Tier 1 core	Prior knowledge and grade-level standard	Prior knowledge and grade-level standard	Prior knowledge and grade-level standard	Prior knowledge and grade-level standard	Prior knowledge and grade-level standard
Intervention time	**Tier 3** Foundational reading or numeracy	**Tier 3** Foundational reading or numeracy	**Tier 3** Foundational reading or numeracy	**Tier 3** Foundational reading or numeracy	**Tier 3** Foundational reading or numeracy
Week 2					
Tier 1 core	Prior knowledge and grade-level standard	Prior knowledge and grade-level standard	**Common assessment**	**Tier 2 Flex day—**Re-engage with grade-level standard	Prior knowledge and grade-level standard
Intervention time	**Tier 3** Foundational reading or numeracy	**Tier 3** Foundational reading or numeracy	**Tier 3** Foundational reading or numeracy	**Tier 3** Foundational reading or numeracy	**Tier 2** Re-engage with grade-level standard

Source: Kramer & Maeker, 2022.

FIGURE 6.2: Example of ten-day learning cycle showing Tier 1, Tier 2, and Tier 3 interventions.

In addition to a scheduled time of day for interventions, consider how to allow collaborative teams to teach subjects or courses at the same time of day so teachers can share students for flex days during Tier 1 instruction or regroup students across classrooms. At an elementary school, if mathematics is taught for seventy-five minutes two days a week, teachers might teach a lesson for forty-five minutes and use the last thirty minutes as a Tier 2 intervention time across the team. At the secondary level, schools could schedule two eighth-grade science classes during the same period to allow the teachers to share students if needed. These options are only available when teachers on the same grade-level or course team are teaching similar subjects or courses at the same time.

Finally, collaborative teams need time to meet and plan for acceleration and interventions. This often happens during collaborative team meetings but cannot be the sole focus of collaborative team meetings week to week because a focus on Tier 1 core instruction is most important when working to prevent students from needing additional time and support to learn. Teams may need to carve out additional time to meet during the school day by utilizing a common planning period, also a consideration in the master schedule.

It is not easy to revamp a master schedule to account for interventions, but MTSS with a focus on acceleration is more effective when teams have the additional time to work with students and time to plan the intervention and extension groups. Find examples of schedules that accommodate intervention time and collaborative team meetings at AllThingsPLC (www.allthingsPLC.info/evidence) as part of each Model PLC's profile. Such change is critical for intervention and extension options to meet students' needs and accelerate learning.

Respond as a Team to Student Learning Data

To create meaningful intervention learning experiences, teams use data. Teachers plan for learning in learning cycles (see chapter 3, page 33) and gather data from common and progress-monitoring assessments to determine students' specific learning needs. Teachers intentionally plan and respond in real time to student learning as a collaborative team.

There are several types of data teachers and teams use when planning for student learning in the three tiers. Daily classroom data teachers generate from observations during lessons informs differentiation and intentional grouping (Tier 1). Data from common formative assessments during a unit of instruction inform the use of such interventions as a flex day during instruction for re-engagement strategies, station work, or the sharing of students during core instruction to accelerate learning. Such interventions are called *Tier 2* because teachers pause core instruction, but these interventions do happen during core instruction time. Regardless of the name, teachers target the interventions specific to student needs. Data from common end-of-unit assessments inform Tier 2 interventions for priority standards, although teachers may also implant them during core instruction. Typically, Tier 3 includes data from common assessments, progress-monitoring assessments, district benchmark assessments, or interim assessments. Varied data from classroom formative assessments to larger-scale assessments inform strategic groupings for all three tiers.

As teachers across a team gather learning evidence, they work together to identify the students in need of intervention or extension and uncover each student's targeted and specific needs. Grouping students based on what the data reveal is essential to accelerating learning and more critical than worrying about the number of students in any intervention group. Many teachers would rather work with thirty students in an intervention setting focused on a targeted skill than five students needing intervention on five different skills.

As mentioned in chapter 4 (page 61), the primary ways teachers and collaborative teams collect student learning data are as follows.

- ▶ Daily formative checks for understanding and observations during lessons
- ▶ Common formative assessments on specific learning targets or skills teachers across a collaborative team give mid-unit
- ▶ Common end-of-unit assessments on specific learning targets or skills teachers across a collaborative team give
- ▶ Progress-monitoring assessments, benchmark or interim assessments, universal screeners, or diagnostic measures
- ▶ End-of-year state-assessment data

Teams may start with progress-monitoring data from the end of the previous school year to inform intervention groups at the beginning of the year and then use classroom and team assessments or future progress-monitoring assessments to determine needs for Tier 2 and Tier 3 moving forward. Teams discuss how to use activities during lessons when most students did not yet learn, small-group minilessons when a few students have not yet learned, and flex days for in-class interventions when some students have learned and others have not yet learned. This is not intervention by individual teachers; this is systemic intervention and a promise that regardless of teacher, all students will receive the instruction they need to accelerate learning to grade level or beyond. The *team* makes plans for students across the grade level or course.

Remember, teams design interventions first for grade-level priority standards and the prerequisite skills that lead to proficiency with each priority standard. As such, it is helpful for teams to keep track of student proficiency with each priority standard. Figure 6.3 (page 116) shows an example of a priority-standards tracker. Teams record data for each common formative assessment by target within the priority standard, with a final column showing overall proficiency, or they may just track the overall proficiency using their own assessments and any progress-monitoring assessments. Teams calculate the percentage of students proficient with each priority standard in each class and across the whole team to determine which priority standards they still need to address in Tier 1 or Tier 2. The team might also choose an essential standard to address before a vacation, rather than starting a new unit, using the information in the tracker—all with the intention of having more students learn the priority standard to grade level.

When analyzing data from common assessments, teams must go beyond proficient or not proficient and investigate what the student work says about student learning on each target. Consider the following questions.

- ▶ What are the common trends in student thinking or strategies used?
- ▶ Are there any misconceptions that seem to be trends across a class or the entire team?
- ▶ What are the strengths in reasoning to build from?

The data protocol in figure 6.4 (page 117) is one process teams can use as they make sense of student work and create interventions and extensions for students. Teachers use the data protocol for common assessments related to a specific learning target or priority standard. This tool uses asset-based thinking. The teams analyze work from students who are proficient or exceed proficiency first to name what students can do and the trends in thinking. Then, teams look at the data for those students close to proficiency to name trends in student work to see what targeted intervention might move students to proficiency. Last, they analyze student work for those students far from proficiency or in need of support. They identify trends (if any) and determine next steps to accelerate learning to close to proficiency and eventually, to proficiency. Teams agree on the learning to address during small-group instruction. They determine how teachers should use any additional intervention time during the week, whether carved out of core instruction or at an alternate time in the daily schedule. As a result of the data and discussion, a team might also identify additional practice during class or as homework to reinforce and practice the learning students need.

When analyzing data from progress-monitoring or district-benchmark assessments, consider looking more closely at the priority standards. The protocol in figure 6.5 (page 118) helps initiate a team discussion and plan for addressing data from these types of assessments (which teachers give a few times during the year), with a focus on the priority standards they have taught and assessed at the time of the progress-monitoring assessment.

		RL.1.1: Ask and answer questions about a text.					RL.1.2: Retell stories, including key details, and demonstrate understanding of their central message or lesson.					L.1.1K: Print all upper- and lowercase letters with proper letter formation.			
		Answer Questions September 18	Answer Questions September 25	Ask Questions October 30	Winter Data January	Full Standard	Key Details October 15	Retell Stories October 25	Central Message November 10	Winter Data January	Full Standard	Uppercase August 30	Lowercase September 15	District Benchmark December	Full Standard
Teacher A	Adam F.	3	3	2	3	3	2	3	1	1	2	3	3	3	3
	Jantae R.	4	3	2	3	3	2	3	4	3	3	3	3	3	3
	(List all students.)														
Teacher B	Molly B.	2	2	1	1	2	2	3	2	2	2	3	3	3	3
	Javier D.	2	2	3	3	3	2	3	2	2	3	3	2	3	3
	(List all students.)														
Teacher C	Kathy G.	1	2	1	2	2	1	2	2	1	2	2	2	2	2
	Laticia C.	3	4	3	3	3	3	3	2	3	3	3	3	3	3
	(List all students.)														
Team	Percentage Proficient or Exceeding	50	50	25	54	66	17	83	17	42	50	83	66	76	83

Source for standards: NGA & CCSSO, 2010a.

FIGURE 6.3: Team priority-standards tracker.

Visit go.SolutionTree.com/priorityschools for a free reproducible version of this figure.

Data-Analysis Protocol

1. Identify the priority standard or learning target assessed.

2. Identify the students who demonstrated learning at levels of advanced, proficient, close to proficient, or far from proficient. Total the number of students in each level for the team.

Advanced	Proficient	Close to Proficient	Far From Proficient

3. Look at samples of student work. What are the trends in thinking or reasoning unique to the advanced students? What are the trends unique to the proficient students? Continue with each level and write down the trends in student work for each.

Advanced	Proficient	Close to Proficient	Far From Proficient

4. Determine a collective plan to target interventions or extensions for each group of students. Which teacher will be responsible for the learning of each group? When will teachers re-evaluate the close-to-proficient and far-from-proficient groups to see if learning occurred?

Advanced	Proficient	Close to Proficient	Far From Proficient
Teacher:	Teacher:	Teacher:	Teacher:
		Date for re-evaluation:	Date for re-evaluation:

Source: Adapted from Kramer & Schuhl, 2017.

FIGURE 6.4: Common formative assessment data analysis for a learning target or standard.

*Visit **go.SolutionTree.com/priorityschools** for a free reproducible version of this figure.*

Priority-Standards Assessment Analysis

School:	Team:

Priority Standards: Identify which priority standards teachers taught and assessed, partially taught and assessed, or have not yet taught and assessed at the time of the progress-monitoring assessment. Check the appropriate box.

Priority Standard	Taught and Assessed	Partially Taught and Assessed	Not Yet Taught or Assessed

Analysis

Proficiency With Priority Standards: Determine the percentage of students demonstrating proficiency or higher with each priority standard on the assessment by teacher and as a team.

Priority Standard	Teacher A	Teacher B	Teacher C	Team

Analysis of the Priority Standards Taught and Assessed	
1. Which priority standards have students learned most deeply? Which instructional practices contributed to the results?	
2. What surprises do you see in the data? Why?	
3. Which priority standards (if any) do you need to revisit? How will your *team* plan to re-engage students in learning?	
4. How closely does the data match your team common assessment results?	
Analysis of the Priority Standards Partially or Not Yet Taught and Assessed	
1. Which priority standards (if any) are students already showing they know and can do?	
2. What surprises do you see in the data? Why?	
3. For the priority standards students will learn this term, what are some team instructional practices to use?	
Team Goal for Next Progress-Monitoring Assessment and Action Steps	
Goal:	Team Action Steps:

FIGURE 6.5: Progress-monitoring data protocol for priority standards.

*Visit **go.SolutionTree.com/priorityschools** for a free reproducible version of this figure.*

As teams create intervention groups and plan targeted lessons (whether for Tier 2, Tier 3, or small groups or flex days in Tier 1), consider how to document the intervention plan and monitor its effectiveness. Figure 6.6 shows one possibility. As with figure 6.4 (page 117), teams determine the intervention or extension for each group of students using data, the resources needed, and the person responsible for teaching each group. The student names for each group are written on the second page for the entire team. Once the intervention concludes, teachers place check marks next to the names of students who are now proficient or moved from far from proficient to close to proficient. This enables teachers to see the effectiveness of their plan for accelerating student learning.

Using data to create *team* intervention and extension plans is critical to accelerating student learning. Teachers also need time during the school day to implement targeted and specific interventions when students need additional support beyond Tier 1 core instruction. Data protocols help document student learning and assist teachers in creating a plan for continued learning this year and in future years as they teach units again with new students.

Focus on Student Growth

Teams and teachers work to have every student proficient or beyond with each of the priority standards. Along the way, teachers and students may feel defeated if not enough students are meeting or exceeding expectations. How might teams and students celebrate small wins along the way? Monitoring student growth (in addition to current proficiency levels) and having students understand their growth using student trackers and goal-setting tools generates hope for teachers and students alike. Focusing on growth also contributes to a strength- or asset-based mindset by recognizing what students can do and challenging them to continue growing to proficiency.

After each progress-monitoring assessment (or common formative assessment for priority standards that extend or recur throughout the year), identify the students who are showing growth. Celebrate each victory with an understanding that students have accelerated their learning toward grade-level proficiency. The teams might celebrate after school in a staff meeting as they share their successes with one another. They can name students in an assembly or in their class. Sharon visited a school where teams created a display of a tree trunk and branches and students wrote their names on paper leaves to put on the tree when they grew or achieved proficiency or beyond. Students took great pride in showing others their leaves. When teachers, teams, and school communities celebrate growth, confidence across the collaborative teams and within each student increases, sparking even more success and growth.

Teams should also identify any students who have shown no growth (or declined) since the previous progress-monitoring assessment (or common assessment). As a team, identify individual students by name. Discuss why there is no evidence of growth for each student. Each will vary—and the reasons may at times be outside the classroom, such as family trauma or absences. However, once the team names and claims the students, teachers can implement intentional instructional strategies to develop growth in student learning. Students might get preferential seating or teachers may check in on the students' learning during lessons and provide more frequent feedback. Additionally, teachers re-evaluate small-group and intervention placement for these students to grow learning more effectively.

Celebrating and working toward growth for every student does not mean accepting only growth, but rather acknowledging students need growth if acceleration is to occur. Keep the

WIN Data Sheet

Grade level: _____ Dates: _____ Priority Standards: _____ Learning Targets: _____

Proficiency Level	Students	Resources	Persons Responsible	Plan
Above Proficient	See attached list.			
Proficient	See attached lis.t			
Close to Proficient	See attached list.			
Far From Proficient	See attached list.			

Students

Above Proficient	Proficient	Close to Proficient	Far From Proficient

Source: © 2014 by Newhall School District. Adapted with permission.

FIGURE 6.6: Intervention and extension team plan.

Visit go.SolutionTree.com/priorityschools for a free reproducible version of this figure.

focus on creating learning experiences for students to grow to proficiency or beyond with each grade-level priority standard, but celebrate progress too!

Utilize Blended Learning

Blended learning for interventions means using software programs in partnership with in-person learning experiences. As we shared earlier in this chapter, effective intervention for acceleration occurs with teachers using learning data from common assessments, not simply through the purchase of a program. However, when teachers use blended learning intentionally, computer programs can contribute to acceleration. Consider the following questions when utilizing software programs as part of an intervention plan.

- ▶ If the program uses an assessment to determine student placement, is the placement accurate based on classroom evidence of learning? How will the student track growth in the program?

- ▶ How can teachers assign modules or lessons to students so they are working on prior knowledge and skills leading to a current (or future) grade-level priority standard?

- ▶ How can teachers assign modules or lessons to review priority standards or as additional practice toward learning a grade-level priority standard?

- ▶ When in the school day (or week) will students utilize a computer-intervention program, and when will students receive live instruction with real-time feedback?

- ▶ How will students reflect on their learning and track progress toward learning a priority standard?

- ▶ How will students receive live feedback or instruction (if needed) to access the learning in any computer program?

Teams consider how live instruction will truly blend with any computer program. An intentional computer program might be one station for small groups to cycle through during Tier 1 or Tier 2 learning experiences, with remaining stations being small-group practice or a minilesson with the teacher. As part of a secondary support class, half the group might utilize a computer program while the other half engages in live instructional experiences with the teacher before switching midway through the class period. Ideally, the computer is never the only source of instruction or feedback available—there is an adult in the room to monitor and answer questions, so students stay actively engaged in learning.

Computer programs are not good or bad, but teams' use of them can be. Teams must analyze whether a computer program truly provides an opportunity for students to learn through feedback and track their learning progress to grade-level priority standards, and how teachers will blend those computer-assisted lessons with interpersonal learning experiences.

Create Small Groups

Earlier, we shared the importance of small groups for engagement, differentiation, minilessons, and interventions. In MTSS, small groups provide opportunities for targeted supports. Teachers can use small groups of students as part of Tier 1 instruction or during any Tier 2 or Tier 3 intervention.

Heterogeneous small groups of students can work collectively on a classroom activity during a lesson. For example, students might work together to solve a higher-level mathematics task or complete a Venn diagram to compare characters in a novel or play. Each small group working on the same activity provides an opportunity for the teacher to observe students and provide feedback. The teacher can prepare scaffolding questions to accelerate learning for students in need of support during the activity, as well as an extension question should a group finish the task early and need meaningful extension. The small groups can share their work with one another as part of the closure of the activity.

Often, teachers use small groups for interventions, with each small group focused on a targeted skill. In this case, the students in each small group are homogeneous in terms of ability or need based on data. Teachers and teams determine from data what the targeted focus of each small group should be and how students will engage in learning through a minilesson or practice with feedback during each small-group experience. In such a case, the teacher might form small groups after core instruction—whether still in Tier 1 as part of the lesson or a flex day, or in Tier 2 or Tier 3 interventions. For example, after an initial grade-level lesson, teachers might then group students during reading time, so each small group is reading a designated and purposeful text at their reading level. The teacher spends time working with each small group to further the students' reading skills. Other times, small groups may rotate through stations that include learning games or additional practice related to priority standards, intentional learning via a computer program, and a targeted minilesson with the teacher. Teachers change small groups as needed based on the data and standard students are learning. Paraprofessionals may help support the small groups, or teachers might even combine classes so there are two adults with the small groups to monitor and advance learning.

Develop and Use Peer Tutors

Some schools and districts have formal peer-tutoring programs, which teach qualified students how to teach and work with other students. In these schools and districts, peer tutors can help with interventions. Peer tutors are typically high school juniors or seniors, and teachers assign them to work in K–10 classes. Often, these peer tutors earn elective or career and technical education credits for peer tutoring as a course.

Generally, the peer tutor is assigned to a class, learns with the class, and then helps students during any work time. The teacher of the class works with the peer tutor to make sure the peer tutor is sitting with students, supporting small-group work, and asking questions of students to support them in making sense of the subject matter. Teachers sometimes loan peer tutors to other teachers if the class they are assigned to is taking a test and there isn't any need for support during that test time or if another teacher requests a peer tutor based on intervention and small-group needs.

Another option is to create an after-school tutoring center. This practice could exist at the elementary, middle, or high school level, with teachers from core-subject areas taking turns to lead the center. Teachers can train high school juniors and seniors as peer tutors, who see their efforts as an extracurricular activity, or the school might utilize student volunteers from the National Honor Society or similar groups, who then earn community service hours. The peer tutors go to the tutoring center and answer students' questions or work with specific students, as the teacher on duty directs.

The mathematics rubric in figure 6.7 (page 124) is an example of a rubric to evaluate a peer tutor when the peer tutor is enrolled in a course. Teachers fill it out for their peer tutors each week, and the peer tutors justify each score. Notice how the rubric shares with the peer tutor how to support learning, which in turn provides additional help in the classroom to accelerate learning.

Score	Teacher Communication	Student Interaction	Mathematics Understanding
5	• Asks for clarification • Interacts with teacher daily to determine where services are useful • Communicates student progress • Engages in lectures and other activities	• Sits with students • Initiates conversations about mathematics • Responds to students with questions • Students appreciate and learn from the help	• Asks questions which lead to student learning • Able to break problems into understandable pieces • Tries to find new ways for students to understand and solve problems • Demonstrates with, finds, or creates additional examples
4	• Asks for clarification but may still have questions • Usually interacts with the teacher to determine where needs for the day are • Usually communicates student progress • Often engages in lectures and other activities	• Usually sits with students • Sometimes initiates conversations about mathematics • Often responds to students with questions • Students often appreciate and learn from the help	• Often asks questions which lead to student learning • Often able to break problems into understandable pieces • Often tries to find new ways for students to understand and solve problems • Often demonstrates with, finds, or creates additional examples
3	• Asks for clarification but is still unclear • Sometimes interacts with the teacher to determine where needs for the day are • Sometimes communicates student progress • Sometimes engages in lectures and other activities	• Sometimes sits with students • Seldom initiates conversations about mathematics • Sometimes responds to students with questions • Students sometimes appreciate and learn from the help	• Asks questions that tell students each step without internalizing the problem • Sometimes able to break problems into understandable pieces • Sometimes tries to find new ways for students to understand and solve problems • Sometimes demonstrates with, finds, or creates additional examples
2	• Asks for clarification but translates the information incorrectly • Seldom interacts with the teacher to determine where needs for the day are • Seldom communicates student progress • Seldom engages in lectures and other activities; distracted	• Seldom sits with students • Initiates conversations about mathematics when the teacher tells them to • Seldom responds to students with questions • Students seldom appreciate and learn from the help	• Asks students questions, but implies the answer • Seldom able to break problems into understandable pieces • Seldom tries to find new ways for students to understand and solve problems • Seldom demonstrates with, finds, or creates additional examples
1	• Never asks for clarification when needed • Never asks the teacher to determine where needs for the day are • Never communicates student progress • Never engages in lectures or other activities (but does homework, writes notes, and so on)	• Never sits with students • Initiates conversations about math when told to • Never responds to students with questions • Students don't want assistance because it isn't helpful	• Never asks questions which lead to student learning—gives the answer in each step • Never able to break problems into understandable pieces • Never tries to find new ways for students to understand and solve problems • Never demonstrates with, finds, or creates additional examples

FIGURE 6.7: Mathematics peer tutor rubric example.

If using peer tutors, teachers ask students how the peer tutor helped them learn. This provides insights on how to utilize peer tutors most effectively for acceleration. Also, teachers ask the peer tutors what types of questions students had to inform future instruction. In general, whether during the school day or before or after school, peer tutors may be an additional source of support to accelerate student learning.

Implement Support Classes or Learning Labs

As mentioned previously, *support classes* are separate courses that students take in addition to their grade-level classes when they have significant needs in a foundational area (usually reading or mathematics). Teachers assign students to these intervention classes when a combination of data—such as state-assessment scores, progress-monitoring scores, and common-assessment results—show students need more than two years of learning to reach grade-level standards.

Support classes are more common at the secondary level. Students enroll in the grade-level core class and simultaneously enroll in the support class (as an elective course) as an intervention to help accelerate learning. Teachers of support classes collaboratively plan with the corresponding core class teachers to preteach prerequisite skills students might need or accelerate learning for current priority standards. While support classes usually focus on foundational skills and are, therefore, a Tier 3 intervention, at times these classes offer additional Tier 2 support and intervention for the current priority standards in the core class.

The goal of any support class is that, with the additional targeted time and support, students can be successful in their core ELA or mathematics course and deepen their reasoning skills. Students exit the support course when the data show they are being successful in their core class.

Sometimes, high schools create study hall periods when students need them based on their common assessment results. Highly qualified teachers staff these periods so students have open reading and mathematics labs or periods in the corresponding field teachers assign students to instead of study hall. Teachers assign students to the learning lab to receive intervention when needed; when these students have caught up, they go back to their study hall. Within a given period of time (for example, two weeks), teams use data to determine which students they should assign to the learning lab.

Engage Students in Learning Behavior Expectations

MTSS or RTI includes not only academic interventions and extensions but also behavior interventions and extensions. Sometimes, students act out when they are bored, frustrated, or believe they cannot academically succeed in class. Sometimes students have not had the opportunity to learn appropriate behaviors at home and come to school not understanding the social or academic skills they need to be successful. In a learning-centered school culture, teachers and administrators approach behavior the same way they do academics. When students do not learn, teachers intervene to help them succeed, but too often when students misbehave teachers are quick to punish (Buffum et al., 2018). Implementing MTSS means addressing academic *and* behavioral learning with an eye on student growth and grade-level achievement.

To begin, as a school, clarify those behaviors required for students to be successful and contribute to the positive school culture. How should they look and sound in classrooms, the cafeteria, the hallways, the restrooms, the playground, the gym or fields, and the bus loading or parent drop-off area? Name the desired behaviors and calibrate staff tolerance for acceptable and unacceptable behaviors to create a consistent environment for students. Next, *teach* students (through examples and counterexamples) the desired behaviors in each school space. Be careful to phrase desired behaviors in positive language, such as, "Walk in the hallway," instead of negative statements, such as, "Don't run in the hallway." Students are clever and will skip or jump to push boundaries while not running. By stating students should walk, the desired behavior is clear. Solidify the campus behavior expectations in writing.

When developing an intervention system for behavior, the guiding coalition, learning team, or a separate behavior task force explores the current reality related to behavior and plans for teaching, intervening, and extending student understanding and actions about the desired behaviors students need to learn. Consider the following questions to improve schoolwide systems.

- ▸ What are the behaviors getting in the way of student learning?
- ▸ When during the school day (or school year) does each behavior happen most often?
- ▸ How well do students understand how a person should behave in various social situations?

When students do not meet behavior expectations, teachers need to refocus and teach appropriate behavior, rather than punish or escalate situations. Consider the following questions regarding teachers' response to behavior.

- ▸ How can students learn strategies to behave given the triggers that may occur during the school day?
- ▸ How can students learn to connect their behaviors with positive social and academic experiences?
- ▸ How will your school encourage and celebrate positive behaviors?

In addition to proactively defining expected behaviors, Tier 1 should include classroom reteaching when students misbehave. At times, students need Tier 2 or Tier 3 behavior interventions, often with a counselor or administrator to clarify expectations and train students to act in ways that promote and accelerate learning. Such interventions occur in small groups or one on one, and involve finding the root cause of the behavior and helping students know how to act in the future if a similar trigger happens again.

Conclusion

Accelerating learning using asset-based thinking means growing student learning toward proficiency of priority standards. What has the student already learned? How can a student access grade-level learning in core Tier 1 instruction? What does student work demonstrate students understand, and what is their next step? Teams answer these questions and work together to develop targeted and specific interventions and extensions to accelerate student learning based on what students have already learned.

When designing academic interventions to accelerate learning, the intervention should be required during the school day, allow for flexible grouping, be targeted and specific, be led by a highly qualified teacher, and show evidence of effectiveness (Buffum et al., 2018). Teams use small groups, frequent common assessments, and progress-monitoring assessment data to determine any intervention needs. Whether the intervention then happens during an allocated flex day during a learning cycle, the last twenty minutes of core instruction two days a week, or during an intervention block, what matters is teams are responding to common assessment data and working collaboratively to guarantee grade-level learning for every student. And, most importantly, teachers and students celebrate gains in learning leading to proficiency.

Discussion Questions for Reflection and Action

As a team, discuss the following questions. Visit **go.SolutionTree.com/priorityschools** for a free reproducible version of these questions.

- ▶ How are Tier 1, Tier 2, and Tier 3 defined in a pyramid of interventions?

- ▶ What distinct tiers of interventions do your educators and staff utilize schoolwide?

- ▶ What shifts in practice do teachers need to make to have more effective interventions and extensions?

- ▶ How are academic and behavior interventions related?

- ▶ How are teams analyzing data to identify which students have learned and still need to learn?

- ▶ What intervention or extension strategies will you try to strengthen student learning in your school?

- ▶ What behaviors do teachers need to teach on your campus? How will students learn them?

- ▶ How will you know if the interventions or extensions you use are effective and grow learning? What data will you collect?

CHAPTER 7

Leadership Practices That Accelerate Learning

As is often the case when embarking on a journey to continuously improve student learning, one of the biggest questions for accelerating learning is, How do leaders provide the direction and supports students need for learning to truly accelerate to grade level or beyond? Sharon grappled with this question when she worked with a district in Minnesota. When she arrived, the district leaders had distributed an implementation plan and action steps designed to grow student learning, which included schedule revisions at the elementary, middle, and high school levels to allow time for collaborative teams to meet during the school day. The leaders' plan also required teams to produce certain deliverables during their collaboration time. Although these deliverables were the same products and artifacts that teams typically develop as they answer the four critical questions of learning, the teachers did not perceive them as such. For one thing, every deliverable in the process involved a form to complete and turn in to the principal. Principals were expected to monitor this work and collect the documents for each deliverable (meeting agendas, meeting minutes, collaborative logs, data protocols, standards documents, collaborative formative and summative assessments, and so on) from every teacher team.

The problem was not the actual expected work, but the way the leaders rolled out and monitored the work. The word *deliverable* developed a negative connotation among the teachers and they often used it as a slur to describe school and district leadership. Even worse, teachers came to define the collaborative team process as complying with deliverable requirements, rather than view the deliverables as protocols to record the meaningful conversations teachers have to ensure the learning of all students. The collaborative team meetings became sessions to complete whatever was due now. The collaborative discussions rarely engaged members in looking deeply at standards, assessments, data, instructional practices, or interventions. This heavy focus on compliance resulted in resentment and teams describing their collaborative time as "worthless." Teachers often asked to go back to their classrooms to get the "real work" done! It was obvious that deliverables were not moving the work forward or increasing student achievement as the school had intended.

Leadership really matters when working to create systems for accelerating learning—from creating a school culture focused on learning to developing high-functioning

> [Leaders in gap-closing schools and districts] have seen the power schools have to change lives . . . They aren't waiting for the cavalry to teach the kids; they are the cavalry.
>
> —KARIN CHENOWETH

collaborative teams to strengthening teacher instruction. Leading acceleration is bigger than any one person. Leading acceleration requires a shared leadership model, with feedback and supports for teams and teachers.

The Shift to Shared Leadership

All stakeholders must be involved in the culture of learning and the process of acceleration, but it also takes effective leadership to generate change. Sometimes individual leaders feel the urgency to change and try to take it all on themselves. But even if initially successful, this approach is not sustainable because it is solely dependent on one person. Should that person leave or move to a different position, the change loses momentum and those left are often unable to continue or deepen the work. No one person has all the knowledge, skills, patience, and resilience to meet the needs of every student in a class, so teachers work collaboratively in grade-level or content-specific teams to support one another in the challenges of meeting all the diverse needs of students. In the same vein, even the most charismatic and knowledgeable principal or superintendent cannot do the work alone of ensuring student learning accelerates. *Leading acceleration requires a team.*

Furthermore, any attempt to improve schools must be done *with* teachers, not *to* teachers. Involving teachers as valued partners in the work increases their level of commitment (Covey, 2013). Speaker and former teacher and administrator Luis F. Cruz (2022) often says, "Teachers are less likely to tear down a fence they helped build." All too often, schools and districts turn to compliance because it can be easier to give mandates and directives to employees, as we demonstrated earlier in this chapter. It is far more difficult to ensure staff are engaging in the work with commitment to the process because they know it is the right work and will result in more learning for students. Compliance is *first-order change* (a change in strategies), while commitment requires *second-order change* (a shift in beliefs and philosophies; Kramer & Schuhl, 2017). The shift from compliance to commitment creates the culture necessary to improve. So, how can leaders *lead* change, not merely impose it?

First, leaders must share and widely disperse leadership. It resides not solely in the individual at the top, but in every person at every level who, in some way, acts as a leader to others. Leaders are administrators, instructional coaches, teachers, staff, and students, to name a few. Schools and districts are filled with leaders. Second, leaders must not let gaining universal acceptance before initiating change sidetrack them. In too many instances, leaders work to ensure buy-in to any new idea or initiative. Buy-in rarely comes before implementation because others often use this absence as an excuse to slow improvement efforts. Rather than wait for buy-in, especially from extremely resistant individuals, it is much more effective for leaders to build a solid rationale and share knowledge. Building a vision, rationale, and understanding creates a pathway for the work to begin.

Schools accelerating learning for both staff and students shift their understanding and implementation of leadership. Table 7.1 highlights some critical shifts.

Schools and districts are filled with leaders. Every individual in a school has an enormous opportunity to lead in a way that impacts students for life.

Leadership Practices to Accelerate Learning

In learning organizations where learning is required, everyone is a learner, and everyone is a leader. It takes a village to ensure all students learn at high levels. Shared leadership is an outcome

TABLE 7.1: Shifts in Leadership to Accelerate Student Learning

SHIFT FROM . . .	SHIFT TO . . .
Authoritarian leadership	Shared leadership
A focus on management	A focus on learning and instruction
Buy-in as a prerequisite for change	Clear rationale and research for change and acceptance that buy-in will come with results and celebrations
Leadership teams that focus on managerial tasks	Leadership teams that focus on learning
Majority of time spent on urgent issues	Majority of time spent on important issues related to learning
Compliance-focused monitoring	Celebration-based monitoring

of the deeply held belief that each person plays a role in a learning organization. Public education leader and best-selling author Phillip C. Schlechty (2001) describes shared leadership this way:

> Shared leadership . . . is less like an orchestra, where the conductor is always in charge, and more like a jazz band, where leadership is passed around . . . depending on what the music demands at the moment and who feels most moved by the spirit to express the music. (p. 178)

Create a Guiding Coalition or Learning Team

As mentioned previously, the district and school *guiding coalition* or *learning team* leads the mission of learning (DuFour et al., 2016). Unlike a more traditional leadership team that focuses on managerial tasks associated with the smooth operation of the school or district, the responsibility of the guiding coalition or learning team is to lead the learning of adults as the adults lead the learning of students. The team accepts the responsibility of reciprocal accountability: for every task, teachers, collaborative teams, and students are asked to engage in, the necessary supports are in place, along with an understanding of *why*. Bill Hall (2022), a former school district director of educational leadership and professional development, describes the *guiding coalition* (or learning team) as "an alliance of staff from within a school who have the responsibility of leading a change process through the many challenges and barriers of implementation" (p. 9). Coauthors Terri L. Martin and Cameron L. Rains (2018) state, "The guiding coalition identifies necessary changes and develops implementation plans. Its members understand the change process, help move staff forward positively, and challenge the status quo when necessary" (p. 29). Support always precedes accountability. Support is the work of the guiding coalition or learning team so teachers can successfully accelerate learning.

Support begins by creating coherence and clarity. Too often systems focus time on structural change, as did the Minnesota school district Sharon worked with at the beginning of this chapter. Schools and districts can often describe all the processes and structures in place, such as standards, assessments, professional development, teacher preservice training, and so on. But such knowledge is structural alignment, not coherence, and although necessary, will not improve student learning unless there is an underlying sense of system coherence. *System coherence* is a shared mindset throughout the organization; everyone can articulate the same story in terms of goals, strategies, and progress (see chapter 2, page 17). This means everyone understands and can articulate the *why* and *how* to accelerate learning. The mission, vision, collective commitments, and goals are clear and compelling. Building coherence is essential to ensuring commitment (rather than compliance) to the process.

The guiding coalition or learning team develops coherence by communicating purpose, priorities, and goals clearly and consistently with one voice and engaging in two-way communication with others. As the process unfolds, insist on a learning-through-action approach. Remember, as part of a learning organization, educators learn by trying different approaches, keeping what works, and revising or stopping what does not work well. Westover and Steinhauser (2022) ask, "What if the solution was not for educators to be better consumers of research but for educators to become better action researchers?" (p. 107). This work is a journey of continuous improvement, not a destination or a program to implement. When done correctly, this work is a process that results in more learning for students.

Leadership sustains the focus on the right work. Teams and teachers often suffer from initiative fatigue. Many times, there are so many programs and curricula it is difficult for teachers to focus on the most important work—learning. When everything is important, then nothing really is.

Since the quality of any school system cannot exceed the quality of the people within it, accelerating student learning is about growing people over programs or curricula. It requires the people within a school to learn together because adult learning is essential to student learning. Reporter and educational writer Karin Chenoweth (2021) states:

> It is long past time to acknowledge that it is impossible for individual educators to know all there is to know about making kids smarter. There is simply too much to know. It is only by pooling their knowledge and learning from expertise that educators can possibly expect to help all kids. (p. 137)

If adults are not learning, students will make little progress (Barth, 1991).

The guiding coalition or learning team serves as a model for the work the school or district expects from each team. To support teachers, the guiding coalition or learning team answers similar questions to those that collaborative teams use to support student learning (see page 21; DuFour et al., 2016; Schuhl, 2021).

1. What do we expect *collaborative teams* to know and be able to do?

2. How will we know if each *collaborative team* has learned it and is effective?

3. How will we respond if some *collaborative teams* have not learned it or are not yet working effectively?

4. How will we extend learning for *collaborative teams* that have demonstrated proficiency and are effective?

Figure 7.1 outlines the work of collaborative teams and the guiding coalition or learning team.

For every expectation, the primary job of the guiding coalition or learning team is to ask what teams and teachers need to meet the expectation. In addition, giving support often requires the guiding coalition or learning team to remove barriers impeding progress at the team and school

Guiding Coalition	Collaborative Teams

Lead Creation of School Foundations
 	
• Create a mission.
• Create a vision.
• Create collective commitments.
• Create schoolwide SMART goals.
 	
Analyze Data
 	
• Monitor progress toward SMART goals and the accompanying action steps.
• Monitor student learning and behavior data.
• Plan celebrations.
 	
Remove Roadblocks
 	
• Identify roadblocks and brainstorm solutions. Consider possible issues with the following.
  ◦ Master schedule
  ◦ Collaboration time
  ◦ Resource allocation
  ◦ Protected time for Tier 1 core instruction
  ◦ Time and personnel for Tier 2 interventions
  ◦ A plan for Tier 3 remediations
• Identify needed staff professional development.
• Keep focused on the tights, or non-negotiables.
 	
Identify Academic and Behavior Consistencies
 	
• Identify core instructional practices needed across the school.
• Identify schoolwide expected behaviors.
 	
Monitor the Work of Collaborative Teams
 	
• Share artifacts and provide feedback.
• Celebrate student learning resulting from the work of teams.
• Determine what is tight and loose for all teams.
• Identify next steps and any interventions or extensions for teams.
	Create Team Foundations
	
	• Create a vision.
	• Create norms.
	• Create SMART goals with action steps.
	
	Question one: What is it we want our students to know and be able to do?
	
	• Identify essential standards.
	• Unwrap essential standards and plan for the common assessments of each.
	• Create proficiency maps (pacing guides) to include every course or subject state or provincial standard.
	• Create unit plans for instruction and assessment of standards in each unit.
	• Create student learning targets for each unit.
	
	Question two: How will we know if each student has learned it?
	
	• Create common mid-unit and end-of-unit assessments before the unit begins.
	• Determine scoring agreements for common assessments and clarify student proficiency.
	• Calibrate scoring of common assessments.
	• Analyze data from common assessments as a team by standard or learning target.
	
	Questions three and four: How will we respond when some students do not learn it and how will we extend learning for students who have demonstrated proficiency?
	
	• Collectively respond to common assessment data by answering the following.
	  ◦ Which instructional practices worked?
	  ◦ Which students learned or did not learn?
	  ◦ What are the trends in learning as shown in work?
	  ◦ How will students reflect on their learning and set goals?
	• Create a team plan to re-engage students in learning identified targets whether they need intervention or extension.

Source: Adapted from Buffum et al., 2018; DuFour et al., 2016; Kramer, 2021b; Kramer & Schuhl, 2017.

FIGURE 7.1: Leading the right work.

*Visit **go.SolutionTree.com/priorityschools** for a free reproducible version of this figure.*

levels. The questions that guide these teams are: What is getting in the way of student or team learning? What can we do about it?

Most importantly, the guiding coalition or learning team celebrates progress. The only way to effect change is to celebrate small wins every day. Celebrations are a form of communication. Celebrations announce to everyone what is valued, encouraged, and supported in any organization. Celebrate students, teachers, parents, community, teaching assistants, bus drivers, food service personnel, custodial staff, nurses, counselors, and collaborative teams. The best way to do this is to catch people doing the right work and celebrate it in every way possible using photos, videos, social media, email, public meetings, and individual notes. These celebrations demonstrate and acknowledge what your school values, promotes, and stands for. In a process of change that can be tumultuous, celebrations tell everyone to stay the course because they are making a difference.

In addition to school-level guiding coalitions or learning teams, it is important that districts also establish guiding coalitions to support the work of the schools. This team is usually composed of the principal and perhaps others members from each of the schools plus the district office staff. A district guiding coalition is tasked with looking at all their policies, practices, and procedures to determine if they support learning or create challenges to the important work of schools. The focus is also on learning and the district guiding coalition often builds the structural supports each school needs to improve. For example, the district guiding coalition sets the stage for collaboration by building a districtwide schedule that supports collaboration and interventions. In some instances, this involves working with the community to understand the need to extend the day or release students early to build in collaborative time. The district guiding coalition ensures coherence throughout the system.

Utilize Instructional Coaches

The role of instructional coaches (or facilitators) has evolved. In the past, the expectations for this position were often *teacher-centered coaching*, meaning that coaches worked with teachers to improve instructional practices or content knowledge—especially if a teacher was struggling. At times, coaching was also relationship driven, primarily focusing on helping teachers who requested support. Schools and districts did not expect teacher-centered and relationship-driven coaches to directly improve student learning. The hope was that by improving teachers, improved student results would naturally follow. Unfortunately, this was not always the case (Sweeney & Harris, 2020). This was not due to a lack of effort, knowledge, or desire to improve student learning on the part of instructional coaches or teachers. Rather, it was a function of the instructional coach's job description the principal or district office determined, which too often had a negative connotation to teachers (Sweeney & Harris, 2020). Instead, instructional coaching must be student centered and link to student data and results, involving both collaborative teams and teachers.

Since the engine that drives the work of school improvement is the collaborative teams (DuFour et al., 2016), instructional coaches or facilitators are the direct line of support to these teams as they respond to the individual needs of the teacher members. Coaches differentiate their support based on an agreed-on outcome and need. Student data and information are major components of the process. Importantly, instructional coaches work with the entire teaching staff, not solely a subset of struggling teachers. Coaches are not seen as people who "fix" teachers, in which case few teachers want to work with them. Similarly, coaches are not a support only for those who actively seek the support. Rather, coaches are a required and available support to grow every team and every teacher. Instructional coaches do this through the establishment of team and teacher coaching cycles.

To accelerate learning, *student-centered coaching cycles* simultaneously involve collaborative teams and the teachers on those teams. The following outlines the student-centered coaching process for a collaborative team (Sweeney & Harris, 2020).

1. Create a plan for instructional coaches to work with each team at least once during the year (ideally once per semester).

2. Determine the team SMART goal for the priority standard students are learning during the coaching cycle (Conzemius & O'Neill, 2014).

3. Unpack the priority standard into learning targets (see chapter 3, page 33) and clarify the instructional strategies teachers will use.

4. Create common assessments the team will use to assess student learning of the priority standard (see chapter 4, page 61).

5. Monitor the progress of student learning by analyzing the assessment results as a team to collectively determine next instructional steps (see chapter 6, page 87).

6. At the end of the cycle, have teachers share their learning from their individual coaching cycles, as well as their learning from the team coaching, to identify how to implement effective practices in future units of study.

Use the following steps for student-centered coaching cycles for individual teachers within the team (Sweeney & Harris, 2020).

1. Select a specific student learning goal with the teacher, which ties to the team SMART goal (Conzemius & O'Neill, 2014), as a focus for the coaching cycle. Discuss how to measure student learning relative to that goal.

2. Coach the teacher each week during the cycle. Ensure coaching sessions include the following.

    a. Planning a lesson

    b. Co-teaching or observing the lesson

    c. Debriefing the impact of the lesson on student learning tied to the goal

3. At the end of the cycle, discuss progress toward the identified goal and reflect with the teacher on the learning and next steps.

Coaching is an effective way to support all teams as they hone their knowledge and skills. The coaching of collaborative teams builds collective efficacy and is equity in action since all grade-level and content-area teachers engage throughout the process. As all teams and teachers grow in their lesson design and team practices, learning for all students improves.

It is important to clarify the role of the coach to staff so everyone understands the ways the instructional coach might support teachers. Figure 7.2 (page 136) shows an example of a flier coaches might share with staff at the start of the school year. It provides a menu of options teams or teachers might choose from as they engage in student-centered coaching, whether through a formal coaching cycle or by request.

INSTRUCTIONAL COACHES can help you answer the **four critical questions** of a PLC.

What do we want all students to know and be able to do?

We can support you in:

- Reviewing and modifying your proficiency maps
- Unpacking your standards to identify necessary content and skills
- Writing learning targets
- Aligning and integrating reading, writing, or mathematics standards in your lessons

How will we know if they learned it?

We can support you in:

- Aligning assessments with standards and learning targets
- Developing common assessments
- Collecting and using assessment resources
- Analyzing common assessment data to inform instruction

How will we respond when some students do not learn?

How will we extend the learning for students who are already proficient?

We can support you in:

- Designing and refining lesson plans to meet specific learning needs
- Creating differentiated lessons and activities
- Learning and strengthening your use of instructional strategies
- Designing team interventions and extensions using common assessment data

We can support you by . . .

- Facilitating group work sessions and meetings
- Conducting one-to-one coaching sessions to meet teacher-identified goals
- Modeling instructional strategies with your students
- Co-teaching lessons
- Finding resources and information to meet specific needs
- Watching student learning while you teach and providing targeted feedback

Who can support you?

- Literacy coach
- Mathematics coach
- Language coach

Source for PLC questions: DuFour et al., 2016.

Source: © 2005 by Sarah Schuhl and Rita Ramstad. Adapted with permission.

FIGURE 7.2: Instructional coaching flier example.

Coaching cycles will be most effective if they last three to six weeks (although to accommodate all teams, the duration is most often three to four weeks) and are embedded in the actual units or learning cycles teams are using in the classroom. Figure 7.3 (page 138) shares an example of a coaching plan and the roles of the principal, instructional coach, and teachers. Coaches may adjust a schedule during the year if unexpected situations arise or data indicate the need to change the schedule.

Collaborative teams choose the subject and content focus (based on data) and a determined problem of practice they are struggling to address. Once teams select a focus, the coach assists team members with creating a standards-based goal that relates to what teachers expect students to know and be able to do for a current priority standard. As teams engage in the learning cycle for the priority standard, they discuss their work during collaborative team meetings with the instructional coach. The team co-plans with student evidence in mind. They collaboratively answer the question, What evidence will we accept that students are learning the priority standard? The team begins to plan daily check-ins, common formative assessments, and the end-of-unit assessment.

Each teacher may have a slightly different concern about teaching the current priority standard in the classroom, which the team can discuss when planning the learning cycle together. One teacher might describe the need for more time for small-group work due to the academic diversity of her students. Another teacher on the team may wonder how to make the time students spend in small groups more effective. Someone else may wonder how to increase active engagement or student discourse to formatively assess learning of the target during a lesson. Still another teacher may ask what other strategies the team should include to teach the priority standard. As these questions and discussions occur, the coach plans how to address the individual needs of each member of the team.

The coach differentiates support for each individual teacher during a coaching cycle. Support can be in the form of lesson planning, building background knowledge, co-teaching lessons, observing teacher lessons and providing feedback, whisper coaching, problem solving, and providing new learning. This process is not evaluative, but rather designed for both the coach and teacher to learn together how to strengthen instructional practices so more students learn grade-level standards (or beyond) and implement acceleration strategies as needed.

The next step in the process is to measure the impact on student and teacher learning during the coaching cycle. Teams analyze student data and artifacts to target any student misconceptions and plan for interventions. The instructional coach helps the team make sense of the data and asks strategic questions so teachers come to collective realizations about current student learning. Similarly (and depending on the strength of the team), the coach helps members reflect on their learning, record the most effective instructional strategies, revise the assessments, and archive the misconceptions they need to address as they approach this same standard next year. This is continuous improvement in action.

Figure 7.4 (page 139) shares a template the instructional coach might use with each teacher on a collaborative team when planning for a three-week coaching cycle. To summarize, using figure 7.4 (page 139), the instructional coach and teacher meet ahead of the three-week cycle. They establish a goal related to student learning that fits within the unit the team is planning. Together, they determine what the coach will do, what the teacher will do, and what they will do together to reach the learning goal. They also determine how they will measure the effectiveness of the coaching using student learning data. Will they use assessment data related to a specific

Three-Week Coaching Cycles

At Smith Elementary, Ms. X and Mr. Z are instructional coaches on campus to support teams and teachers as they collaboratively answer the four critical PLC questions and plan lessons. Following is a description of three-week coaching cycles for teachers and teams, which focus on improving student learning.

Teachers will

- Complete a three-week coaching plan with Ms. X or Mr. Z with a specific goal that ties to a priority standard to improve student learning.
- Engage in collaborative team meetings each week.
- Work with Ms. X or Mr. Z to plan a lesson together, teach the lesson, and discuss what worked well during the lesson and what needs to be strengthened in future lessons. Planning lessons will focus on student learning of the priority standard or target, as well as independent reading, engagement, or student discourse.
- Schedule each lesson-planning, classroom-observation, and reflection time during the three weeks with Ms. X or Mr. Z.
- Reflect on progress related to student learning at the end of the cycle.

Ms. X and Mr. Z will

- Continue to meet with teachers when requested or for planning purposes and perform duties already assigned.
- Meet with designated teachers during a three-week cycle.
- Meet with the designated teachers' collaborative team each week.
- Schedule teachers for lesson planning and observation each week of three-week cycle.

Principal will

- Introduce the plan to teachers.
- Meet with each teacher before the end of the year to reflect on the coaching process and the experience.

Schedule

Dates	Ms. X	Mr. Z
October 4–22	Grade 1	Grade 4
October 25–November 12	Grade 2	Grade 5
November 15–December 10	Grade K	Grade 6
January 3–21	Grade 1	Grade 4
January 24–February 11	Grade 2	Grade 5
February 14–March 4	Grade K	Grade 6
March 7–April 1	Grade 1	Grade 4
April 4–22	Grade 2	Grade 5
April 25–May 13	TBD	TBD

FIGURE 7.3: Sample plan for three-week instructional coaching cycles.

Teacher Goals in Three-Week Coaching Cycle

Teacher: _____   Date: _____

1. What is your goal for student learning during the three-week coaching cycle?

2. The plan: How will you reach your goal?

Coach	Together	Teacher

3. What resources will you need and what possible roadblocks do you need to plan for?

4. How will we know you have reached your goal and students have learned?

5. When will we meet each week? Put the date and time in each box.

	Plan the Lesson	Teach the Lesson	Debrief
Week One			
Week Two			
Week Three			

FIGURE 7.4: Example of organizer for coach-teacher work during the three-week coaching cycle.

Visit go.SolutionTree.com/priorityschools for a free reproducible version of this figure.

implemented strategy? Observational data generated from watching students in the classroom during a lesson? Or perhaps they might gather student work samples during the coaching cycle to show learning growth over time. The teacher and coach consider and plan around any potential roadblocks. Finally, they clarify when they will meet during the three-week cycle to co-plan lessons, teach, and debrief.

To ensure their coaching is effective, coaches can survey teachers about what the most effective parts of the coaching model are and what parts coaches could improve for greater learning. The survey might also ask what the teacher learned or how the coaching improved student learning. Additionally, instructional coaches meet weekly with the principal (or other appropriate administrators) throughout the coaching cycles. Without naming individual teachers, coaches share instructional practices teachers have learned or are trying, share student results from coaching, and recommend any needed professional development. During guiding coalition or learning team meetings, instructional coaches may share universal strategies that work to improve learning (as evidenced through coaching sessions), so other teams can learn from each experience, too (again, keeping teacher names and specific experiences confidential). It is important to celebrate the evidence-based practices that are working so everyone can learn from them.

Student-centered coaching allows teams to learn the priority standards together, create quality assessments and common scoring practices, engage in purposeful data discussions that result in targeted instruction, and improve their individual practice. Because the team- and teacher-coaching processes require evidence of student learning on a grade-level priority standard, opportunities arise to identify lesson strategies that accelerate student learning to grade level or beyond (see chapter 5, page 87). Then, share those strategies throughout the school or district. The deepest insights and understandings come from reflection on actions.

Build a System of Instructional Support

It is no secret: educators are in great demand, especially in priority schools or underperforming schools. Teacher recruitment and retention challenges are real. While teacher shortages existed before the COVID-19 pandemic, the pandemic worsened them. At the start of the 2022–2023 school year, the National Education Association estimated there were three hundred thousand vacancies, many of them in rural areas and in the STEM fields (National Public Radio, 2022). To deal with the shortage, some states began allowing noncredentialed adults to serve as teachers (Querolo, Rockeman, & Ceron, 2022). As a personal example of the shortage, Sharon's granddaughter had four different teachers in second grade! The reasons for this were varied and it was not anyone's fault, but nonetheless, the turnover is disconcerting.

It is a challenge for teachers who are not highly qualified, are unfamiliar with the standards, or have not mastered pedagogy to effectively accelerate learning for students. Even highly qualified teachers working in isolation only impact the learning of a few students, rather than all students (DuFour, 2015). The teacher shortage and high turnover in schools accentuate the need to build a system of instructional supports that will attract, support, and grow the instructional practices of all teachers in a school or district.

The answer to the question, How can we recruit, retain, and grow our staff? is not to provide random supports, but rather to provide focused, targeted, specific supports that foster individual and collective teacher efficacy. Teaching is one of the most difficult and multifaceted professions, and one of its most difficult aspects is just keeping up with all that is required instructionally.

Every school should focus on the most effective instructional practices that support and accelerate learning—not all strategies, but the few with the greatest impact. These core instructional practices should be evident in every class, regardless of the grade level or content area. Once a school collaboratively establishes the core instructional practices, the school must communicate, support, and celebrate those practices.

The guiding coalition or learning team determines the focus of core instruction as they respond to these questions.

- ▶ How can research inform our practice?

- ▶ What do those who have studied and selected the most effective strategies for learning tell us?

- ▶ Based on our current needs, what specific practices do we want to focus our time and attention on?

- ▶ What instructional practices might we try, and how will we determine their effectiveness (action research)?

Many books and resources describe a variety of research-informed instructional practices to use in core instruction. For students not yet learning at grade or course level, instructional strategies must accelerate learning by intentionally incorporating prior-knowledge standards and grade- or course-level standards so students can make sense of and learn each priority standard. Closing or eliminating learning gaps occurs with focused and increased attention on the most impactful strategies, since the gap in achievement clearly indicates a need for more growth than is typical in a year. The following list is a sampling of effective instructional practices for accelerating learning that align with the work in this book and *School Improvement for All: A How-to Guide for Doing the Right Work* (Kramer & Schuhl, 2017).

- ▶ **Collective teacher efficacy:** Learning by collaborating in teams
- ▶ **Clear goal intentions:** Creating daily learning targets students understand
- ▶ **Cognitive-task analysis:** Unpacking or unwrapping standards for rigor
- ▶ **Classroom discussions:** Ensuring student voice and students learning from peers
- ▶ **Feedback:** The most effective being student to teacher
- ▶ **Response to intervention:** Providing focused Tier 1, Tier 2, and Tier 3 interventions during the school day
- ▶ **Scaffolding:** Building a learning ladder of instruction from least complex to most complex
- ▶ **Micro-teaching:** Using short, targeted lessons and video review
- ▶ **Prior knowledge and transfer strategies:** Tapping into previous learning and students making connections
- ▶ **Spaced versus massed practice:** Conducting continuous spiral review with focused instruction
- ▶ **Student self-reported grades:** Using student data trackers, goal setting, and reflection
- ▶ **Student self-efficacy:** Promoting student confidence in learning

As the guiding coalition or learning team builds shared knowledge on the most impactful instructional practices, they work together to brainstorm a list of effective components that should be evident in every classroom. The team can use variations on the four critical PLC questions (DuFour et al., 2016) to guide their conversation.

1. What do we want teachers to know and be able to do related to high-quality instruction?

2. How will we know if teachers are implementing high-quality instruction?

3. How will we respond when some teachers are not providing high-quality instruction?

4. How will we celebrate and challenge teachers who are providing high-quality instruction?

What Do We Want Teachers to Know and Be Able to Do Related to High-Quality Instruction?

As a guiding coalition or learning team answers the first question, they are defining the core instructional practices for the school. Figure 7.5 demonstrates the thinking of Anna Strong Learning Academy, an elementary school in Arkansas that spent time reflecting with Sarah on the most effective instructional practices and built their first draft of core instructional practices. You should not necessarily replicate this list; each guiding coalition or learning team will need to respond by collectively determining the greatest areas of need at their school. Also consider the lesson design elements we shared in figure 5.1 (page 93).

Once the guiding coalition or learning team identifies core instructional practices, the entire staff works together to clarify what each practice looks like, sounds like, and feels like in every class and subject area. For example, a school may decide its focus is to improve student engagement during instruction. *Student engagement* has a variety of definitions and includes multiple practices, so defining it is critical. Is student engagement passive (observers cannot tell if students are or are not fully engaged in the task) or active (student learning is observable in real time), or both? If a student is reading a text during a lesson, is this engagement? The English teacher in a middle or high school may respond *yes*. The science teacher may describe discussions or lab work as engagement since the students are working with others. As the staff discuss and clarify what student engagement means, it requires everyone to reflect on their practices and determine ways to improve instruction. It also creates agreed-on commitments that increase teacher effectiveness and student learning.

How Will We Know If Teachers Are Implementing High-Quality Instruction?

The next question to answer is, How will we know if teachers are implementing the core instructional practices our school selected? Just as collaborative teams collect evidence about learning, analyze the results of that evidence, and then plan actions to improve results, this same process of gathering evidence and responding to it applies to improving instructional practices. The collaborative team is applying formative (not evaluative) practices when they do this. Formative feedback is nonevaluative. In this same manner, formative walkthroughs (or *instructional sweeps*) are not about specific teachers or classes, and anyone (not just the principal) can gather these data and information. *Formative walkthroughs* provide a snapshot of instruction and learning with a specific focus on the predetermined core instructional practices; they give a picture of the current reality and trends with the purpose of improving the instructional process across the school.

When beginning to utilize walkthroughs, it is important to calibrate observations by debriefing after classroom visits. Additionally, to gather thorough evidence, engage in walkthroughs during various times in lessons (beginning, middle, and end). The guiding coalition or learning team,

Core Instructional Practices

Classroom

☐ Student learning target posted and relevant.

☐ Language objective posted.

☐ Classroom is clean, organized, and inviting.

☐ Classroom has anchor charts on walls to support learning.

☐ Ten-day learning cycle or unit posted outside the door.

Teacher Actions

☐ Uses the curriculum in the lesson

☐ Provides grade-level instruction

☐ Uses gradual release

    ☐ I do

    ☐ We do

    ☐ You do

☐ Monitors (while walking around the classroom) and gives feedback to students while they are working

☐ Differentiates instruction with small groups

☐ Provides evidence of routines and smooth transitions

☐ Closes the lesson by having students reflect on the target

Student Actions

☐ Verbalizes what they are learning

☐ Actively engages in learning

    ☐ Participates in discussions

    ☐ Works in small groups and learns from others

    ☐ Responds to direct teacher instructions

    ☐ Listens and takes notes

    ☐ Presents or performs

    ☐ Takes a test or quiz

    ☐ Reads silently

    ☐ Answers questions

    ☐ Practices an activity

    ☐ Writes

    ☐ Uses computer intervention

    ☐ Uses small-group intervention

    ☐ Other (provide)

Source: © 2022 by Anna Strong Learning Academy. Used with permission.

FIGURE 7.5: Elementary school example of core instructional practices.

instructional coaches, administrators, and any other interested staff member who is willing to assist can conduct walkthroughs. Frequency of walkthroughs is important, and many schools recommend each person visit and record walkthrough data in ten classrooms per week. Data are reported for each school, collaborative team, and department or content-area team, not each teacher. This creates a culture of instruction with an emphasis on the specific practices most effective in improving learning.

The instructional leadership team (administrators, instructional coaches, or other staff who focus on supporting teachers and teams) can discuss the data and use the results to focus future coaching cycles or professional development. Similarly, the instructional leadership team can share information with the guiding coalition or learning team and teachers to celebrate and choose an area of focus to continue working on. Continue to ask, "What are the instructional strategies that accelerate learning and how should we implement them during lessons?"

How Will We Respond When Some Teachers Are Not Providing High-Quality Instruction?

The data from walkthroughs inform and answer the last two instructional questions: How will we respond when some teachers are not providing high-quality instruction? and How will we celebrate and challenge teachers who are providing high-quality instruction? Much like the schoolwide system of support teams and teachers employ to respond to student learning needs, improving instructional practices also requires a system of support.

In chapter 6 (page 107), we discussed three-tiered systems of support for responding when students are not learning, such as RTI or MTSS (Buffum et al., 2018; Navo & Williams, 2023). We also discussed how educators utilize the tiers to accelerate student learning. Just as educators can ensure and support student learning using the three tiers, leaders can support teachers using a three-tiered model of increasingly intensive support that builds collective efficacy and improves core instructional practices. This system provides support for teachers on their specific individual needs.

Tier 1 consists of the core instructional practices that the entire staff agrees to implement in every classroom. As teachers and teams dig deeply into the core instructional practices and gain clarity, they support one another and build collective efficacy. Tier 1 describes the common instructional expectations, such as posting learning targets and referencing them throughout the lesson, giving all students opportunities to work in small groups every day, or making sense of the predetermined core instructional practices the guiding coalition or learning team identified (see figure 5.1, page 93, and figure 7.5, page 143). Instructional coaches utilize their team and teacher coaching cycles focused on student learning as part of the Tier 1 practices designed to strengthen instruction.

Tier 2 supplemental support is specific and targeted for individual teachers to build their skills in implementing the expected instructional practices or collaborative team actions. Teachers who need Tier 2 support might include any teacher who needs instructional support beyond coaching cycles to be effective in the classroom. A collaborative team might request Tier 2 support for the group or for an individual teacher when data indicate an area they need to improve practices. Individual teachers might seek out Tier 2 support after conducting a self-assessment or reflection. Instructional coaches may recommend Tier 2 support for specific teachers still working to effectively implement the agreed-on instructional practices. Principals may also suggest the need for support as they conference with individual teachers. Tier 2 support can take many forms. An instructional coach or administrator may work with a teacher or team to implement an instructional strategy and monitor progress. Coaches or administrators may facilitate team meetings to grow a team's ability to impact learning through their planning and implementation of each learning cycle. Regardless of the specific situation, Tier 2 involves clear outcomes for the specific teacher or team and targeted supports to ensure those outcomes.

Tier 3 is reserved for teachers who need intensive instructional support. They may include some early-career teachers, teachers moving to a new grade level or content area, emergency-certified teachers, permanent substitutes, teachers in departmentalized structures moving to self-contained classes, teachers implementing new courses, or teachers new to the state, district, or school. Learning a new system, new content, or new pedagogy is time intensive and stressful for anyone. Intensive support may include, but is not limited to, mentoring from an experienced teacher; providing micro-learning or short bursts of just-in-time information; discussions of exactly how to introduce, teach, and review content as a regular part of collaborative team meetings; intensive work with an instructional coach; robust preservice training; and opportunities for professional learning throughout the year.

A support system where all three tiers work in concert and are available to all teachers and teams as needs are identified improves instructional practices and team actions so more students learn. The support system is not intended to evaluate teachers or designate good and not-so-good teachers or teams; the support system is intended to assist as the entire school community works to be the best it can be for the students it serves. It is intended to grow individual and collective teacher efficacy so every student learns at grade level or beyond.

How Will We Celebrate and Challenge Teachers Who Are Providing High-Quality Instruction?

Finally, the most effective way to monitor any system of support is to intentionally celebrate strategies that work and people who are doing things well. Monitoring often has a punitive connotation and indicates something is not working, but it is also an opportunity to catch individuals and teams succeeding. The work of learning is not about good or bad; instead, it is about *better*. The question is, How can we do this better? Monitoring through celebrations is a way forward that encourages and supports everyone. Formative instructional walkthroughs are a great way to capture moments of success through pictures, videos, and recordings. One or more of the core instructional strategies can be the focus over a two-to-three-week period, so everyone knows exactly what to look for and celebrate.

Celebrate publicly and privately as often as possible using email, social media, bulletin boards, and personal notes. Guiding coalitions, administrators, and instructional coaches should share success stories and collectively celebrate staff achievements.

Engage the Community and Stakeholders

Just as it is important to engage parents as partners in the education of their children, school leaders must also engage the greater community in support of their work. Schools are the foundation of every community, and often one reason families choose to live in a community. It is important to include community stakeholders in a variety of ways. For example, some schools gather commitment statements from community members that describe their role in making sure the school requires students learn. Community members may state that because the school requires learning, they will volunteer a specified numbers of hours per week to tutor students. Other community members may state that because the school requires learning, they will provide school supplies to those students in need. Include these commitments on the district website, along with the commitments from students, teachers, administrators, and parents that describe what they are willing to do to support the school's mission.

Every community has a variety of resources that can bring the real (or outside) world into schools. Districts and schools often ask businesses and other entities to fund projects and provide other resources to support their efforts in creating and sustaining excellent schools. Community and stakeholder engagement are more than donations, however. For example, a high school could create a business council that advises and supports pathways for students beyond secondary education. The council works with a school task force (or guiding coalition or learning team) to identify the knowledge, skills, competencies, and dispositions necessary to be successful in the workforce. The council also shares opportunities for internships or determines how to institute student job shadowing. These are just a few options for engaging the community to create greater opportunities for students.

To support schools, community members must receive clear communication. There has never been more information available but, unfortunately, it often comes without common understanding or clear communication. Districts, schools, teachers, and parents must work together to strengthen the information flow and build shared knowledge. They can improve and enhance communication between principal and teacher, teacher and student, teacher and parents, educators and community members, and students and peers. Communication is not always about quantity; quality is the key. When it comes to community engagement, consider the following questions.

▶ Is our message clear and respectful even when we disagree?

▶ Do we seek first to understand or be understood?

▶ Do we communicate the information in a timely manner or at the last minute?

When calling students' homes or working with an outside agency, being respectful and assuming good intentions are important. Additionally, listening to parent or guardian concerns and celebrations—whether real or perceived—and working to understand shows empathy and begins to build trust. Finally, leaders are as proactive as possible and communicate frequently with stakeholders. The community around the school impacts the learning of the students inside the school. Engage the community in accelerating learning to grade level or beyond for every student.

Conclusion

Successful schools and districts share and widely disperse the leadership for accelerating learning. Structures are in place to support the learning of students and teachers alike. Collaborative teams, guiding coalitions or learning teams, instructional coaches, a tiered instructional support system that differentiates support for individual teachers, and a culture of formative (not evaluative) practices exist to ensure learning for all. The critically important aspect is to engage the entire staff in defining a vision of high expectations for all students and building a culture where all adults in the system feel it is incumbent on them to improve student learning. This creates a system that undergirds the improvement process and moves the work from compliance to shared commitment. This is leadership in action and the reason leadership really, really matters!

Discussion Questions for Reflection and Action

As a team, discuss the following questions. Visit **go.SolutionTree.com/priorityschools** for a free reproducible version of these questions.

- ▸ How does your school share and widely disperse leadership?

- ▸ What is the focus of the work of your guiding coalition or learning team?

- ▸ How does your school support collaborative teams to improve their effectiveness?

- ▸ How does your school or district allocate the time of instructional coaches? What data inform and validate the fact that student and teacher learning are improving?

- ▸ What core instructional practices will result in accelerating learning and eliminating the achievement gap?

- ▸ What supports exist to improve instructional practice in every classroom?

- ▸ How will you recruit and retain teachers? What structures of support must be in place to grow each teacher based on specific needs?

- ▸ What are the good things happening in your school and district? How does your school or district communicate and celebrate them?

CHAPTER 8

Continuous Improvement That Accelerates Learning

We have seen schools work to impact student learning year after year through the practices we share in this book. Like elite athletes always striving to accomplish more, these schools are not content to just celebrate their growth and reach initial goals; they learn from the prior year and continue to stretch to reach even more students the next year by working with their collaborative teams to identify the instructional, assessment, and intervention and extension practices that accelerate student learning. They thrive with focused leadership in a healthy learning culture. And they celebrate along the way. Since the quality of any school system cannot exceed the quality of the people within it, *continuous improvement* is about growing people over programs or curricula. Educational consultants and coauthors Kenneth C. Williams and Tom Hierck (2015) write:

> The research and evidence support the fact that schools make the difference—not where students are from; what they look like; their race, culture, or language; and who their parents are or aren't. What matters is what you do in school from the time students arrive until the time they leave. (p. 11)

When those minutes focus on the learning of staff and students every day, more learning happens and improvement results.

One example of continuous improvement in schools is the Glendale Elementary School District. The mantra in Glendale is "We are *all* in for *all* kids!" The entire district understands that continuous improvement never ends. This journey is much like climbing a mountain. If you reach the top of a mountain, the only way to go is down. Glendale Elementary School District realizes that if you are on a continuous-improvement journey, you are always climbing. They continue to grow and challenge themselves to reach more students and grow educator learning across the district on an ongoing basis. Specifically, the district annually reviews data to create a plan for each year based on the district's experiences and learning from previous years and the results of multiple measures of achievement. This collaborative review includes an examination of any challenges and barriers and determines the immediate focus for the work with the goal of increasing student learning and success. Quarterly reviews of the data for each school and the overall district monitor progress and determine adjustments needed immediately. Schools and

Excellence is not a destination; it is a continuous journey that never ends.
—BRIAN TRACY

districts that embrace continuous improvement do not wait for next year or next semester to make needed changes; they have a sense of urgency that requires immediate actions. Continuous improvement does not reinvent the wheel or just do more of the same every year. It requires a district and each school to determine what's working and what needs to change to achieve even better results for the students they serve. This is the reflective continuous-improvement journey Glendale Elementary School District engages in and the reason achievement improves each year.

Continuous improvement means constantly evaluating practices, policies, and procedures, and celebrating the wins the school or district creates while being willing to use collective inquiry and action research to try new ones or evolve existing ones, as the need arises. Cognia (formerly AdvancED) President and CEO Mark A. Elgart (2017) defines *continuous school improvement* as "an embedded behavior within the culture of a school that constantly focuses on the conditions, processes, and practices that will improve teaching and learning" (p. 55). Elgart (2017) further states:

> Among the high-performing schools we have visited, there often is a common thread: a culture of continuous learning that permeates all levels and stakeholders. In these schools, that culture is supported by high expectations and accountability. While school leaders must emphasize and embody these values, for schools to be successful, they must be embraced by everyone— teachers, students, and other stakeholders alike. That kind of culture cannot be legislated. It must be developed and nurtured over time. (p. 58)

Continuous improvement is contingent on working collectively to reach a goal and learning from collective organizational experiences along the way.

In schools that have moved from compliance to embracing continuous improvement, leaders shape the culture through clear expectations and ensure all stakeholders understand the goals and expectations, while making sure the actions stakeholders take improve the learning of both students and adults. Chenoweth (2021), from her work analyzing six school districts that have beaten the odds to grow student learning, concludes:

> The common elements of these districts are *leadership* that defines a vision of high expectations for all students and builds a culture where all adults in the system feel it incumbent to make kids smarter; a *process* to guide the adults in the district to making better decisions while growing their ability to do so using the scientific method; and *systems* to undergird that improvement process. (p. 148)

To guide continuous improvement, leaders must be persistent, limit initiatives, analyze team products and processes in light of student learning, and be willing to drill deeper and make adjustments every day (Eaker, 2020). Recall from chapter 7 (page 129) that leadership for acceleration maintains a relentless focus on learning for both students and staff—"*perpetual learning for the purpose of continuous improvement*" (Eaker, 2020, p. 135).

Regarding process, Chenoweth (2021) emphasizes the scientific method of identifying a problem and a potential solution, implementing the solution, and using data and evidence to determine if the solution worked, needs to be revised, or a new solution needs to be tried. Knowing whether learning is improving from year to year requires frequent analysis of student learning data and behavior data, as well as analysis of the adult team actions and learning that contribute to improved student learning. As the process unfolds, insist on a learning-through-action approach. The time spent learning through reading and attending professional development opportunities must turn into purposeful actions. Teachers then keep what works, and revise or stop what does not work well.

Westover and Steinhauser (2022) ask, "What if the solution was not for educators to be better consumers of research but for educators to become better action researchers?" (p. 107).

The systems that support the improvement process include effective teamwork, common assessments, a culture of trust, and using research about how people learn (Chenoweth, 2021). We have addressed these important topics throughout this book. In a healthy culture steeped in vulnerability and openness to learning from one another, working together to accelerate student learning, and using data to inform next instructional steps, continuous improvement is more than a possibility—it is a reality. Continuous improvement is ongoing and relentless, with the lives and learning of students at its heart.

The Shift to Continuous Improvement

Schools that accelerate student learning to grade level or beyond live in the flow of continuous improvement. Unfortunately, some schools fall short of reaching their goals despite their best efforts. There are many reasons for schools giving up or stalling in the continuous school-improvement cycle. Table 8.1 shares some shifts schools need to tackle from all angles, every day for continuous improvement with student learning results.

TABLE 8.1: Shifts for Continuous Improvement

SHIFT FROM . . .	SHIFT TO . . .
Pivoting to new initiatives or programs that look promising to improve student learning	Holding firm to a few initiatives, one of which is creating a PLC with collaborative teams that answer the four critical questions using priority standards
Engaging in deficit thinking by focusing on what students cannot do	Engaging in asset-based thinking by identifying what students can do and accelerating learning from there
Analyzing data only after progress monitoring and state assessments	Analyzing student learning and behavior data frequently from team common assessments, progress-monitoring assessments, and state assessments
Celebrating individual teacher successes to grow student learning in a classroom	Celebrating the work of collaborative teams to collectively grow student learning across a grade level or course
Celebrating when goals are reached in a way that suggests victory or the end of a process	Celebrating teacher and student learning often and continuing to set new goals
Storing documents and team artifacts in individual teachers' personal computer files	Creating a schoolwide system for teams to store and access documents and artifacts
Making program adjustments from one year to the next without input from preceding or subsequent grade levels	Engaging in vertical conversations and sharing with the next grade-level or course teachers what students learned or did not learn for stronger planning from the start of the school year

Continuous improvement builds on collaboration. When schools operate with teachers isolated from one another—each working hard alone to improve learning—it is exhausting, and continuous improvement fails. Accelerating every student to grade-level learning or beyond is larger than any one person. Schools need to analyze systems, create a culture with all stakeholders, and strengthen instructional practices to continuously improve student learning.

The work of collaborative teams is critical to continuous improvement as teams analyze their learning data from one year to the next and look for student growth in their grade level or course. Teachers working in collaborative teams unpack standards, design common assessments, and use the data from common assessments to determine interventions and extensions as well as document the instructional practices that are working for students. Teams engage in collective inquiry and action research to discover other instructional practices to use when students are not learning. Teams develop their tools and strategies from one year to the next and can collectively articulate what students learned and what they may still need to learn in the next grade level or course. Teachers across the school share their effective acceleration strategies.

Similarly, the guiding coalition or learning team and administrators work to remove roadblocks, frequently and relentlessly analyze student learning and behavior data, and lead the work of continuous improvement. They look for celebrations and determine how to recognize the learning of educators and students in meaningful ways. They clarify best practices for all teachers to use as they work to improve student learning. They also look in the mirror to find solutions rather than blame others when student learning stalls. Together with teachers, the guiding coalition or learning team and administrators create the school's vision and work to make it a reality in a healthy culture.

Continuous improvement is multifaceted and requires a healthy culture and practices steeped in the PLC process with leaders who are clear about the school's goals and what they frequently monitor along the way. For many schools, this requires another look at the policies, practices, and procedures that are contributing to—or possibly derailing—continuous improvement.

Acceleration Strategies in Continuous Improvement

Successful schools look under every rock to analyze their data and policies, procedures, and practices supporting student learning or hindering it. When they have successes, these schools celebrate those successes and then challenge themselves to create more wins for student and adult learning. When an action born from research-affirmed practices, collective inquiry, or action research fails to generate learning results, schools focused on continuous improvement are not derailed, but rather readjust and try something new. Schools learn as much from actions that do not continuously improve learning as those that do.

We have shared many actions that support acceleration throughout this book. Schools shifting mindsets (see chapter 1, page 5), creating healthy cultures (see chapter 2, page 17), working in collaborative teams to address the four critical PLC questions (see chapters 3–6), and using effective leadership (see chapter 7, page 129) are all part of acceleration. These practices will grow stronger from year to year in a continuous-improvement cycle. Additionally, continuous improvement requires an organized archive of team artifacts so teams can grow their resources and plans from one year to the next. It requires teachers to teach until the last day of school to maximize learning time. Continuous improvement also requires teams to know what priority standards students have learned and the instructional strategies and practices that supported the learning so they can share them with the next grade-level or course teams for intentional planning. And, finally, continuous improvement requires a robust system of celebration to contribute to a positive and healthy culture where teachers know the impact they have on student learning.

Archive Team Products Systematically

We have seen many situations when teams lost precious time because they could not quickly locate their artifacts. As one example, a high school English team met to analyze an assessment. One teacher had created the assessment and sent it to the team for review via email. However, she left one team member off the email, so another member forwarded the email to that person. As each team member replied, some feedback went to only one person and some feedback went to the incomplete team email. It took forty-five minutes to ensure the team had the most recent version of the assessment and the meeting was only fifty-five minutes long.

At a fourth-grade collaborative team meeting, the members were quietly sitting with nothing in front of them. When the principal asked for the agenda, the teachers said they did not know the agenda or what they were supposed to work on next. The principal suggested the team look at the next priority standard and common assessment. The teachers agreed, but confessed their absent team leader had all the team's products on her own computer and they did not have access to any team documents.

In another school, a fifth-grade team was composed of three first-year teachers. At that school, teachers did not store products electronically, but rather on paper in three-ring binders. Unfortunately, the previous fifth-grade teachers had taken their binders with them when they left for other schools. Although the principal had asked them to make copies and return the binders, the teachers never did. Now, three brand-new teachers needed to re-create the products necessary to address student learning as a team without the wisdom and experience of those former fifth-grade teachers.

It is important for teachers to archive their products in a team folder the school owns, rather than any individual teacher. This enables teams to quickly find their products so they can spend their meeting minutes revising and strengthening their work instead of searching for lost documents, even when someone is absent. Furthermore, it enables continuous improvement from year to year, as teams can continue to develop resources from prior years, even when there is staff turnover. If done systematically, leaders, the guiding coalition or learning team, and other collaborative teams can also access teams' work for feedback and continued learning. The grade-level or course team from one year to the next can use the folder and strengthen the products to grow teacher and student learning.

Figure 8.1 (page 154) shows some of the products teams should be creating and storing as they address the four critical PLC questions.

To do the work of acceleration and share artifacts with other educators in the building or district efficiently, teams need an organized system of folders. There are many ways to organize team folders—not one "right" or "wrong" way. However, it is extremely helpful to have a schoolwide organizational structure so if teachers move from one grade or course to another, they can seamlessly find the team products they need for their learning cycles throughout the year.

Often teams will create a folder for unpacked standards, a folder for common assessments, a folder for data analysis, a folder for instruction and activities, and a folder for interventions and extensions. While definitely organized, we find that teams struggle unit to unit or ten-day

Team Foundations

☐ Norms

☐ Audacious Team SMART Goal

☐ Rolling Agenda for Team Meetings

1. What do we want students to know and be able to do?	**2. How will we know if they learned it?**
☐ Create a proficiency map (yearlong plan) with team-identified prior-knowledge standards.	☐ Determine proficiency criteria for each standard.
☐ Determine priority standards.	☐ Create common formative assessments with scoring agreements.
☐ Unpack priority standards and determine the learning progression.	☐ Create common end-of-unit assessments with scoring agreements.
☐ Create unit plans with team pacing calendars to include grade-level and prior-knowledge standards.	☐ Create a pretest on prior-knowledge standards in a unit if needed.
☐ Create a student-reflection tool with student-friendly I can statements to use during the unit.	☐ Utilize classroom formative assessments during daily lessons (showing the assessments in lesson plans).
	☐ Analyze data from common formative and end-of-unit assessments using a protocol and data tracker.
	☐ Engage students in self-reflection after common assessments.
3. How will we respond when some students do not learn?	**4. How will we extend learning for students who are already proficient?**
☐ Use data and student work from common assessments to create targeted and specific team interventions.	☐ Use data and student work from common assessments to create team extensions.
☐ Identify students in need of intervention by target and need.	☐ Identify students in need of extension.
☐ Create interventions for students who did not yet learn specific targets.	☐ Create extension activities for students showing they learned the target or priority standard.
☐ Utilize small groups, part of core instruction (for example, flex days or thirty minutes of class time twice a week), or additional intervention time built into the school day when responding to student learning as a team.	☐ Utilize small groups, part of core instruction (for example, flex days or thirty minutes of class time twice a week), additional intervention time built into the school day, or end-of-class periods when some students have finished early and learned.
☐ Evaluate the effectiveness of interventions using student-progress data.	☐ Evaluate the effectiveness and meaningfulness of the extension activity.

FIGURE 8.1: The work of collaborative teams to archive.

learning cycle to ten-day learning cycle because the documents they need are in five different folders. We suggest it is more efficient if a team can open one folder for each unit or learning cycle and find all the needed artifacts. In this organizational system, it is especially important to label each unit folder by unit name or each learning-cycle folder by the priority standard it addresses. That way, if the curriculum or the order in which teachers teach the standards changes, the teams can quickly find the products and reorder them to match the changes without starting all over.

Figures 8.2 and 8.3 show sample organizational systems, one for elementary by grade level and one for secondary by department. In both figures, each subject-area folder contains subfolders for each unit. The folder labeled *General* holds such products as the team meeting rolling agenda, grade or course proficiency map, list of priority standards, state standards, team norms, team SMART goals, and a priority-standards data tracker by student and by teacher.

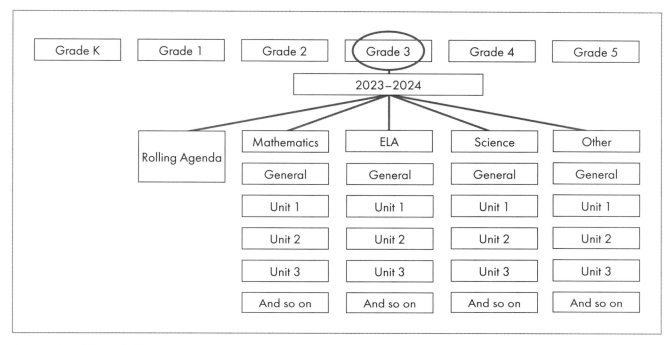

Source: Adapted from Schuhl et al., 2021.

FIGURE 8.2: Elementary grade-level digital folder organization example.

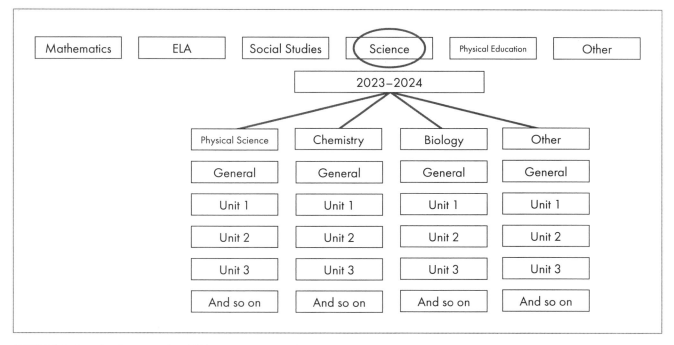

FIGURE 8.3: Secondary department digital folder organization example.

To accelerate learning in a systematic and effective way, teams may need to share their proficiency maps and priority standards with other educators on campus who also serve the students across grade-level or course-alike teams. Using a consistent structure to organize folders expedites sharing.

Teach Until the Last Day of School

With the stresses of the school year nearly behind them and the excitement of summer on the horizon, teachers sometimes—with the best intentions—turn to fun projects or activities after the state assessment or the spring progress-monitoring assessment, even if there are still three or four weeks of school left (10 percent of the school year). Much like accelerating learning starts on day one of the school year, it also ends on the last day of the school year. The weeks after end-of-year assessments are the optimal time to prepare students to be as ready as possible for the next grade level or course—and teams can still make it fun!

The teachers across a collaborative team might teach content they were not yet able to address. Another option is to use common assessments to give students reassessment opportunities on topics for which they did not demonstrate proficiency earlier in the year. However, teams also might reference their priority-standards tracker (see figure 6.3, page 116) to determine which priority standards students learned and which they have not learned yet (which may include students reading at grade level). Armed with this information, the teachers can share students, with each taking a priority standard to work on with a group of students, share the workload of creating stations for the priority standards students still need to learn with intentional minilessons, or choose some critical priority standards to re-engage students in learning in preparation for next year. Team members may also want to invite the next grade-level or course teachers into the conversation for additional feedback when determining how to end student learning for the year. Teachers might fill out a quick plan like the one in figure 8.4.

Some schools and teams give end-of-year assessments to prepare for instruction at the start of the following year. For example, kindergartners may have exit assessments on foundational skills related to letters, sounds, and reading, as well as numbers, addition, subtraction, and shapes. Kindergarten teachers often assess these students and send the information to the first-grade teachers. Sometimes the first-grade teachers see different results than they expect when students return the next year and may think the kindergarten teachers assessed inaccurately or with some bias. Instead, consider having the first-grade teachers assess the kindergartners so they can already begin to plan for intervention groups (based on the data) and better understand any learning differences they observe after the summer vacation. The kindergarten and first-grade teachers might share students in creative ways to work on priority standards while some students are assessing with the next grade-level teachers.

Engage in Step-Up Transition Planning

Continuous improvement requires learning, which means it also requires reflection. As Brown (n.d.) says, "Anyone that is too busy to reflect is too busy to learn." Collaborative teams stop to reflect on the instructional practices, pacing, and common assessments to determine which contributed to student learning and which they could improve or drop to strengthen learning next year. They do this after each unit or learning cycle, as well as at the end of the year.

At the end of the year, teachers across a collaborative team reflect on the priority standards they taught and assessed, and develop a plan to teach any priority standards they may not have been

1. Review your priority standards. Which ones do you need to review? Which ones need more teaching?

2. Which priority standards do you need to teach at the end of the year so students are ready for next year?

3. Identify what to review or teach related to priority standards each day, and what lessons (if any) you need to address on the calendar. What are the learning targets for each day?

Week	Priority Standard to Teach	Priority Standard to Review
Dates:		
Dates:		
Dates:		
Dates:		

Calendar to the End of the Year—Which priority standards will students continue to learn in preparation for next year? What is the learning target or lesson for each day? Block off days for state or district testing, holidays, students' last day of school, professional development days, and so on.

Monday	Tuesday	Wednesday	Thursday	Friday
Date:	Date:	Date:	Date:	Date:
Date:	Date:	Date:	Date:	Date:
Date:	Date:	Date:	Date:	Date:
Date:	Date:	Date:	Date:	Date:
Date:	Date:	Date:		

FIGURE 8.4: End-of-year plan.

Visit go.SolutionTree.com/priorityschools for a free reproducible version of this figure.

able to address this year for next year's students. They reflect on the priority standards and make needed adjustments to their proficiency map and time spent on lessons. This learning not only helps the team but also supports the planning of the teachers in the next grade level or course. Teams then engage in *step-up transition planning*, which refers to ensuring a smooth transition to the next year or level for teachers and students.

Step-up transition planning is a vital activity that uses the knowledge of those teachers who taught students in a grade level or course *this year* to document what worked and did not work. That way should any members of the team change for *next year*, continuous improvement can still occur. During step-up transition planning, teams plan to transition students to the next grade level or course and also strengthen their own program. The planning involves the following.

> ▸ Identify which priority standards students learned or have not yet learned using data (use the priority standards–data tracker in figure 6.3, page 116).

> ▸ Identify instructional strategies, activities, or lessons that contributed to student learning.

> ▸ Write any comments to remember or share with the next grade-level or course teachers. Comments might relate to instruction, student misconceptions, or the learning in core versus intervention in units related to priority standards.

Teams complete a document for themselves and one they can share with the next grade level or course in a step-up transition meeting. Figure 8.5 is an example of a step-up transition planning document teams complete as they engage in reflective conversations. If needed, elementary grade-level teams can use separate copies of this form for each subject area. Department teams should fill out this form separately for each course.

A team shares this information and data with the next grade level or course. The next grade-level or course collaborative team uses this information (including proficiency maps) to embed and spiral in the standards teams still need to teach or review. As we previously shared, beginning the school year teaching last year's missed standards before teaching the grade-level curriculum will only serve to create even larger learning gaps, so the next year's teams must plan to deliver just-in-time learning for acceleration. Once the planning documents are complete, teams can schedule step-up transition meetings to share their information with one another and plan for next year.

Apply Learning at Vertical Step-Up Transition Meetings

Teams need time to share their step-up transition planning documents with the team from the next grade level or course. We refer to these as *vertical step-up transition meetings*. Kindergarten teams meet with first-grade teams, first-grade teams meet with second-grade teams, and so on. If the middle school is grades 6–8, the fifth-grade team still shares, but with the appropriate subject-area teams in sixth grade. Additionally, throughout secondary schools (including between the middle or junior high school and the high school), teachers within a department share from one course to the next. The next grade-level or course teams ask clarifying questions about the information in the step-up transition planning documents related to academic learning and about any proactive strategies to minimize any behavior problems or student clashes.

Once teams share the information, the next grade-level or course teams begin to plan for the next year. The teachers on these teams identify any priority standards from the previous grade or course that will become prior-knowledge standards, and determine in which unit it most makes sense to

Grade and Subject or Course: _____

Step-Up Transition Planning

Team Priority Standards and Strategy Reflection for the Current Year

1. **Which priority standards have your students learned this year? Which have they not learned yet? What evidence (common assessment, progress monitoring, or other) do you have to support your thinking?**

Priority Standards Learned (80+ Percent Students Proficient)	Priority Standards Taught But Not Yet Learned	Priority Standards Not Taught

2. **Special notes to our team for next year and the next grade-level or course team** (include strategies teams used that impacted student learning, connections teachers should use when teaching next year, common misconceptions, and so on.).

Priority Standard	Successful Strategies the Team Used	Comments

FIGURE 8.5: Step-up transition planning document.

*Visit **go.SolutionTree.com/priorityschools** for a free reproducible version of this figure.*

address them. Teams identify any of their own content they might need to de-emphasize to make time for the content they still need to address from last year to accelerate learning most effectively. Teams might also use spring learning data or the previous grade level's priority standards data tracker to tentatively form intervention groups that can start on day one of the next school year.

Some questions to guide the discussion at vertical set-up transition meetings include the following.

- ► What should the next grade-level teachers expect students to know and be able to do?

- ► What should the next grade-level teachers expect to review or teach from your grade level?

- ► What should the next grade-level teachers know about some of the students they will work with next year (which students the teacher may need to separate, how students best work together, and so on)?

- ► What are your recommendations for interventions on targeted skills at the start of next year for students currently in your grade? What data support these recommendations?

Figure 8.6 shares a vertical step-up transition meeting document for the team gathering information from the prior grade level or course to record notes for their own planning next year. For example, for a meeting between a seventh-grade team and a sixth-grade team, the seventh-grade teachers would use this form (see figure 8.6). As with the step-up transition-planning document, fill out a copy of this form for each subject area or course.

Teachers take time to update their proficiency maps for next year, so they know when to best embed prior-knowledge priority standards (see figure 3.6, page 46, and figure 3.7, page 48). They begin to plan their first unit, as well as possible initial intervention groups with a targeted focus.

Vertical step-up transition meetings take time so teachers can adequately share the information with the next team. Vertical teams need to begin planning. Some schools engage in this planning during professional development days at the end of the school year, others find time in May, and still others might do their planning at the start of the summer. These meetings are most effective when current team members are present to fully share the picture of the year with the next grade-level or course teachers with the year still fresh on their minds.

Step-up transition planning and vertical planning meetings are a catalyst to continuous improvement. Teachers celebrate the teacher and student learning that occurred throughout the year and leave school with a tentative plan to start the next year strong.

Celebrate!

Accelerating student learning with priority standards to grade level or beyond, and learning together as collaborative teams is meaningful and challenging work—work worthy of celebrating! In fact, celebrations contribute to a healthy culture focused on the right work and continuous improvement. In his book *In Praise of American Educators*, DuFour (2015) writes, "Constantly search for evidence that students are learning at higher levels, call attention to the progress, and seek every opportunity to express appreciation and admiration for the individual and collective efforts that are contributing to that progress" (p. 242). Coauthors and PLC experts Mike Mattos, Richard DuFour, Rebecca DuFour, Robert Eaker, and Thomas W. Many (2016) further state, "Celebration is an important part of sustaining any continuous improvement process" (p. 149). And Timothy D. Kanold (2011), an award-winning educator, in-demand motivational speaker, and educational leader, shares in *The Five Disciplines of PLC Leaders*, "Something very valuable

Grade and Subject or Course: _____

Vertical Step-Up Transition Meeting

Team Priority Standards and Strategy Reflection for the Next Year

1. Identify the priority standards that students did not learn (whether taught or not) in the previous grade level or course (prerequisite knowledge). What is your team's plan to embed these standards into your proficiency map, pacing, and calendar for next year?

Priority Standard (Not learned in previous grade level or course)	Timing (Where does this fit into your progression for next year?)
Ideas for Standards to Drop or De-Emphasize Next Year	

Special Notes From the Discussion to Remember When Teaching Next Year

Unit	Teaching Notes

FIGURE 8.6: Vertical step-up transition meeting document.

*Visit **go.SolutionTree.com/priorityschools** for a free reproducible version of this figure.*

occurs in families, schools, and corporations when we bring people together for social support and celebrations. We promote the health and well-being of others and ourselves" (p. 71). Administrators, the guiding coalition or learning team, and all other collaborative teams should celebrate wins and understand each win is a stepping stone to the ultimate mission of ensuring high levels of learning for every student. Success builds on success, and continuous improvement uses celebrations as a catalyst for more learning. Celebrations are for the staff, the students, and the collaborative teams.

Celebrations do not need to be large parties. Celebrations for collaborative teams can be acknowledgments in weekly newsletters from the principal, team products on a bulletin board in the staff room or where collaborative teams meet, feedback teams receive on their products, or recognition of how they are embracing the school's collective commitments. Celebrations can be an announcement on the school website, Facebook page, or Twitter feed when student learning across a team increases or a team meets their SMART goal (Conzemius & O'Neill, 2014). Celebrations can also be larger when staff, students, and collaborative teams reach milestones.

Also consider *how* to celebrate students throughout the year based on their learning data. How can your school celebrate this growth? Reaching proficiency? Exceeding proficiency? Students create and use student-data trackers so they can visually see their learning progress and even share it with parents at parent conferences. Schools might acknowledge students in an assembly or class awards ceremony with a certificate or small prize for growth or proficiency or higher on a progress-monitoring assessment or state assessment. Teachers might call parents when students demonstrate all they have learned on their common assessments.

Also celebrate individual teachers for acts of excellence. Students might write letters of appreciation to teachers who contributed to their learning. Teachers might nominate one another for special acknowledgments when they observe a colleague supporting a teacher, team, or student learning by going beyond expectations.

In our book *School Improvement for All*, we write:

> Celebrations act as an antidote to constant change. They indicate what an organization values. They shape the stories that the people in a school tell themselves and others about their school, students, teachers, parents, and administration. Stories can feed the cycle of failure or describe a culture of success. (Kramer & Schuhl, 2017, p. 37)

Figure 8.7 is a template for guiding coalitions or learning teams to plan celebrations. Leaders can also survey parents, students, and staff to generate ideas for celebrations.

Celebrations tell the story of your school. They contribute to a healthy culture when they are meaningful and sincere. Celebrations energize ongoing continuous improvement and challenge collaborative teams, teachers, and students to learn and grow. When students' learning accelerates to grade level or beyond, a school has much to celebrate! Celebrations bring the fun into learning and spark joy. They create the type of school parents, students, and educators want to be part of. Schools in continuous improvement create a celebratory culture.

Conclusion

Continuous improvement is forward motion in a school—looking ahead and making each day and each year stronger for educator and student learning. As schools improve practices, policies, and procedures, more students learn and the gaps prompting the need to accelerate learning to

Celebration Planning

Brainstorm different ways to celebrate teachers, collaborative teams, and students throughout the year. When during the year should each celebration occur? Is the celebration a public or private experience? What is your plan for the celebration and who is responsible for ensuring it occurs?

Celebration	Time of Year and Frequency	Plan
Collaborative Teams		
Students		
Teachers		

FIGURE 8.7: Celebration plan template.

*Visit **go.SolutionTree.com/priorityschools** for a free reproducible version of this figure.*

grade level or beyond narrow. Collaborative teams, administrators, and guiding coalitions or learning teams keep continuous improvement in mind as they work to accelerate learning for the priority standards. Teams archive their team products in a systematic digital folder schema, teach until the last day of school, reflect on their practices and student learning through step-up transition planning and vertical meetings, and celebrate along the way. Teams are ready with intervention groups at the start of the next school year and have a learning plan for embedding prior-year priority standards—all to improve student learning.

Continuous improvement does not mean perfection. There will be times when mistakes are made and teams need to revise actions, but learning happens in those moments too. Through continuous improvement, schools grow each year and move toward becoming the great schools they envision, and the great schools students deserve.

Discussion Questions for Reflection and Action

As a team, discuss the following questions. Visit **go.SolutionTree.com/priorityschools** for a free reproducible version of these questions.

- ▶ What are some ways your school shows it is on a continuous-improvement journey?

- ▶ How does your team store team products so they are easy to find and learn from the next year?

- ▶ How might your team plan for student learning of the priority standards until the last day of school?

- ▶ When near the end of the year can teams engage in step-up transition planning and vertical team conversations?

- ▶ What does your team want to learn about incoming students so you can better plan for next year and begin teaching grade-level standards on day one of school?

- ▶ How will your team use data from incoming students to plan for targeted interventions at the start of school next year?

- ▶ What are ways you might celebrate teachers, collaborative teams, and students?

- ▶ How will you celebrate learning at your school to prioritize its importance and make it fun?

EPILOGUE

Dare to Dream and Then Dare to Do

Change is difficult for everyone, especially if engaging in second-order change, which requires deep changes in beliefs and philosophies. Acceleration is the path less traveled because doing so requires shifts in mindsets. For too long, educators have struggled with prioritizing state standards students are supposed to learn and instead try to teach everything. Acceleration can only occur when the most essential of the standards (priority standards) become the focus of teaching and learning in combination with the corresponding prior-knowledge standards each day. Less is more, and letting go of special units and past practices is necessary. Assessment practices must change from occasional tests to daily *show what you know* opportunities. Interventions must be universal and support grade- and course-level curriculum and build the prerequisite skills of the priority standards. Given the pronounced need to close learning gaps, acceleration is the only way. These changes require a leap of faith and a belief that every student can learn and succeed.

Though we have shared many strategies in this book, it would be impossible to present an exhaustive resource. Educational researchers continue to examine best practices related to acceleration, and teachers and teams constantly learn more through their own action research. Learn new strategies. Try new strategies. Continue to grow a toolkit that accelerates student learning of priority standards to grade level or beyond.

Now is the time to build equitable practices that close the achievement gap in every school. There is no time for complacency. Accelerating learning requires action and that action starts today. It starts with one step and then another over the course of time. From your reading, consider where you might begin your journey. Use the graphic organizers in figure E.1 (page 166) and table E.1 (page 168), which list the acceleration strategies and tools and protocols in this book, to start your planning.

This book is a call to all dreamers who won't accept poverty, language, or class size as reasons for failure. In fact, they won't accept anything other than their students' success. To achieve this, they are willing to change the way they teach, the way they think, and even the way they behave—whatever it takes to make sure every student learns and succeeds. Dare to dream and then dare to do!

Acceleration Strategies	Next Step	Time Line
Chapter 1: The Case for Acceleration		
• Mindset one: Schools and districts are learning organizations (page 11). • Mindset two: All students can learn grade- and course-level standards (page 12). • Mindset three: Formative assessment is integral to learning (page 12). • Mindset four: Schools must systematically intervene to accelerate learning (page 12). • Mindset five: Instructional strategies should create forward-moving learning (page 13). • Mindset six: Everyone is a leader of learning (page 14).		
Chapter 2: Culture That Accelerates Learning		
• Students co-create learning contracts (page 18). • Teachers engage and learn in collaborative teams (page 21). • Administrators stay focused on learning (page 22). • Parents and community members shift their thinking to learning (page 22). • Symbols and artifacts show learning is required (page 25). • SMART goals are audaciously attainable (page 25).		
Chapter 3: Priority Standards and Learning Cycles That Accelerate Learning		
• Identify priority standards (page 35). • Unpack priority standards to create learning progressions (page 38). • Embed prior-knowledge standards into units (page 43). • Focus acceleration in ten-day learning cycles within units (page 45).		
Chapter 4: An Assessment System That Accelerates Learning		
• Audit current assessment practices (page 64). • Create a balanced assessment system (page 66). • Create common assessments unit by unit (page 68). • Implement common formative assessment strategies (page 71).		

Acceleration Strategies	Next Step	Time Line
Chapter 5: Daily Grade-Level Instruction That Accelerates Learning		
• Design quality lessons tied to grade-level learning every day (page 90). • Plan for massed and spaced practice (page 93). • Utilize whole-group and small-group learning (page 95). • Teach conceptually (page 96). • Incorporate reading and writing every day (page 99). • Engage students actively (page 101). • Utilize error analysis (page 102). • Give meaningful feedback (page 103). • Empower student learning through reflection and goal setting (page 104).		
Chapter 6: An Intervention System That Accelerates Learning		
• Repurpose time in the master schedule for intervention (page 112). • Respond as a team to student learning data (page 114). • Focus on student growth (page 120). • Utilize blended learning (page 122). • Create small groups (page 122). • Develop and use peer tutors (page 123). • Implement support classes or learning labs (page 125). • Engage students in learning behavior expectations (page 125).		
Chapter 7: Leadership Practices That Accelerate Learning		
• Create a guiding coalition or learning team (page 131). • Utilize instructional coaches (page 134). • Build a system of instructional support (page 140). • Engage the community and stakeholders (page 145).		
Chapter 8: Continuous Improvement That Accelerates Learning		
• Archive team products systematically (page 153). • Teach until the last day of school (page 156). • Engage in step-up transition planning (page 156). • Apply learning at vertical step-up transition meetings (page 158). • Celebrate (page 160)!		

FIGURE E.1: Action plan for accelerating learning graphic organizer.

*Visit **go.SolutionTree.com/priorityschools** for a free reproducible version of this figure.*

TABLE E.1: Tools and Protocols for Next Steps

If you want to . . .	Protocol or Tool
Chapter 1: The Case for Acceleration	
Explore current reality related to acceleration	Figure 1.1: Learning is required discussion tool (page 11) Figure 1.2: Assessment discussion tool (page 13) Figure 1.3: Intervention discussion tool (page 14)
Chapter 2: Culture That Accelerates Learning	
Create classroom agreements for learning	Figure 2.1: Sample learning contract (page 20)
Clarify the work of teams	Figure 2.2: Work of teams in recurring learning cycles (page 21)
Reflect and plan actions to be an instructional leader	Figure 2.3: Administrator learning-focus planning tool (page 23)
Analyze the school's visual story	Figure 2.4: Symbol and artifact walk recording sheet (page 26)
Create audaciously attainable goals	Figure 2.5: Safe SMART goal example (page 28) Figure 2.6: Audaciously attainable SMART goal example (page 29) Figure 2.7: Audaciously attainable goals for diverse populations (page 30) Figure 2.8: SMART goal data board (page 31)
Chapter 3: Priority Standards and Learning Cycles That Accelerate Learning	
Clarify a guaranteed and viable curriculum that focuses on priority standards for acceleration	Figure 3.1: Standards acceleration diagram (page 36) Figure 3.2: Critical knowledge and skills for acceleration (page 37) Figure 3.3: Priority standards and time frames (page 39) Figure 3.6: Proficiency map—Grade 5 mathematics (page 46) Figure 3.7: Proficiency map—Grade 3 ELA (page 48)
Unpack standards to create acceleration learning progressions	Figure 3.4: Example of an unpacked standard in reading (page 41) Figure 3.5: Example of unpacked standard in mathematics (page 42)
Clarify a unit learning cycle	Figure 3.8: Learning cycle (page 50) Figure 3.9: Example of unit plan and calendar (page 52) Figure 3.10: Ten-day cycle planning template (page 56)
Chapter 4: An Assessment System That Accelerates Learning	
Examine assessments	Figure 4.1: Assessment audit template (page 65) Figure 4.2: Balanced assessment system (page 67)

If you want to . . .	Protocol or Tool
Create team common assessments	Figure 4.3: Creating common assessments checklist (page 69) Figure 4.4: Common assessment rubric (page 70) Figure 4.5: Common assessment and daily formative assessment connection in each unit (page 71) Figure 4.11: Kindergarten rolling assessment for letter recognition (page 80)
Create student-reflection and tracker tools	Figure 4.6: During-the-unit student-reflection tool (page 74) Figure 4.7: End-of-unit student-reflection tool (page 75) Figure 4.8: Student-reflection tool for standards over time (page 76) Figure 4.12: Student learning passport example (page 83)
Create a pretest to assess entry learning	Figure 4.9: Grade 3 pretest—addition and subtraction (obtrusive) (page 77) Figure 4.10: Grade 3 pretest—addition and subtraction (unobtrusive) (page 78)
Chapter 5: Daily Grade-Level Instruction That Accelerates Learning	
Create a quality lesson to accelerate learning	Figure 5.1: Questions to guide lesson design (page 93) Figure 5.2: Example of spaced and massed practice to balance grade-level and prior-knowledge standards (page 94) Figure 5.3: Example of clarifying concepts students are learning (page 98)
Create classroom posters or anchor charts to build student perseverance	Figure 5.4: Examples of posters for students to reference when they get stuck (page 99)
Chapter 6: Intervention System That Accelerates Learning	
Clarify intervention tiers and a plan for learning in each	Figure 6.1: RTI pyramid of interventions (page 108) Figure 6.2: Example of ten-day learning cycle showing Tier 1, Tier 2, and Tier 3 interventions (page 113)
Collect and analyze data as a team to make targeted intervention plans	Figure 6.3: Team priority-standards tracker (page 116) Figure 6.4: Common formative assessment data analysis for a learning target or standard (page 117) Figure 6.5: Progress-monitoring data protocol for priority standards (page 118) Figure 6.6: Intervention and extension team plan (page 121)
Utilize student peer tutors	Figure 6.7: Mathematics peer tutor rubric example (page 124)
Chapter 7: Leadership Practices That Accelerate Learning	
Clarify the work of the guiding coalition and collaborative teams	Figure 7.1: Leading the right work (page 133)

If you want to . . .	Protocol or Tool
Utilize instructional coaches	Figure 7.2: Instructional coaching flier example (page 136)
	Figure 7.3: Sample plan for three-week instructional coaching cycles (page 138)
	Figure 7.4: Example of organizer for coach-teacher work during the three-week coaching cycle (page 139)
Clarify instructional expectations for feedback	Figure 7.5: Elementary school example of core instructional practices (page 143)
Chapter 8: Continuous Improvement That Accelerates Learning	
Clarify collaborative team products and how to organize them	Figure 8.1: The work of collaborative teams to archive (page 154)
	Figure 8.2: Elementary grade-level digital folder organization example (page 155)
	Figure 8.3: Secondary department digital folder organization example (page 155)
Plan for learning at the end of the year and beginning of next year	Figure 8.4: End-of-year plan (page 157)
	Figure 8.5: Step-up transition planning document (page 159)
	Figure 8.6: Vertical step-up transition meeting document (page 161)
Plan for celebrations	Figure 8.7: Celebration plan template (page 163)
Epilogue: Dare to Dream and Then Dare to Do	
Create a plan for acceleration	Figure E.1: Action plan for accelerating learning graphic organizer (page 166)

Visit **go.SolutionTree.com/priorityschools** for a free reproducible version of this table.

References and Resources

Accelerate. (n.d.). In *Merriam-Webster's online dictionary*. Accessed at https://merriam-webster.com/dictionary/accelerate on December 4, 2022.

Accelerated Schools Plus. (2006). *Welcome to Accelerated Schools plus*. Accessed at https://www.acceleratedschools.net/asp/Accelerated_Schools_Plus/aboutus.html on November 25, 2022.

Ainsworth, L. (2003). *"Unwrapping" the standards: A simple process to make standards manageable*. Englewood, CO: Advanced Learning Press.

Ainsworth, L. (2004). *Power standards: Identifying the standards that matter most*. Englewood, CO: Advanced Learning Press.

Bandura A. (1995). *Self-efficacy in changing societies*. Cambridge, England: Cambridge University Press.

Barth, R. S. (1991). *Improving schools from within: Teachers, parents, and principals can make a difference*. San Francisco: Jossey-Bass.

Benson, J. (2021). *Improve every lesson plan with SEL*. Alexandria, VA: ASCD.

Black, P., & Wiliam, D. (1998). Inside the black box: Raising standards through classroom assessment. *Phi Delta Kappan, 80*(2), 139–148.

Bleiberg, J., Brunner, E., Harbatkin, E., Kraft, M. A., & Springer, M. (2021). *The effect of teacher evaluation on achievement and attainment: Evidence from statewide reforms* (EdWorkingPaper: 21–496). Accessed at https://doi.org/10.26300/b1ak-r251 on December 19, 2022.

Boaler, J. (2016). *Mathematical mindsets: Unleashing students' potential through creative math, inspiring messages, and innovative teaching*. San Francisco: Jossey-Bass.

Boaler, J. (2019). *Limitless mind: Learn, lead, and live without barriers*. New York: HarperCollins.

Boaler, J., & Foster, D. (2021, August). *Raising expectations and achievement: The impact of two wide scale de-tracking mathematics reforms*. Accessed at https://www.youcubed.org/wp-content/uploads/2017/09/Raising-Expectations-2021.pdf on August 9, 2021.

Brown, T. (n.d.). *PLC is common sense*. Global PD Video. Accessed at https://app.globalpd.com/search/content/MTI2 on April 17, 2022.

Brown, T., & Ferriter, W. M. (2021). *You can learn! Building student ownership, motivation, and efficacy with the PLC at Work Process*. Bloomington, IN: Solution Tree Press.

Buffum, A., Mattos, M., & Malone, J. (2018). *Taking action: A handbook for RTI at Work*. Bloomington, IN: Solution Tree Press.

Butterfield, L. H., & Friedlaender, M. (Eds.). (1973). *The Adams papers: Adams family correspondence* (Vol. 3, pp. 310–313). Cambridge, MA: Harvard University Press.

Chappuis, J. & Stiggins, R. (2020). *Classroom assessment for student learning: Doing it right—using it well* (3rd ed.). New York: Pearson.

Chenoweth, K. (2021). *Districts that succeed: Breaking the correlation between race, poverty, and achievement*. Cambridge, MA: Harvard Education Press.

Conzemius, A. E., & O'Neill, J. (2014). *The handbook for SMART school teams: Revitalizing best practices for collaboration* (2nd ed.). Bloomington, IN: Solution Tree Press.

Council of the Great City Schools. (2020, June). *Addressing unfinished learning after COVID-19 school closures.* Accessed at https://www.cgcs.org/cms/lib/DC00001581/Centricity/Domain/313/CGCS_Unfinished%20 Learning.pdf on September 12, 2020.

Covey, S. R. (2013). *The 7 habits of highly effective people: Powerful lessons in personal change.* New York: Simon & Schuster.

Cruz, L. F. (2022, August). *Reset and refresh as a guiding coalition leading a PLC at Work.* Professional development workshop for Walla Walla Public Schools, Walla Walla, WA.

Darling-Hammond, L., Flook, L., Cook-Harvey, C., Barron, B., & Osher, D. (2020). Implications for educational practice of the science of learning and development. *Applied Developmental Science, 24*(2), 97–140. Accessed at https://tandfonline.com/doi/full/10.1080/10888691.2018.1537791 on December 4, 2022.

Deal, T. E., & Peterson, K. D. (2016). *Shaping school culture: Pitfalls, paradoxes, and promises* (3rd ed.). San Francisco: Jossey-Bass.

Dimich, N. (2015). *Design in 5: Essential phases to create engaging assessment practice.* Bloomington, IN: Solution Tree Press.

DuFour, R. (2014). *Common formative assessment: The lynchpin of the PLC process* [Breakout session presentation]. PLC at Work Institute, Minneapolis, MN.

DuFour, R. (2015). *In praise of American educators: And how they can become even better.* Bloomington, IN: Solution Tree Press.

DuFour, R., DuFour, R., Eaker, R., Many, T. W., & Mattos, M. (2016). *Learning by doing: A handbook for Professional Learning Communities at Work* (3rd ed.). Bloomington, IN: Solution Tree Press.

Dweck, C. S. (2016). *Mindset: The new psychology of success* (Updated ed.). New York: Ballantine Books.

Dyer, K. (2015, September 17). *Research proof points: Better student engagement improves student learning* [Blog post]. Accessed at https://www.nwea.org/blog/2015/research-proof-points-better-student-engagement -improves-student-learning/ on November 29, 2022.

Eaker, R. (2020). *A summing up: Teaching and learning in effective schools and PLCs at Work.* Bloomington, IN: Solution Tree Press.

Eaker, R., & Keating, J. (2015). *Kid by kid, skill by skill: Teaching in a Professional Learning Community at Work.* Bloomington, IN: Solution Tree Press.

Elgart, M. A. (2017). Can schools meet the promise of continuous improvement? *Phi Delta Kappan, 99*(4), 54–59.

Erkens, C., Schimmer, T., & Dimich, N. (2017). *Essential assessment: Six tenets for bringing hope, efficacy, and achievement to the classroom.* Bloomington, IN: Solution Tree Press.

Erkens, C., Schimmer, T., & Dimich, N. (2018). *Instructional agility: Responding to assessment with real-time decisions.* Bloomington, IN: Solution Tree Press.

Friziellie, H., Schmidt, J. A., & Spiller, J. (2016). *Yes we can! General and special educators collaborating in a professional learning community.* Bloomington, IN: Solution Tree Press.

Graham, S., Bruch, J., Fitzgerald, J., Friedrich, L., Furgeson, J., Greene, K., et al. (2016). *Teaching secondary students to write effectively* (NCEE 2017-4002). Washington, DC: National Center for Education Evaluation and Regional Assistance (NCEE), Institute of Education Sciences, U.S. Department of Education. Accessed at https://ies.ed.gov/ncee/wwc/Docs/PracticeGuide/508_WWCPG_SecondaryWriting_122719.pdf on April 11, 2022.

Greenwood, S. C., & McCabe, P. P. (2008). How learning contracts motivate students. *Middle School Journal, 39*(5), 13–22.

Guskey, T. R. (2015). *On your mark: Challenging the conventions of grading and reporting.* Bloomington, IN: Solution Tree Press.

Hall, B. (2022). *Powerful guiding coalitions: How to build and sustain the leadership team in your PLC at Work.* Bloomington, IN: Solution Tree Press.

Harlacher, J. E., & Rodriguez, B. J. (2018). *An educator's guide to schoolwide positive behavioral interventions and supports: Integrating all three tiers.* Bloomington, IN: Marzano Resources.

Hattie, J. (2009). *Visible learning: A synthesis of over 800 meta-analyses relating to achievement.* New York: Routledge.

Hattie, J. (2012). *Visible learning for teachers: Maximizing impact on learning.* New York: Routledge.

Hattie, J. (2017, August). *Visible Learning Plus: 250+ Influences on student achievement.* Accessed at https://visible-learning.org/wp-content/uploads/2018/03/250-Influences-Final-Effect-Size-List-2017_VLPLUS.pdf on November 28, 2022.

Hattie, J., Fisher, D., & Frey, N. (2017). *Visible learning for mathematics, grades K–12: What works best to optimize student learning.* Thousand Oaks, CA: Corwin.

Hattie, J., & Smith, R. L. (Eds.). (2020). *10 mindframes for leaders: The visible learning approach to school success.* Thousand Oaks, CA: Corwin.

Hattie, J., & Yates, G. (2014). *Visible learning and the science of how we learn.* New York: Routledge.

Hopfenberg, W. S., Levin, H. M., Meister, G., & Rogers, J. (1990, August). *Accelerated schools* (ERIC Number ED375471), Accessed at https://files.eric.ed.gov/fulltext/ED375471.pdf on December 19, 2022.

Ingle, A. (2019, September 25). 4 ways to foster positive student relationships. *Edutopia.* Accessed at https://edutopia.org/article/4-ways-foster-positive-student-relationships on December 20, 2022.

Kanold, T. D. (2011). *The five disciplines of PLC leaders.* Bloomington, IN: Solution Tree Press.

Kanold, T. D., Kanold-McIntyre, J., Larson, M. R., Barnes, B., Schuhl, S., & Toncheff, M. (2018). *Mathematics instruction and tasks in a PLC at Work.* Bloomington, IN: Solution Tree Press.

Kanold, T. D., & Larson, M. R. (2015). *Beyond the common core: A handbook for mathematics in a PLC at Work, leader's guide.* Bloomington, IN: Solution Tree Press.

Kanold, T. D., Schuhl, S., Larson, M. R., Barnes, B., Kanold-McIntyre, J., & Toncheff, M. (2018). *Mathematics assessment and intervention in a PLC at Work.* Bloomington, IN: Solution Tree Press.

Kilpatrick, J., Swafford, J., & Findell, B. (Eds.). (2001). *Adding it up: Helping children learn mathematics.* Mathematics Learning Study Committee, Center for Education, Division of Behavioral and Social Sciences and Education. National Research Council. Washington, DC: National Academy Press.

Kramer, S. V. (2015). *How to leverage PLCs for school improvement.* Bloomington, IN: Solution Tree Press.

Kramer, S. V. (Ed.). (2021a). *Charting the course for collaborative teams: Lessons learned from priority schools in a PLC at Work.* Bloomington, IN: Solution Tree Press.

Kramer, S. V. (Ed.). (2021b). *Charting the course for leaders: Lessons learned from priority schools in a PLC at Work.* Bloomington, IN: Solution Tree Press.

Kramer, S. V., & Maeker, P. (2022, June 11–12). *Priority schools training* [Presentation]. Bloomington, IN.

Kramer, S. V., & Schuhl, S. (2017). *School improvement for all: A how-to guide for doing the right work.* Bloomington, IN: Solution Tree Press.

Kuhfeld, M., Soland, J., & Lewis, K. (2022). *Test score patterns across three COVID-19-impacted school years* (EdWorkingPaper 22–521). Accessed at https://doi.org/10.26300/ga82-6v47 on February 9, 2022.

Maeker, P. (2021, June). *Gaining ground* [Keynote address], RTI at Work Virtual Summit, Bloomington, IN.

Martin, T. L., & Rains, C. L. (2018). *Stronger together: Answering the questions of collaborative leadership.* Bloomington, IN: Solution Tree Press.

Marzano, R. J. (2003). *What works in schools: Translating research into action.* Alexandria, VA: ASCD.

Marzano, R. J. (2010). *Formative assessment and standards-based grading.* Bloomington, IN: Marzano Resources.

Marzano, R. J. (2017). *The new art and science of teaching.* Bloomington, IN: Solution Tree Press.

Marzano, R. J., & Pickering, D. J. (2011). *The highly engaged classroom.* Bloomington, IN: Marzano Resources.

Marzano, R. J., Warrick, P. B., Rains, C. L., & DuFour, R. (2018). *Leading a high reliability school*. Bloomington, IN: Solution Tree Press.

Mattos, M., DuFour, R., DuFour, R., Eaker, R., & Many, T. W. (2016). *Concise answers to frequently asked questions about Professional Learning Communities at Work*. Bloomington, IN: Solution Tree Press.

Mollenkamp, D. (2022, October 24). *NAEP 'Nation's Report Card' shows steep fall in math scores*. Accessed at https://edsurge.com/news/2022-10-24-naep-nation-s-report-card-shows-steep-fall-in-math-scores on December 20, 2022.

National Commission on Excellence. (1983, April). *A nation at risk: The imperative for educational reform: An open letter to the American people—A report to the nation and the Secretary of Education*. Accessed at https://files.eric.ed.gov/fulltext/ED226006.pdf on December 20, 2022.

National Council of Teachers of Mathematics. (2014). *Principles to actions: Ensuring mathematical success for all*. Reston, VA: Author.

National Council of Teachers of Mathematics & National Council of Supervisors of Mathematics. (2020, June). *Moving forward: Mathematics learning in the era of COVID-19*. Accessed at https://nctm.org/uploadedFiles/Research_and_Advocacy/NCTM_NCSM_Moving_Forward.pdf on May 23, 2022.

National Governors Association Center for Best Practices & Council of Chief State School Officers. (2010a). *Common Core State Standards for English language arts and literacy in history/social studies, science, and technical subjects*. Washington, DC: Authors. Accessed at https://learning.ccsso.org/wp-content/uploads/2022/11/ADA-Compliant-ELA-Standards.pdf on October 18, 2022.

National Governors Association Center for Best Practices & Council of Chief State School Officers. (2010b). *Common Core State Standards for mathematics*. Washington, DC: Authors. Accessed at https://learning.ccsso.org/wp-content/uploads/2022/11/ADA-Compliant-Math-Standards.pdf on October 18, 2022.

National Mathematics Advisory Panel. (2008). *Foundations for success: The final report of the National Mathematics Advisory Panel*. Washington, DC: U.S. Department of Education. Accessed at https://files.eric.ed.gov/fulltext/ED500486.pdf on December 20, 2022.

National Public Radio. (2022, September 13). *The teacher shortage is testing America's schools* [Radio broadcast]. Accessed at https://npr.org/2022/09/13/1122819873/the-teacher-shortage-is-testing-americas-schools on November 23, 2022.

Navo, M., & Williams, A. (2023). *Demystifying MTSS: A school and district framework for meeting students' academic and social-emotional needs*. Bloomington, IN: Solution Tree Press.

Payne, R. K. (2005). *A framework for understanding poverty* (4th rev. ed.). Highlands, TX: aha! Process.

Peters, W. H. (1994). The empowering process of accelerated schools: An essential link in school reform. *The English Journal, 83*(7), 62–65.

Peterson, K. D. (2002). Positive or negative? *Journal of Staff Development, 23*(3), 10–15.

Popham, W. J. (2011). Formative assessment—A process, not a test. *Education Week*. Accessed at https://edweek.org/teaching-learning/opinion-formative-assessment-a-process-not-a-test/2011/02 on January 3, 2023.

Querolo, N., Rockeman, O., & Ceron, E. (2022, September 2). *America's broken education system: Part 1—Why teachers are quitting*. Accessed at www.bloomberg.com/features/2022-america-teachers-great-resignation on November 23, 2022.

Reeves, D. (2002). *The leader's guide to standards: A blueprint for educational equity and excellence*. San Francisco: Jossey-Bass.

Reeves, D. (2016). *Elements of grading: A guide to effective practice* (2nd ed.). Bloomington, IN: Solution Tree Press.

Reeves, D. (2019). *Fast feedback* [Video file]. Accessed at https://www.youtube.com/watch?v=UFNsFEt-oXY on April 11, 2022.

Remediation. (n.d.). In *Merriam-Webster's online dictionary*. Accessed at https://merriam-webster.com/dictionary/remediation on January 12, 2022.

Rogers, P., Smith, W. R., Buffum, A., & Mattos, M. (2021). *Best practices at tier 3: Intensive interventions for remediation, secondary*. Bloomington, IN: Solution Tree Press.

Schimmer, T. (2016). *Grading from the inside out: Bringing accuracy to student assessment through a standards-based mindset*. Bloomington, IN: Solution Tree Press.

Schlechty, P. C. (2001). *Shaking up the schoolhouse: How to support and sustain educational innovation*. San Francisco: Jossey-Bass.

Schuhl, S. (2016, July). *Creating useful common assessments* [Conference presentation]. Professional Learning Communities at Work Institute, Atlanta, GA.

Schuhl, S. (2021). Providing feedback on the right work. In S. V. Kramer (Ed.), *Charting the course for leaders: Lessons from priority schools in a PLC at Work* (pp. 163–179). Bloomington, IN: Solution Tree Press.

Schuhl, S., Kanold, T. D., Barnes, B., Larson, M. R., Jain, D. M., & Mozingo, B. (2021). *Mathematics unit planning in a PLC at Work, high school*. Bloomington, IN: Solution Tree Press.

Sweeney, D. R., & Harris, L. S. (2017). *Student-centered coaching: The moves*. Thousand Oaks, CA: Corwin.

Sweeney, D. R., & Harris, L. S. (2020). *The essential guide for student-centered coaching: What every K–12 coach and school leader needs to know*. Thousand Oaks, CA: Corwin.

Takabori, A. (2021, June 7). *Learning acceleration, not remediation, for a fantastic school year*. Carnegie Learning Blog. Accessed at https://carnegielearning.com/blog/learning-acceleration-not-remediation on April 10, 2022.

TNTP. (2021, May). *Accelerate, don't remediate: New evidence from elementary math classrooms*. Accessed at https://tntp.org/assets/documents/TNTP_Accelerate_Dont_Remediate_FINAL.pdf on December 9, 2022.

TNTP. (2022, August). *Unlocking acceleration: How below grade-level work is holding students back in literacy*. Accessed at https://tntp.org/assets/documents/Unlocking_Acceleration_8.16.22.pdf on November 25, 2022.

Toth, M. D. (2021, March 17). *Why student engagement is important in a post-COVID world—and 5 strategies to improve it* [Blog post]. Accessed at https://learningsciences.com/blog/why-is-student-engagement-important on November 28, 2022.

University of Oregon Center on Teaching and Learning. (n.d.). *Big ideas in beginning reading*. Accessed at http://reading.uoregon.edu/big_ideas/au/au_programs.php on January 29, 2022.

U.S. Bureau of Labor Statistics. (2021, October 8). *Current employment statistics highlights*. Accessed at www.bls.gov/ces/publications/highlights/2021/current-employment-statistics-highlights-09-2021.pdf on October 18, 2022.

Weldmeskel, F. M., & Michael, D. J. (2016). The impact of formative assessment on self-regulating learning in university classrooms. *Tuning Journal for Higher Education, 4*(1), 99–118.

Westover, J., & Steinhauser, C. (2022). *Schools on the move: Leading coherence for equitable growth*. Thousand Oaks, CA: Corwin.

Wiggins, G. (2012, September 1). Seven keys to effective feedback. *Educational Leadership*. Accessed at https://ascd.org/el/articles/seven-keys-to-effective-feedback on April 11, 2022.

Wiggins, G., & McTighe, J. (1998). *Understanding by design*. Alexandria, VA: ASCD.

Wiggins, G., & McTighe, J. (2011). *The understanding by design guide to creating high-quality units*. Alexandria, VA: ASCD.

Williams, K. C., & Hierck T. (2015). *Starting a movement: Building culture from the inside out in professional learning communities*. Bloomington, IN: Solution Tree Press.

Index

A

academic enrichment, 7
Accelerated Schools Project, 7
acceleration
    as an alternative to remediation, 6–8
    assessment system, 61–86
    continuous improvement, 149–164
    daily grade-level instruction, 87–106
    defined, 9
    discussion questions, 15
    intervention system, 107–127
    is a mindset, 2
    leadership practices, 129–147
    learning cycles, 33–59
    priority standards, 33–59
    rationale for, 3, 5–6
    shift to, 8–11
    strategies based on new mindsets, 11–15
    vs. remediation, 2, 13–14
achievement gaps. *See* learning gaps
active engagement, 101–102
    vs. passive, 101
Adding It Up (Kilpatrick et al.), 97
*Addressing Unfinished Learning After COVID–19 School
        Closures* (Council of the Great City Schools), 97
administrators
    focus on learning, 22
    learning-focus planning tool, 23
all students can learn, 10, 12, 89, 109
All Things Assessment, 62
AllThingsPLC, 114
Anna Strong Learning Academy (Marianna, Ark.), 142–144
archiving team products, 153–156
    digital folder examples, 155
    what to archive, 154
The Assessment Center, 62
assessment practices, 2, 135
    acceleration strategies, 166
    acceleration through, 64–66
    assessment audit template, 65
    checklist, 69
    common assessment and daily formative assessment
        connection in each unit, 71
    common rubric, 70
    creating a balanced system, 66–68
    creating unit by unit, 68–71

    defined, 62
    discussion questions, 86
    formative, 3, 10, 12-13, 58, 111, 114
implementing common formative assessment strategies, 71–86
    key to acceleration, 3
    progress-monitoring, 151
    sample balanced system, 67
    shift from learning to, 62–64
    that accelerate learning, 61–62
    tools and protocols for next steps, 168–169
asset-based thinking, 126–127, 151
    vs. deficit-based thinking, 2
auditing current assessment practices, 64–66
    template, 65
awareness of psychological and emotional states, 73

B

balancing assessments, 66–68
    defined, 66
    sample, 67
Bandura, A., 72–73
Benson, J., 92
Bingo, 85
Black, P., 71
blended learning, 122
Boaler, J., 97
Brown, T., 105
Buffum, A., 35, 81, 108
building a system of instructional support, 140–142
    example of core instructional practices, 143
    four questions, 142–146
building coherence, 132

C

celebration-based monitoring, 131
celebrations, 24, 134
    collaborative teams, 151
    continuous improvement, 152, 160–163
    planning template, 163
    student growth, 120
    teachers who provide high-quality instruction, 145
Chappuis, J., 62, 67, 73
Chenoweth, K., 132, 150
clarifying concepts, 98–99
classroom discussions, 90, 141
clear goal intentions, 141

closure, 92–93

cognitive-task analysis, 141

cohort goals
    defined, 27

collaborative teams, 2, 90
    celebrating, 151
    intervention, 113–114
    leadership practices, 129–130, 137
    priority standards, 33–34
    responding to student learning data, 114–120
    shared leadership, 130–134

collective teacher efficacy, 141

commitment, 130, 132

community members
    engaging, 145–146
    shifting their thinking to learning, 22–24

compliance, 130

compliance-based monitoring, 131

concentration, 101–102

conceptual understanding, 96–99

continuous improvement, 3, 149–151
    acceleration strategies, 152–153, 167
    archiving team products systematically, 151–156
    celebrating, 160–163
    defined, 150
    discussion questions, 164
    shift to, 151–152
    step-up transition planning, 156–158
    teaching until the last day of school, 156
    tools and protocols for next steps, 168
    vertical step-up transition meetings, 158–161

cooperative vs. individualistic learning, 90

Council of the Great City Schools, 97

COVID-19 pandemic
    exacerbated teacher burnout, 109
    exposed and exacerbated learning gaps, 7
    unfinished learning, 1
    worsened teacher shortages, 140

creating common assessments unit by unit, 68–71
    checklist, 69
    common assessment and daily formative assessment
        connection in each unit, 71
    common rubric, 70

critical knowledge and skills, 37–38

Cruz, L. F., 130

culture of learning, 3
    acceleration strategies, 166
    administrators focus on learning, 22
    discussion questions, 32
    learning behavior expectations, 125–126
    parents and community members focus on learning, 22–24
    shift to, 17–18
    SMART goals are audaciously attainable, 25–30
    SMART goals data board, 31
    students co-create learning contacts, 18–21
    symbols and artifacts show learning is required, 25
    teachers collaborate in teams, 21–22
    tools and protocols for next steps, 168

curriculum-based learning vs. student-centered learning, 8–9

D

daily formative checks, 114

daily grade-level instruction, 3, 87–88
    acceleration strategies, 89–90, 167
    designing lessons, 90–93
    discussion questions, 106
    engaging students, 101–102
    incorporating reading and writing, 99–101
    massed and spaced practice, 93–95
    meaningful feedback, 103–104
    questions to guide lesson design, 93
    reflection and goal setting, 104–105
    shift to, 88–89
    teaching conceptually, 96–99
    tools and protocols for next steps, 169
    using error analysis, 102–103
    whole-group and small-group learning, 95–96

deficit thinking vs. strengths-based thinking, 8, 28

deliverables, 129

designing quality lessons, 90–93
    questions to guide, 93

diagnostic approach vs. coverage and teaching lessons, 8

differentiation, 92–93, 105, 108, 111

Dimich, N., 63

discussion questions
    assessment that accelerates learning, 86
    continuous improvement, 164
    culture of learning, 32
    daily grade-level instruction, 106
    intervention, 127
    leadership practices, 147
    priority standards and learning cycles, 59
    rationale for acceleration, 15

DuFour, Rebecca, 21, 160

DuFour, Richard, 21, 79–81, 90–91, 108, 111, 160

Dyer, K., 101

E

Eaker, R., 21, 45, 66, 160

education gaps. *See* learning gaps

effect size, 9

Elgart, M. A., 150

end-of-unit assessments, 114

engaging students, 101–102

engaging the community and stakeholders, 145–146

equity in learning, 3–4
    acceleration a matter of, 7

Erkens, C., 62, 92

error analysis, 102–103
    defined, 102

essential standards, 35

establishing high expectations, 88–89

everyone is a leader of learning, 10, 14–15

extension plans, 120

F

FAST feedback, 103

feedback, 9, 111, 141
    generating, 91

giving, 103–104
    importance of, 92–93
Ferriter, W. T., 105
find the mistake, 85
Findell, B., 97
first-best instruction, 89–90
Fisher, D., 105
504 Plans, 109
The Five Disciplines of PLC Leaders (Kanold), 160
flex days, 51
focusing on student growth, 120–122
Formative Assessment and Standards-Based Grading (Marzano), 71
formative assessment practices, 3
    assessment discussion tool, 13
    integral to learning, 10, 12
    intervention, 111, 114
    ten-day learning cycles, 58
formative walkthroughs, 142–144
forward-moving learning, 10, 13–14
foundational skills, 89
    massed and spaced practice, 95
    RTI, 108
four questions of the PLC process, 2, 136, 152, 154, 142
Frey, N., 105

G
gallery walks, 85
games, 85
Glendale (Ariz.) Elementary School District, 82, 149–150
goal setting, 104–105
grade-level instruction. *See* daily grade-level instruction
grade-level standards
    reviews vs. instruction, 8
Graham, S., 99
graphic organizers, 165–168
grouping
    ability vs. differentiation, 8, 10
    heterogeneous, 8, 10, 96, 122–123
    homogeneous, 96, 123
guaranteed and viable curriculum, 3, 33–59
guiding coalition, 131–134
Guskey, T. R., 81

H
Hale, B., 131
Hattie, J., 9, 12, 62, 72–73, 95, 101, 105
heterogeneous groups
    intervention, 122–123
    small-group learning, 96
    vs. leveled groups, 8, 10
Hierck, T., 149
higher-order reasoning tasks, 92
homogeneous groups
    intervention, 123
    small-group learning, 96

I
implementing common formative assessment strategies, 71–72
    learning passports, 82–86
    opportunities for reassessment, 79–81

pretests, 73–79
    rolling assessments, 79
    student self-efficacy, 72–73
    test talks, 81–82
In Praise of American Educators (DuFour), 160
incorporating reading and writing every day, 99–101
    example, 100
    terminology, 100
individualized education programs (IEPs), 109
Inside the Black Box (Black & Wiliam), 71
Instructional Agility (Erkens et al.), 92
instructional coaches, 134–140
    teacher goals in three-week coaching cycles, 139
    three-week coaching cycles, 138
instructional support. *See* building a system of
    instructional support
intervention, 3, 107–109
    acceleration strategies, 111, 167
    blended learning, 122
    discussion questions, 127
    focusing on student growth, 120–122
    learning behavior expectations, 125–126
    peer tutors, 123–125
    repurposing time in the master schedule, 112–114
    responding to student learning data, 114–120
    shift to multitiered systems of support, 109–111
    small groups, 122–123
    support classes and learning labs, 125
    team plan, 121
    tools and protocols for next steps, 168
iReady progress-monitoring tool, 68

J
just-in-time instruction, 2, 73

K
Kanold, T. D., 81, 160
Keating, J., 45, 66
Kid by Kid, Skill by Skill (Eaker & Keating), 45
Kilpatrick, J., 97
Kramer, S. V., 5–6, 17, 36, 102, 104, 129, 131–132, 141, 162
Kuhfeld, M., 7
KWL charts, 78

L
labeling students, 90
leadership practices, 129–130
    acceleration strategies, 167
    administrators focus on learning, 22–23
    building a system of instructional support, 140–146
    creating a guiding coalition or leadership team, 131–134
    discussion questions, 147
    everyone is a leader of learning, 10, 14–15
    leading the right work, 133
    practices, 3
    shift to shared leadership, 130–131
    to accelerate learning, 130–131
    tools and protocols for next steps, 168–169
    using instructional coaches, 134–140
learning at this point in time, 9

learning behavior expectations, 125–126
learning contracts
    defined, 18
    sample, 20
    students co-create, 18–21
learning cycles
    acceleration strategies, 166
    example, 50
    sample ten-day, 113
    teachers engage in collaborative teams, 21–22
    ten-day, 45–58
    that accelerate learning, 3, 33–59
    tools and protocols for next steps, 168
learning from assessments, 62–64
learning gaps
    equity and, 7
    marginalized communities, 1–2
learning is required, 18–21
    parents and community members, 22–24
    symbols and artifacts reflect, 25
learning labs, 125
learning passports, 82–86
    example, 83–84
learning progressions, 3
    creating, 38–43
    vs. increased pace, 8
learning standards
    common formative assessment data analysis, 117
learning targets
    choosing, 135
    students name them, 104
learning team, 131–134
lesson goals, 91, 93
leveled groups vs. heterogeneous groups, 8, 10
Lewis, K., 7
low-income students. *See* marginalized communities

M

Malone, J., 35
Many, T. W., 21, 160
marginalized communities
    achievement gaps, 1–2
    first-best instruction, 89–90
    more likely to experience remediation
Martin, T. L., 131
Marzano, R. J., 45, 71, 73, 81, 101
massed practice, 90, 141
    defined, 93
    planning for, 93–95
mastery experiences, 73
Mattos, M., 21, 35, 160
metacognitive strategies, 90
micro-teaching, 141
mindsets, 10
    all students can learn, 12
    assessment discussion tool, 13
    everyone is a leader of learning, 14–15
    formative assessment is integral to learning, 12
    instruction should create forward-moving learning, 13–14

intervention discussion tool, 14
    learning is required discussion tool, 11
    schools and districts are learning organizations, 11
    systematic intervention accelerates learning, 12–13
mission statements, 17–19
mixed-ability classrooms, 89
Model PLC, 114
model-practice-reflection cycle, 99
Mollenkamp, D., 7
multitiered systems of support (MTSS), 108–111, 144–145

N

Nation's Report Card (Mollenkamp), 7
National Council of Supervisors of Mathematics (NCSM), 34
National Council of Teachers of Mathematics (NCTM), 34, 72
National Education Association, 140
National Research Council, 97
New Teacher Project, 7

O

obtrusive tests, 77
opportunities for reassessment, 79–81
    sample, 80

P

pair shares, 95–96, 102
parents
    shifting their thinking to learning, 22–24
partner sharing, 95
passive engagement
    vs. active, 101–102
peer tutors, 123–125
    evaluation rubric, 124
perpetual learning for the purpose of continuous
        improvement, 150
perseverance, 101–102
Peterson, K. D., 18
plausible distractors, 81
Popham, W. J., 62
power standards, 35
pretests, 73–79
    during-the-unit student-reflection tool, 74
    end-of-unit student reflection tool, 75
    samples, 77–78
    student-reflection tool for standards over time, 76
prevention, 111
Principles to Action (NCTM), 72
prior knowledge
    activating, 9
    determining standards, 91–92
    embedding into units, 43–45
    embedding vs. reteaching, 35
    massed and spaced practice, 94
    transfer strategies, 141
priority standards
    acceleration strategies, 34–35, 166
    assessment analysis, 118–119
    critical knowledge and skills for acceleration, 37
    defined, 35

determining, 91–92

discussion questions, 59

embedding prior-knowledge standards into units, 43–45

example of standards and time frames, 39

examples of proficiency maps, 46–49

examples of unit plan and calendar, 53–55

examples of unpacked standards, 41–43

focus acceleration in ten-day learning cycles, 45–58

focusing on, 9

identifying, 35–38

learning cycle, 50

massed and spaced practice, 93–94

RTI, 108

sample tracker, 116

shift to focusing on, 34–35

standards acceleration diagram, 36

ten-day cycle planning template, 57–58

that accelerate learning, 3, 33–34

tools and protocols for next steps, 168

unpacking, 135

unpacking for the ten-day cycle, 56

unpacking to create learning progressions, 38–43

professional learning community (PLC) process, 2

common assessments at the heart, 6

creating, 151

four questions, 2, 136, 152, 154, 142

proficiency maps, 35, 44

program goals

defined, 27

progress-monitoring assessments, 114

promise standards, 35

Q

quantitative vs. qualitative data, 111

R

Rains, C. L., 131

rationale for acceleration, 3, 5–15

acceleration strategies, 166

discussion questions, 15

tools and protocols for next steps, 168

ReadWorks, 7

reassessment, 79–81

Reeves, D., 38, 81, 103–104

relay races, 85

remediation

defined, 6

vs. acceleration, 2, 8, 13–14

acceleration as an alternative, 6–8

repurposing time for intervention, 112–114

sample ten-day learning cycle, 113

responding to student learning data, 114–120

response to intervention (RTI), 90, 108–109, 141, 144–145

rolling assessments, 79

S

scaffolding, 10, 19, 105, 141

Schimmer, T., 63., 81

Schlechty, P. C., 131

school culture. *See* culture of learning

School Improvement for All (Kramer & Schuhl), 36, 104, 141, 162

schools and districts

are learning organizations, 10–11

becoming learning communities, 17–18

learning is required discussion tool, 11

Schuhl, S., 33, 36, 61, 81, 87, 102–104, 107, 141, 162

self-assessment. *See* student self-assessment

self-efficacy. *See* student self-efficacy

self-reported grades. *See* student self-reported grades

shared leadership, 130–131

shift to acceleration, 8–11

show what you know opportunities, 165

small groups, 111

creating, 122–123

small-group learning, 93, 95–96

SMART goals

audaciously attainable, 25–30

creating, 19

data board, 31

defined, 27

determining, 135

examples, 28–29

for diverse populations, 30

social persuasion, 73

software programs, 122

Soland, J., 7

spaced practice, 90, 141

defined, 93

planning for, 93–95

spiral review, 91

stakeholders

engaging, 145–146

stations, 82

Steinhauser, C., 15, 132, 151

step-up transition planning, 156–158

defined, 158

Stiggins, R., 62, 67, 73

strengths-based thinking vs. deficit thinking, 8, 28

student discourse, 92–93

student engagement, 91, 93, 101–102

defining, 142

in learning behavior expectations, 125–126

promoting, 101–102

student expectations, 90

student learning data. *See* responding to student learning data

student motivation, 14

student reflection, 91, 93, 104–105

student self-assessment, 104

student self-efficacy, 141

assessments, 72–73

importance of, 11

student self-reported grades, 90, 141

student-centered coaching cycles, 135

student-centered learning vs. curriculum-based learning, 8–9

students co-creating learning contracts, 18–21

students of color. *See* marginalized communities

student-student relationships

importance of, 12
    peer tutors, 123–124
student-to-student discourse, 95–96
support classes, 125
supporting standards, 36, 44, 47–49
Swafford, J., 97
symbols and artifacts
    recording sheet, 26
    show learning is required, 25
systematic intervention
    intervention discussion tool, 14
    to accelerate learning, 10, 12–13

T

Taking Action (Buffum et al.), 35
task selection, 92–93
teach until the last day of school, 156
    end-of-year plan, 157
teacher burnout, 109
teacher clarity, 90
teacher shortages, 140–141
teacher-centered coaching, 134
teacher-student relationships, 90
    importance of, 12
teachers engaging in collaborative teams, 21–22
    work of teams in recurring learning cycles, 21
teaching conceptually, 96–99
    example of clarifying concepts, 98
    sample posters, 99
team interventions, 120
ten-day learning cycles, 45–58
    calendar, 57
    continuity between, 153–154
    example, 113
    priority standard unpacking for, 56–57

Test Score Patterns Across Three Covid-19-Impacted School Years
    (Kuhfeld et al.), 7
test talks, 81–82
three reads, 101
three-week coaching cycles, 138
    teacher goals, 139
tiered intervention systems. *See* intervention
tools and protocols for next steps, 168

U

unobtrusive tests, 78
using mascots, 112

V

vertical conversations, 151
vertical step-up transition meetings, 158–161
    planning forms, 159, 161
vicarious experiences, 73
vitamin approach, 112–113
vocabulary programs, 90

W

Westover, J., 15, 132, 151
whole-group learning, 95–96
    feedback during, 95
Wiliam, D., 71
Williams, K. C., 149
WIN data sheet, 121

Y

Yates, G., 95

Z

Zearn, 6
zone of opportunity, 28

School Improvement for All
Sharon V. Kramer and Sarah Schuhl

Sustained school improvement only happens when teachers and administrators collectively ensure all students succeed within a professional learning community. With this practical guide, K–12 educators will discover how to target their school's specific needs with an immediate course of action to improve student achievement. Each chapter includes space for teams to determine action steps and questions to bring greater focus to improvement efforts.
BKF770

Charting the Course for Leaders
Edited by Sharon V. Kramer
Jack Baldermann, Kimberly Rodriguez Cano, Joe Cuddemi, Michelle Marrillia, Rebecca Nicolas, Robin Noble, Gerry Petersen-Incorvaia, Karen Power, Michael Roberts, Tamie Sanders, and Sarah Schuhl

This all-encompassing anthology delivers clear steps that leaders can take throughout the PLC at Work® process to turn their priority school around. Over the course of thirteen chapters, readers will grow in their role as leaders and gain a clear vision of how to evolve their school into a thriving place of learning.
BKF979

Charting the Course for Collaborative Teams
Edited by Sharon V. Kramer
Joe Cuddemi, Diane Kerr, Tammy Miller, Gerry Petersen-Incorvaia, Dana Renner, Michael Roberts, Tamie Sanders, and Sarah Schuhl

Develop the know-how to work collaboratively within the PLC at Work® process to overcome barriers and challenges in your priority school. This anthology gathers numerous expert contributors who share strategies and tools used to successfully turn around their underperforming schools.
BKF978

Stick the Learning
Eric Saunders

Combing through research for effective teaching strategies is a big ask for busy educators. This concise guide bridges brain-based learning theory with instructional practice to maximize teacher effectiveness for visible student achievement. Learn three powerful techniques proven to support long-term retention: spaced repetition, interleaving, and retrieval (SIR). Explore activities designed to improve student retention, application, and transfer by integrating SIR into your classroom.
BKG083

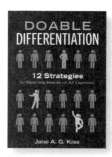

Doable Differentiation
Jane A.G. Kise

Differentiating for students' learning preferences can often seem too complex and complicated for too little gain. Learn a better way forward with the guidance of *Doable Differentiation*. Author Jane A.G. Kise provides a series of straightforward, high-reward strategies that K–12 educators like you successfully use in their daily practice to support, engage, and challenge students with diverse learning styles.
BKF952

a division of

Solution Tree | Press

Solution Tree

Visit SolutionTree.com or call 800.733.6786 to order.

Tremendous, tremendous, tremendous!

The speaker made me do some very deep internal reflection about the **PLC process** and the personal responsibility I have in making the school improvement process work **for ALL kids**.

PD Services

Our experts draw from decades of research and their own experiences to bring you practical strategies for building and sustaining a high-performing PLC. You can choose from a range of customizable services, from a one-day overview to a multiyear process.

Book your PLC PD today!
888.763.9045

Solution Tree